T5-CQA-933

Fodor's InFocus

GREAT SMOKY MOUNTAINS NATIONAL PARK

1st Edition

Where to Stay and Eat
for All Budgets

Must-See Sights
and Local Secrets

Ratings You Can Trust

Fodor's Travel Publications New York, Toronto, London, Sydney, Auckland
www.fodors.com

FODOR'S IN FOCUS GREAT SMOKY MOUNTAINS NATIONAL PARK

Editor: Salwa Jabado

Series Editor: Douglas Stallings

Writers: Michael Ream, Lan Sluder

Editorial Production: Carrie Parker

Maps & Illustrations: David Lindroth, Mark Stroud, *cartographers*; Bob Blake and Rebecca Baer, *map editors*

Design: Fabrizio La Rocca, *creative director*; Guido Caroti, *art director*; Ann McBride, *designer*; Melanie Marin, *senior picture editor*

Cover Photo: Deep Creek Valley, Great Smoky Mountains National Park, NC: Adam Jones/Danita Delimont/Alamy

Production/Manufacturing: Amanda Bullock

SPECIAL SALES

This book is available for special discounts for bulk purchases for sales promotions or premiums. Special editions, including personalized covers, excerpts of existing books, and corporate imprints, can be created in large quantities for special needs. For more information, write to Special Markets/Premium Sales, 1745 Broadway, MD 6-2, New York, New York, NY 10019, or e-mail specialmarkets@randomhouse.com.

AN IMPORTANT TIP & AN INVITATION

Although all prices, opening times, and other details in this book are based on information supplied to us at press time, changes occur all the time in the travel world, and Fodor's cannot accept responsibility for facts that become outdated or for inadvertent errors or omissions. **So always confirm information when it matters,** especially if you're making a detour to visit a specific place. Your experiences—positive and negative—matter to us. If we have missed or misstated something, **please write to us.** We follow up on all suggestions. Contact the Great Smoky Mountains National Park editor at editors@fodors.com or c/o Fodor's at 1745 Broadway, New York, NY 10019.

PRINTED IN THE UNITED STATES OF AMERICA

10 9 8 7 6 5 4 3 2 1

Be a Fodor's Correspondent

Your opinion matters. It matters to us. It matters to your fellow Fodor's travelers, too. And we'd like to hear it. In fact, we *need* to hear it. When you share your experiences and opinions, you become an active member of the Fodor's community. Here's how you can help improve Fodor's for all of us.

Tell us when we're right. We rely on local writers to give you an insider's perspective. But our writers and staff editors also depend on you. Your positive feedback is a vote to renew our recommendations for the next edition.

Tell us when we're wrong. We update most of our guides every year. But things change. If any of our descriptions are inaccurate or inadequate, we'll incorporate your changes in the next edition and will correct factual errors at fodors.com *immediately*.

Tell us what to include. You probably have had fantastic travel experiences that aren't yet in Fodor's. Why not share them with a community of like-minded travelers? Share your discoveries and experiences with everyone directly at fodors.com. Your input may lead us to add a new listing or a higher recommendation.

Give us your opinion instantly at our feedback center at www.fodors.com/feedback. You may also e-mail editors@fodors.com with the subject line "Great Smoky Mountains National Park Editor." Or send your nominations, comments, and complaints by mail to Great Smoky Mountains National Park Editor, Fodor's, 1745 Broadway, New York, NY 10019.

Happy Traveling!

Tim Jarrell, Publisher

CONTENTS

MAPS

ABOUT THIS BOOK

Our Ratings

We wouldn't recommend a place that wasn't worth your time, but sometimes a place is so experiential that superlatives don't do it justice: you just have to be there to know. These sights, properties, and experiences get our highest rating, **Fodor's Choice**, indicated by orange stars throughout this book. Black stars highlight sights and properties we deem **Highly Recommended**, places that our writers, editors, and readers praise again and again for consistency and excellence.

Credit Cards

Want to pay with plastic? **AE, D, DC, MC, V** after restaurant and hotel listings indicate whether American Express, Discover, Diners Club, MasterCard, and Visa are accepted.

Restaurants

Unless we state otherwise, restaurants are open for lunch and dinner daily. We mention dress only when there's a specific requirement and reservations only when they're essential or not accepted—it's always best to book ahead.

Hotels

Unless we tell you otherwise, you can assume that the hotels have private bath, phone, TV, and air-conditioning. We always list facilities but not whether you'll be charged an extra fee to use them, so when pricing accommodations, find out what's included.

Many Listings

★	Fodor's Choice
★	Highly recommended
✉	Physical address
♦	Directions
⌂	Mailing address
☎	Telephone
🖷	Fax
⊕	On the Web
✉	E-mail
☜	Admission fee
☉	Open/closed times
Ⓜ	Metro stations
⊟	Credit cards

Hotels & Restaurants

🏨	Hotel
⟿	Number of rooms
⚲	Facilities
⦿	Meal plans
✕	Restaurant
⌣	Reservations
⬎	Smoking
⊌	BYOB
✕🏨	Hotel with restaurant that warrants a visit

Outdoors

⛳	Golf
⛺	Camping

Other

♺	Family-friendly
⇨	See also
✉	Branch address
☞	Take note

PLANNER

Top Reasons to Go

Witness the wilderness: Get away from civilization in more than 800 square mi of tranquility, with old-growth forests, clear streams, meandering trails, wildflowers, and panoramic vistas from mile-high mountains.

Get your endorphins going: Outdoor junkies can bike, boat, camp, fish, hike, ride horses, go white-water rafting, and even ski cross country.

Experience mountain culture: Visit restored mountain cabins and tour "ghost towns" in the park.

Spot wildlife: You can see black bears, elk, white-tailed deer, wild turkeys, and other wildlife.

Learn something new: Take advantage of the interpretive talks and walks and Junior Ranger programs for kids.

Getting Here

The good news is that it's easy to get to the Great Smoky Mountains National Park. In some ways, that's also the bad news, as the Smokies are within a day's drive of some of America's largest cities, resulting in traffic during peak travel periods such as summer and fall weekends. The closest sizeable cities to the park are Knoxville, TN, to the west and Asheville, NC, to the east.

Coming either from the east or west, I–40 is the main access route to the Smokies; from the north and south, I–75, I–81, and I–26 are primary arteries.

Gatlinburg, TN entrance: From I–40 take Exit 407 to TN 66 South. At the Sevierville intersection, continue straight onto U.S. 441 South and follow it into the park.

Townsend, TN entrance: From I–40, take Exit 386B to U.S. 129 South to Alcoa/Maryville. At Maryville take U.S. 321 North/TN 73 East through Townsend; continue straight on TN 73 into the park.

Cherokee, NC entrance: Follow U.S. 441/U.S. 23 North. At Dillsboro merge on U.S. 74 West/U.S. 441 North. At Exit 74 merge onto U.S. 441 into the park.

A much more pleasant (but slower) route to the Smokies from North Carolina is the **Blue Ridge Parkway**, which has its southern terminus at Cherokee.

By Air: The closest airports with national air service are McGhee-Tyson Airport (TYS) in Knoxville, about 45 mi west of the Gatlinburg entrance to the park, and Asheville Regional Airport (AVL), about 60 mi east of the Cherokee entrance.

Getting Oriented

Tennessee Side. This is where the action is, and also the crowds. Near the western edge of the park are the towns of Gatlinburg and Pigeon Forge, virtually synonymous with the tourist trade, and Sevierville, a little less so. Here you'll find souvenir shops, outlet malls, country music theaters, mini-golf courses, amusement parks like Dollywood and Ober Gatlinburg, chain motels, and plenty of restaurants.

The top attraction on the Tennessee side of the park is Cades Cove. Despite the traffic, Cades Cove is well worth your time, because it's undoubtedly the most beautiful valley in the park, with wide, open fields and many preserved settlers' buildings.

The main road through the park, Newfound Gap Road, also known as U.S. 441, provides an easy window onto the diverse wonders of the Smokies. Many trails and short nature walks beckon, if you have time to stop.

North Carolina Side. Sometimes called "the quiet side of the park," the North Carolina side of the Smokies is edged with a collection of small, low-key towns. The most appealing of these are Bryson City, Sylva, and Waynesville. Except for these towns, and the city of Asheville about 50 mi east, most of the area around the east side of the Smokies consists of national forest lands. On the southwestern boundary of the park is Lake Fontana.

The vast majority of people entering the Smokies from the North Carolina side do so via Newfound Gap Road (U.S. 441) at Cherokee. This paved, two-lane highway, will take you to several of the park's top attractions, including the Mountain Farm Museum at Oconaluftee, Mingus Mill, and to Clingmans Dome, the highest mountain in the park.

Getting Around

A car is virtually a necessity for getting around the park, even if you want to enjoy the Smokies on foot or bike. However, some public transportation is available. For years, the National Park Service looked at introducing shuttle services, and in fall 2008, an experimental shuttle tour of Cades Cove began, operated by Cades Cove Heritage Tours in Townsend (☎ 865/329-2424 ⊕ www.cadescove-heritagetours.org ⛟ $13). Tours in 19-seat buses depart from the Great Smoky Mountains Heritage Center in Townsend (✉ 123 Cromwell Dr., Townsend, TN) and last about three hours. Also, Cherokee Trails, operated by the Eastern Band of Cherokee Indians Public Transit in Cherokee (☎ 828/497-5296 ⊕ www.cherokeetransit.com ⛟ $12-$14, round-trip) runs a shuttle bus between Cherokee and Gatlinburg/Pigeon Forge, with two to four trips daily May–November.

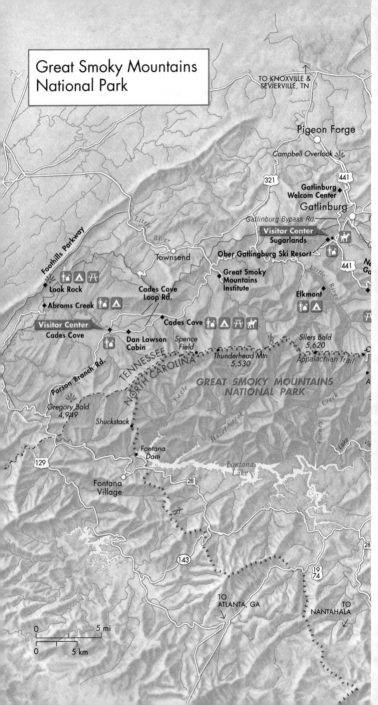

Great Smoky Mountains National Park

TO KNOXVILLE & SEVIERVILLE, TN

Pigeon Forge

Campbell Overlook

321

Gatlinburg Welcom Center

Gatlinburg

441

Gatlinburg Bypass Rd.

Visitor Center
Sugarlands

Ober Gatlinburg Ski Resort

441

Little River

Townsend

Great Smoky Mountains Institute

Elkmont

Foothills Parkway

Look Rock

Abrams Creek

Cades Cove Loop Rd.

Visitor Center
Cades Cove

Cades Cove

Dan Lawson Cabin

Spence Field

Silers Bald
5,620

Thunderhead Mtn
5,530

Appalachian Trail

TENNESSEE
NORTH CAROLINA

Parson Branch Rd.

GREAT SMOKY MOUNTAINS
NATIONAL PARK

Eagle Creek

Forney Creek

Gregory Bald
4,949

Shuckstack

Hazel Creek

Fontana Dam

Lake

129

Fontana Lake

28

Fontana Village

143

19
74

28

TO ATLANTA, GA

TO NANTAHALA

0   5 mi

0   5 km

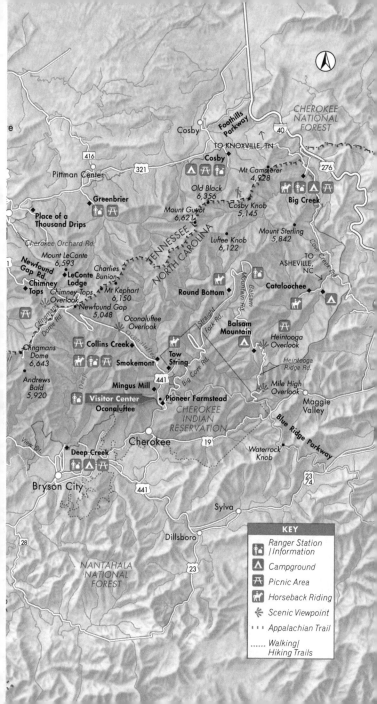

WHEN TO GO

There's no bad time to visit the Smokies, though summer and the month of October are the busiest times. The biggest crowds in the park arrive mid-June to mid-August, and all of the month of October, peak fall color season. There are six times as many visitors in the park in July as in January. Beat the crowds by coming on weekdays and also early in the day, before 10 AM. Late spring is a wonderful time to visit the park, as wildflowers are in bloom, and it's before the heat, humidity, and crowds of summer. Winter in the park can be beautiful, especially when there's snow on the ground or frost on the tree limbs. The air is usually clearer in the winter, with less haze, and with leaves off the trees the visibility is excellent.

Climate

Weather in the park is highly changeable, especially in the spring. On one day it may be a balmy 70°F, and the next bitterly cold and snowy. By mid-June, haze, heat, and high humidity have arrived. In July, highs at the lower elevations average 88°F, but at Clingmans Dome (elevation 6,643 feet) the average high is just 65°F. In September a pattern of warm, sunny days and cool nights sets in. Winters in the park see some snow, especially at the higher elevations.

GATLINBURG, TN (ELEVATION 1462')

	Avg. High	Avg. Low	Precip.
Jan	51	28	4.8"
Feb	54	29	4.8"
Mar	61	34	5.3"
Apr	71	42	4.5"
May	79	50	4.5"
Jun	86	58	5.2"
Jul	88	59	5.7"
Aug	87	60	5.3"
Sep	83	55	3.0"
Oct	73	43	3.1"
Nov	61	33	3.4"
Dec	52	28	4.5"

CLINGMANS DOME, NC (ELEVATION 6643')

	Avg. High	Avg. Low	Precip.
Jan	35	19	7.0"
Feb	35	18	8.2"
Mar	39	24	8.2"
Apr	49	34	6.5"
May	57	43	6.0"
Jun	63	49	6.9"
Jul	65	53	8.3"
Aug	64	52	6.8"
Sep	60	47	5.1"
Oct	53	38	5.4"
Nov	42	28	6.4"
Dec	37	21	7.3"

Welcome to the Great Smoky Mountains

WORD OF MOUTH

"There are so many hiking trails in the Smokies, including the Appalachian Trail. It's a great place . . . to enjoy nature. Numerous peaks over 6,000 ft in the park . . . pretty spectacular. Once you get to even the most basic trails in the park you'll find the crowds quickly evaporate. If you're into backcountry camping, the trails and vistas are endless."

—tmd63

By Lan
Sluder

THE GREAT SMOKY MOUNTAINS NATIONAL Park is one of the great wild areas of the eastern United States and the most visited national park in the entire country. From a roadside lookout or from a clearing in a trail, in every direction you can see the mountains march toward a vast horizon of wilderness.

Some of the tallest mountains in the eastern United States are here, including 16 peaks over 6,000 feet. The highest in the park, Clingmans Dome, was reputedly the original inspiration for the folk song "On Top of Old Smoky." It rises 6,643 feet above sea level and 4,503 feet above the valley floor. These are also some of the oldest mountains in the world, far older than those in the Rockies, the Alps, or the Andes. Geologists say the building of what are now the Great Smokies began about a billion years ago.

In his classic 1913 book, *Our Southern Highlanders*, Horace Kephart wrote about his experience living in the area that he later helped to establish as the national park: "For a long time my chief interest was not in human neighbors, but in the mountains themselves—in that mysterious beckoning hinterland which rose right back of my chimney and spread outward . . . mile after mile, hour upon hour of lusty climbing—an Eden still unpeopled and unspoiled."

Today, the park hosts over 9 million visitors each year, almost twice as many as the second-most visited national park, the Grand Canyon. Even so, with more than 814 square mi of protected land, it's easy to immerse yourself in Kephart's unpeopled and unspoiled wilderness.

Due to a fortuitous combination of moderate climate and diverse geography, the Great Smoky Mountains National Park is one of the most biologically rich spots on earth. Bears are the most famous animal in the park, but elk are also making the Smokies their home for the first time in 150 years. And it is not just large mammals that make it special. The Smokies has been called the "salamander capital of the world," with at least 30 different salamander species. It is also one of the few places on earth where, for a few evenings in June, you can see synchronous fireflies flashing in perfect unison.

The park offers extraordinary opportunities for outdoor activities: it has world-class hiking on more than 850 mi of trails, ranging from easy half-hour nature walks to week-long backpacking treks. While backcountry hiking has its

CLOSE UP

Smoke or Smog?

Air pollution is taking a toll on the Smokies. Fifty years ago, from Clingmans Dome on an average day you could see over 100 mi. Today, you can see only about 25 mi. The whitish haze you see in the Smokies, especially in summer, is not the bluish fog created by moisture in the air that the park was named for. It consists of airborne particles, mostly sulfates from coal-burning power plants as far away as the Ohio Valley, the Gulf Coast, and the Northeast. Sadly, the Great Smokies now has the worst overall air quality of any national park, with sulfur dioxide, nitrogen oxides, ozone, and particulate matter mainly responsible for the unnaturally hazy skies.

wonders, some of the most interesting sights in the park are viewable from the comfort of your car or motorcycle. You can explore old farms and mountain homesteads, or watch cornmeal being ground at a working gristmill, stopping to picnic at one of the park's 11 developed picnic areas. The picnic sites have tables and grills, but of course there's nothing to stop you from finding your own perfect spot beside a cool, shady stream.

HISTORY OF THE PARK

Long before the first Europeans arrived, American Indians inhabited the Smokies. More than 10,000 years ago, nomadic people called Paleo-Indians occupied the mountain valleys. Around 900 BC, Eastern Woodland Indians took up a more agrarian life in the mountains. By around 900 AD, the native cultures of this region were evolving into the highly complex societies of the Mississippian period. At the time the Europeans came in the 16th and 17th centuries, the Cherokee nation, descendants of earlier Indian groups, had a population of about 100,000, spread out over eight southeastern states.

The Spanish adventurer and explorer, Hernando de Soto, came through the Smokies in 1540, seeking gold. In the early 1700s, sizeable numbers of white settlers, mostly from Scotland and Northern Ireland, arrived. They first homesteaded the river bottoms, and then, when the best farmland was taken, moved up the hillsides. Cut off by mountains and lack of roads, the settlers remained isolated from the rest of the country. Long after America began to become homogenized, the mountain people retained their traditions and ways of talking.

During the period of white settlement, many Cherokees died of smallpox and other diseases against which they had no resistance. In 1830, President Andrew Jackson ordered the removal of all Native American people from the Southern states, relocating them to reservations in Oklahoma. The forced march of the Cherokee that took place between 1838–39 is now known as the Trail of Tears or "Nunna daul Isunyi" in the Cherokee language. It is memorialized in the outdoor drama, *Unto These Hills,* in Cherokee, North Carolina.

About 600 Cherokee Indians were allowed to remain in North Carolina, either because they lived on private land or because they had assisted the U.S. Army. They became the basis of the Eastern Band of the Cherokee Nation, based today on the Qualla Boundary reservation adjoining the Great Smokies Park.

In the early 1900s, large lumber corporations moved into the southern Appalachians, clear-cutting the mountains and erecting sawmills and paper factories. Railroads and roads were built ending the area's isolation at considerable cost to the environment and local culture.

With the natural beauty of the land endangered by lumbering and industrialization, many began urging that a new national park be established in the mountains. In 1923, William P. Davis, a prominent Knoxville businessman, began promoting the idea of a park. Fund raising began in 1925. Oil baron and philanthropist John D. Rockefeller gave $5 million, to be matched with state funds from North Carolina and Tennessee. Beginning in 1929, land for the park was acquired from the large timber companies and from more than 6,000 individual landowners. Altogether, the land acquisition cost $12 million, about $200 million today. Even at that, it was a great bargain, and today the value of this scenic wilderness goes far beyond its monetary worth.

On June 15, 1934, the Great Smoky Mountains National Park was officially established. However, it took another 10 years to finalize the purchase of parklands and to resettle most of the landowners outside the park.

CLOSE UP

Did You Know? No Admission Fees

Unlike nearly all other major U.S. national parks, admission to the Great Smoky Mountains National Park is free. Why? The reasons date back to before the park was established, when the land was privately owned. The states of North Carolina and Tennessee, along with some local communities, paid to construct Newfound Gap Road, now officially U.S. Highway 441. Construction was completed in 1932. At that time, before the days of the interstates, Newfound Gap Road was one of the major highways across the Appalachians. When Tennessee transferred ownership of this important road to the federal government in 1936, it stipulated that "no toll or license shall ever be imposed." Official action by the Tennessee legislature would be required to lift this deed restriction. North Carolina imposed no restrictions, but it would be impractical to charge admission to only about one-half of the park. The result? One of the great freebies of the American outdoors.

Today, the once clear cut mountains are filled with a diversity of plant and animal life that 9 million people come to enjoy each year.

75TH ANNIVERSARY. The 75th anniversary of the park is in 2009. Various events are planned to celebrate the event, including a 75th Anniversary Weekend Celebration June 13–15, 2009, and a Rededication Ceremony September 2, 2009. A new Web site has been created for the 75th anniversary: ⊕ *www.great-smokies75th.org.*

GEOLOGY OF THE PARK

The geology of the Great Smokies is a story that's at least a billion years old. It began when giant, continent-sized tectonic plates shifted, moving only inches a year but with immense power. These plates collided, grinding together, buckling over one another. Earthquakes shook the earth, molten lava erupted from deep underground, and chains of mountains were pushed up.

Over millions of years, clay, sand, silt, and pebbles from the highlands of these ancient mountains washed down into the valley basins, leaving sedimentary deposits. These sediments eventually became cemented together, forming a layer of sedimentary rock under the Smokies some 9 mi deep. Geologists say most of the rocks were formed during the Proterozoic Era, 545 to 800 million years ago. About 450 million years ago, the rock underwent a metamorphosis caused by pressure and heat. Throughout the Smokies today, large boulders of metamorphosed sandstone can be seen in the park's 2,115 mi of rivers and streams.

Then, perhaps 245 to 350 million years ago, in the last great wave of evolutionary mountain building, the North American continental plate collided with the African and European plates. This collision pushed up the Appalachian Mountains, which run from modern-day Newfoundland, Canada, down to northern Alabama. The Great Smokies are a range of mountains within the Appalachians.

Among the mountains in the Great Smokies are some of the tallest peaks in eastern America, but they used to be much higher, at least as high as those in the Rockies. Tens of millions of years of ice, wind, rain, and erosion have worn down the mountains to their present height. Erosion continues even now. Scientists estimate that peaks in the Smokies lose about 2 inches every 1,000 years.

FLORA

A profusion of vegetation defines the Great Smoky Mountains; the park has one of the richest and most diverse collections of flora in the world. The park is about 95% forested, home to almost 6,000 known species of wildflowers, plants, and trees.

In the park are five distinct forest ecosystems, mostly based on elevation: the spruce-fir forest grows at the highest peaks, from 4,500 to 6,600 feet, and gets up to 85 inches of rain a year. Also above 4,500 feet is the northern hardwood forest, with predominantly beech and yellow birch trees. Hardwood cove forests—with those fall foliage superstars, the sugar maples, as well as buckeye, basswood, tulip poplar, hickory, and beech adding to the fall color show—appear in sheltered slopes and coves up to 4,500 feet. In the fall, typically in October, hundreds of thousands of visitors jam the roads of the park to view the autumn leaf color. Hemlock forests grow along streams below 3,000 feet and on exposed slopes. Finally, on dry slopes in direct sunlight you'll find pine-and-oak forests, as well as mountain laurel, rhododendron, other trees and shrubs.

Many call the Smokies the "wildflower national park," as it has more flowering plants than any other U.S. national park. You can see wildflowers in bloom virtually year-round, from the ephemerals such as trillium and columbine in late winter and early spring, to the bright red cardinal flowers, orange butterfly weed, and black-eyed Susans in summer, and Joe-pye weed, asters, and mountain gentian in the fall. However, the best time to see wildflowers is spring, especially April and early May. The Spring Wildflower Pilgrimage, in late April, celebrates the blooms with classes, nature walks, and other events. The second-best time to see the floral display is early summer. From mid-June to mid-July, the hillsides and heath balds blaze with the orange of flame azaleas, the white and pink of mountain laurel, and the purple and white of rhododendron. ⚠ **Remember to bring your friend to the flower not the flower to your friend; it is illegal to pick any wildflower, plant, or tree in the park.**

American Chestnut *(Castaneda dentata)*: Until the early 20th century, the American chestnut was the dominant tree in the Smokies and in much of the eastern United States, from Maine to Georgia. It represented one-fourth to one-third of all trees in the Smokies. Its consistent mast provided plentiful food for many different animals. Then, a fungus, *Cryphonectria parasitica,* was accidentally brought in from Asia. The fungus was first discovered in the Bronx Zoological Park in New York in 1904, probably imported with specimens from China or Japan, and it spread throughout the entire range of the American chestnut by the 1930s. In Asia, this fungus and the local chestnuts had evolved to co-exist with each other, but in the United States the American chestnut had no defenses, and the fungus proved to be devastating. By the 1950s, virtually every chestnut tree in the Smokies and indeed the entire country, had been killed. Some 4 billion trees died. The virulent pathogen still remains in the Smokies. Sprouts from wild American chestnut roots still spring up, but as soon as they reach 10 or 20 feet tall, they are killed back by the blight.

Catawba Rhododendron *(Rhododendron catawbiense)*: With its waxy dark-green leaves and brilliant purple flowers, the Catawba rhododendron is one of the showiest flowering shrubs in the park. It thrives on mountain slopes at elevations over 3,500 feet and blooms in June, sometimes extending into July. Mountain people often call rhododendron "laurel," and when any variety of rhododendron or

CLOSE UP

Exotic Threat

The Smokies have been a victim of many alien predators. Hundreds of exotic, non-native plants and a few non-native animals have been introduced in the park.

One of the earliest and still most serious was the chestnut blight, a fungus from Asia that struck the American chestnut. Once the dominant tree in Appalachian forests, by the time the Great Smoky Mountains National Park was officially established the chestnut had been all but wiped out by the fungus. Biologists think 4 billion trees died across the eastern United States. In many areas, oaks and poplars became the successor trees, significantly changing not only the look but also the ecology of the region's forests. More recently, other species from Asia have been killing the firs and hemlocks in the Great Smokies. The balsam woolly adelgid has destroyed many of the Fraser firs in the park, and the hemlock woolly adelgid has infested most of the park's eastern hemlocks. At lower elevations, the southern pine beetle has bored into native pines, quickly turning them brown and leaving piles of fallen dead trees which are a potential fire hazard.

The granddaddy of all the exotics is kudzu, which was introduced into the United States at the 1876 Centennial Exposition in Philadelphia. The Japanese government's pavilion included a garden with kudzu, and American gardeners quickly adopted the plant as an ornamental. Then, in the 1930s, the Soil Conservation Service promoted kudzu for erosion control. Unfortunately, the climate in the Southeast is ideal for kudzu, and it grows all too well here. Kudzu vines can grow over a foot a week and it now covers over 7 million acres in the South. It is a pest in parts of the Smokies, although park workers have been able to control it in most areas.

Other troublesome exotics in the park include the multiflora rose, mimosa, bush honeysuckle, privet, oriental bittersweet, Japanese grass, Japanese spirea, and garlic mustard.

On the mammal side, the wild European hog roots up hundreds of acres of parkland, killing native plants and making the earth look like it was tilled. The hog was brought to a private game preserve in western North Carolina over 100 years ago. Some of the hogs escaped, interbred with domestic hogs, and eventually, in the 1940s, made their way to the Smokies. After years of removing hogs from the park, today only a few hundred remain.

mountain laurel grows in a thick, virtually impenetrable thicket, it's called a "laurel hell" or a "laurel slick."

Eastern Hemlock *(Tsuga canadensis)*: Also known as the Canadian hemlock, the stately eastern hemlock commonly stands as high as a 10-story building. It grows well in shade and likes moist areas near streams. This evergreen has small cones less than an inch in length. It can live hundreds of years, with the oldest known specimen being over 550 years old. The largest known eastern hemlock stands over 156 feet tall, with a diameter of over 4 feet, which it retains as far as 70 feet above the ground. It was found in the Laurel Branch area of the Smokies, at Greenbrier in eastern Tennessee. Sadly, most hemlocks in the Smokies and elsewhere in the region are now infested with the hemlock woolly adelgid, which first arrived in the United States in 1924 from Asia. Individual trees can be treated against this adelgid, but it is impractical to do so in large wild stands. In recent years, tens of thousands of hemlocks have died. A project called "Tsuga Search" is being conducted to save the largest and tallest remaining eastern hemlocks in the Great Smokies.

Flame Azalea *(Rhododendron calendulaceum)*: When in bloom, with its bright orange flowers, this shrub is unmistakable. The native azalea prefers shadier locations, at low to mid-elevations in the park. It is also common along the Blue Ridge Parkway, especially the section near the Oconaluftee entrance to the park near Cherokee. Blooms show up at the lower elevations in April and through July at elevations around 5,000 feet.

Fraser Fir *(Abies fraseri)*: Named after the 18th-century Scottish botanist John Fraser, the Fraser fir is best known for their annual appearances in homes come December. The needles of this fragrant evergreen stay on weeks or even months after harvest, making it an ideal Christmas tree. In the Smokies, it lives only at the highest elevations, typically above 4,000 feet. It is usually mixed with red spruces. The Fraser fir in the Smokies and elsewhere in the highland mountains has been hit by a double whammy: first, acid rain killed many high-altitude trees; then, a tiny immigrant from Asia, the balsam woolly adelgid, led to a rapid decline in its range, and in some areas 90% or more of the evergreens have been killed. The firs regenerate from seedlings, but in a few years the maturing trees also are struck by this destructive adelgid.

Ginseng *(Panax quinquefolius)*: Wild ginseng, or "sang" as it's known locally, is a slow-growing perennial plant native to well-drained hardwood forests. The stem is about a foot high, bearing three leaves, with a few small, yellowish flowers in mid-summer. The fruit is a cluster of bright red berries and ripens in the early fall. The root of the plant is highly valued in traditional Chinese medicine as an aphrodisiac, a stimulant, and as a treatment for adult-onset diabetes. Now fairly rare and even endangered, wild ginseng, dried, can fetch as much as $1,000 a pound. Its collection in the Smokies is strictly prohibited.

Mountain Laurel *(Kalmia latifolia)*: This evergreen shrub, which can grow to 40 feet, is common on mountain slopes in the Great Smokies. It has waxy, star-shaped pink or white flowers in May and June. A good way to distinguish mountain laurel from both rosebay and Catawba rhododendrons is by the leaves. The mountain laurel's leaves are much shorter. There's an old saying to help distinguish laurel from rhododendron: "short leaf, short name; long leaf, long name"—that is, the laurel has a short name and a short leaf while the rhododendron has a long name and a long leaf.

Rosebay Rhododendron *(Rhododendron maximum)*: The most common rhododendron in the Smokies, the rosebay rhododendron is usually found in wet areas along creeks or streams. It has clumps of white flowers, starting in early June at lower elevations, and through August at elevations near 5,000 feet.

Tulip Poplar *(Liriodendron tulipifer)*: The tulip or yellow poplar is one of the tallest trees in the Smokies, sometimes reaching heights of almost 200 feet, though more commonly it stands at 100 feet. The largest specimens in the region are in the virgin stands of the Joyce Kilmer Memorial Forest in Robbinsville, NC, just outside the park. Usually the tulip poplar has no limbs for most of its trunk height, so it is an important tree for lumber. It is not a true poplar but a member of the magnolia family.

Trillium *(Trillium)*: Ten species of trillium grace the Great Smokies. They are easy for even an amateur to identify, since most of the plant comes in threes—they have three bracts (similar to leaves), flowers with three petals, and three-lobed fruit. One of the most common species in the park is the large-flowered trillium *(Trillium grandiflorum)*. This trillium blooms in April and May, showing off a white flower. An unusual aspect of trilliums is that their seeds are spread by ants, which eat the fatty material attached to the seeds and then carry the seeds off to another area. Feral hogs are the biggest enemy of trilliums, because they root up large areas where the plants grow.

FAUNA

Living in the Great Smoky Mountains National Park are some 66 species of mammals, over 200 varieties of birds, 50 native fish species, and more than 80 types of reptiles and amphibians.

The North American black bear is the symbol of the Smokies. Bear populations vary year to year, but biologists think that up to 1,600 bears are in the park, a density of about 2 per square mile. Many visitors to the park see bears, although sightings are never guaranteed.

At one time, bison, elk, mountain lions, gray and red wolves, river otters and peregrine falcons were common in the park. The National Park Service has helped reintroduce elk, river otters, and peregrine falcons to the Smokies. The wild European hog is a non-native species that has caused extensive damage to the park's ecosystem by wallowing and rooting. Wildlife biologists trap or shoot hogs to keep their numbers under control.

Only 2 of the 23 species of snakes that live in the park are venomous—the Northern Copperhead and the Timber Rattlesnake. The chance of your being bitten by one of these snakes is extremely small, and the park has no record of anyone ever dying of a snake bite here.

Because of the high elevation of much of the park, you'll see birds here usually seen in more northern areas, including the common raven and the ruffed grouse.

Bobcat *(Lynx rufus)*: This North American feline is about twice the size of a domestic cat. It is thought to be the only wild cat in the Smokies, although mountain lions are occasionally reported. Bobcats have grayish-brown coats, black-tufted ears, and a short black-tipped tail. They prey primarily on rabbits, but are also known to eat insects, rodents, birds, squirrels, and even deer. Solitary and territorial, they can occasionally be spotted at dawn or at twilight.

CLOSE UP

The Bear Facts

Black Bear attacks in the Great Smokies or elsewhere in the mountains are extremely rare, but they do happen occasionally. Only one human death due to bear aggression has ever been reported in the park, but human–bear incidents occur each year. There are about 1,500 to 1,600 black bears in the Smokies, an average of 2 per square mile. If you see a bear, don't approach too closely. In fact, it is illegal to get closer than 150 feet. Never feed bears or leave food out, as most human–bear conflicts result from bears becoming used to eating human food. Bear-proof dumpsters and garbage cans also help reduce the number of problem bears. When a bear does become a problem, wildlife managers use proactive aversive conditioning that involves capturing, tranquilizing, and examining the bear, and then releasing it back into the same area. While the procedure is harmless to the bear, it's unpleasant and re-instills a fear of humans. This approach allows bears to remain in their home range, but they learn to shy away from developed areas.

In the backcountry, hang food and anything with strong odors (toothpaste, bug repellent, soap, etc.) at least 10 feet off the ground and 4 feet down from a tree branch, or use special food storage boxes and cable systems available at some sites. You can also buy or rent bear-proof food canisters at visitor centers in the park. Do not cook or store food in or near your tent. Pack out your trash—don't bury it for bears to find later.

If a bear comes toward you making loud noises or swatting the ground, it's likely demanding more space. Back away slowly. Don't run—a bear can jog at up to 30 or 35 MPH, much faster than you can. If the bear follows, especially if it is not vocalizing or swatting, stand your ground, shout, and try to intimidate it by throwing rocks. Try to stay uphill of the bear, and raise your arms over your head, which will make you appear larger. If you are carrying any food, quickly rid yourself of it.

Brook Trout *(Salvelinus fontinalis)*: The brookie, or speckled trout as locals call it, is the only native trout in the streams of the Smokies. Actually, it's not a true trout but a char. Rainbow trout and brown trout are more common. The National Park Service hasn't stocked trout streams in the park since 1975, but through natural reproduction many park waters are at maximum trout carrying capacity, with 2,000 to 4,000 trout per mile.

1

Bringing Your Pets

Pets are allowed in some areas of the Great Smoky Mountains National Park. Dogs are allowed in campgrounds, picnic areas, and along roads; however, they must be on a leash at all times (maximum leash length 6 feet). With the exception of service animals, pets are not allowed in park lodging, backcountry campgrounds, or on most park trails because they might carry disease to wildlife populations, chase or threaten wildlife, and disturb the quiet of the wilderness. Pets also can become prey for bears or other large predators. Dogs are allowed on two short walking paths—the Gatlinburg Trail near the Sugarlands Visitor Center and the Oconaluftee River Trail at the Oconaluftee Visitor Center. Pets are not permitted at all in the backcountry. Several nearby federal forest areas have more liberal rules on pets than the Great Smokies. These include the Pisgah National Forest and the Nantahala National Forest.

Common Raven *(Corvus corax)*: The common raven isn't so common in the East and Southeast. It's found mostly in the higher elevations of the Smokies and other mountain areas in the region, and only in small numbers. Ravens are larger than crows, with heavier bills and wingspans over 4 feet. Among their calls is a deep, baritone croak.

Coyote *(Canis latrans)*: Coyotes have returned to the Southeast and can be found in the park. Reddish-gray with a buff underside, coyotes resemble medium-size dogs, but their yellow eyes, alert ears, and bushy, black-tipped tails give away their wild nature. They run in packs or as loners, roam either day or night, and eat nearly anything: fresh meat, carrion, insects, fruits, and vegetables. Coyotes have a diverse vocal repertoire filled with barks, wails, and yips. They are more often heard than seen.

Eastern Yellow Jacket *(Vespula maculifrons)*: This small (about ½ inch long) yellow-and-black wasp is a common pest at picnics in the park. Worse, yellow jackets will sting you repeatedly if you stumble upon their nest and they perceive you as a threat. They nest in the ground or in old logs or stumps. When cold weather comes, yellow jackets die except for mated females, which winter in litter and soil.

Elk *(Cervus canadensis)*: Elk once roamed the southern Appalachians, but the last native elk here was believed to have died over 200 years ago. Beginning in 2001, in an experimental reintroduction program, the park imported more than 50 elk, and a number have since had calves. Today, nearly 100 elk are in the park. During the summer, elk graze almost constantly and will consume as much as 15 pounds of food in one day. Males reach 700 pounds and stand 5 feet tall at the shoulders. They have dark reddish-brown coats with a characteristic white rump patch. Males sport antlers as much as 5 feet wide, which they use when competing with other males during mating season. Their bugling mating call is one of the most distinctive sounds of autumn. The best place to see elk is in the open fields of the Cataloochee Valley in the southeastern part of the park. It is illegal to get closer than 150 feet to elk.

Gray Fox *(Urocyon cinereoargenteus)*: This member of the canid family is primarily nocturnal, but sometimes can be seen foraging during the day. The small fox has grayish-brown fur, sports a white belly and facial markings, and has a black stripe on its back and tail. It can climb trees and feeds on small mammals, insects, birds, eggs, nuts, and berries.

Great Horned Owl *(Bubo virginianus)*: The largest owl in North America, the great horned owl ranges in length from 18 to 27 inches with a wingspan of 49 inches. Their disc-shaped face acts like a radar dish, catching faint sounds in a wide range of frequencies. The owl's hearing is so acute, it generally locates its prey in the dark undergrowth by sound alone, perching and hooting to panic the mice and rabbits into betraying their position. This nocturnal predator can see well in dim light and can swivel its head 270 degrees, which gives it wider range of motion to detect prey without moving and giving away its position.

Groundhog *(Marmota monax)*: Groundhogs, or wood-chucks, are among the most commonly seen mammals in the park. You'll often spot these large ground squirrels, or marmots, by the side of the road or at the edge of clearings. Fat with grass and berries, they can weigh 9 pounds and be over 2 feet in length. Groundhogs hibernate in their burrows in winter. Mountain people used to eat groundhog stew, which only seems fair when you consider groundhogs often ravish vegetable gardens.

Northern Copperhead *(Agkistrodon contortrix)*: This pit viper is, with the timber rattlesnake, one of only two venomous snakes in the park. In color, the copperhead has a pale tan to pinkish tan ground color overlaid with a series of tan or light brown crossbands. Copperheads rarely grow to more than 3 feet in length. It's unlikely you'll see one in the park. Visitors often confuse the northern water snake or other harmless snakes for a copperhead.

North American Black Bear *(Ursus americanus)*: Black bears usually range in length from 5 to 6 feet, standing about 3 to 4 feet at the shoulder, and weigh 250–500 pounds when fully mature. The biggest black bear ever recorded was in North Carolina; it weighed 800 pounds. They can stand and walk on their hindquarters, but usually shuffle along on all fours. These bears sport a shaggy black coat and have a long snout, which gives them an excellent sense of smell. Opportunistic eaters, black bears dine on a variety of foods, including insects, nuts, berries, fish, and small mammals. Contrary to popular belief, they do not hibernate in winter, although they become less active and may sleep for long periods. Black bears in the wild normally live 8 to 12 years, though some live 20 years or longer.

Ruffed Grouse *(Bonasa umbellus)*: Also called the ruffled grouse, you'll likely hear rather than see this near chicken-size bird. Males make a drumming sound, like an engine starting, and if you happen to walk too close they will suddenly explode out of the leaves and fly away. The Smokies are at the far southern end of its range.

Southern Gray-cheeked Salamander *(Plethodon metcalfi)*: The Great Smoky Mountains National Park is known as the "salamander capital of the world." In fact, salamanders outnumber all other vertebrate (backboned) animals in the park. You'll find them in creeks, streams, and other moist areas all over the park. The Southern gray-cheeked salamander, common at higher elevations, is one of 30 species of salamanders in the park. Of these, 24 are in the family *Plethodontidae*, known as lungless salamanders. Mountain people refer to salamanders as "spring lizards," though salamanders are not true lizards.

Synchronous Firefly *(Photinus carolinus)*: The Great Smokies is one of the few places in the world where you can see fireflies blinking in unison. (Among the others are parts of Thailand and China.) For a few short weeks, usually from late May to mid-June, these fireflies put on an amazing light show. Entire hillsides seem to blink in rhythm as if they were covered with Christmas tree lights. In this illuminated mating dance, the male Photinus fireflies blink four to eight times in the air, then wait about six seconds for the females on the ground to return a double-blink response. Elkmont and Cades Cove in Tennessee are two good places to see them in the park. The Joyce Kilmer Memorial Forest just outside the park on the North Carolina side is another great place to watch the show. Altogether, about 20 species of fireflies have been found in the park, including the Blue Ghost Firefly (*Phausis reticulata*), which emits a blue or green glow that can last for over half a minute.

Timber Rattlesnake (*Crotalus homidus*): The timber rattler is one of only two poisonous snakes in the park. The other is the northern copperhead. This rattlesnake is quite variable in color, ranging from yellow and brown to nearly black. It has W-shaped lateral markings across its back. The rattles at the end of the tail distinguish it, but sometimes individual snakes lose their rattles. In the park, these rattlesnakes typically reach about 3 feet in length, but they can be 5 feet or more.

White-tailed Deer (*Odocoileus virginianus*): Biologists estimate there are at least 6,000 deer in the park. They live throughout the park but are most common in areas with open fields, especially Cades Cove and Cataloochee. Deer browse many types of leaves and grass; in the fall, they eat acorns and other nuts. Usually, does give birth to their fawns in June; it takes about two years for the young deer to fully mature. Bucks fight for mating rights in the late summer and November is mating season.

Wild Turkey (*Meleagris gallopavo*): Wild turkeys are plentiful in the park, especially in the Cades Cove area on the Tennessee side and the Cataloochee Valley on the North Carolina side. Turkeys sport a dark-brown body, glossy purplish-bronze wings, and rufus-tipped tail feathers. Like their domesticated counterparts, they have a small bald head. Males have red wattles on their necks. They travel in flocks of up to 60 and roost at night in trees. Males often reach 16 pounds.

IF YOU LIKE

BICYCLING

You can enjoy great bike rides in the Smokies, although heavy traffic on some popular roads can be a problem. Most paved and unpaved roads in the park are open for biking, but there are no mountain biking trails. Bicycles are prohibited on all hiking trails except three: Gatlinburg

Trail, Oconaluftee River Trail, and Lower Deep Creek Trail. The 11-mi paved Cades Cove Loop Road is an easy, scenic ride, and you may spot wild turkeys, bears, and deer. However, this is also one of the busiest roads in the park. Recognizing this, park officials restrict the loop to bikes and pedestrians at certain times, currently early mornings until 10 AM on Wednesdays and Saturdays. Cataloochee on the North Carolina side is another good area for bicycling, and you may see elk here. Other areas suitable for bicyclists include Tremont and Greenbrier roads in Tennessee. Up and back on Clingmans Dome Road (16 mi round-trip) is a test of fitness. The thin air at elevations over 6,000 feet and the steep grade going up make this road difficult for most riders who have not trained for biking in the mountains. Avoid this route on summer weekends and during fall leaf season, when heavy traffic can make it dangerous. Tennessee law requires that children 16 and under wear a helmet when biking, and park officials recommend helmets for all bikers. Bike rentals are available at the Cades Code campground store.

CAMPING

There are 10 developed campgrounds in the park, with more than 940 campsites. They range in size from 12 to 220 sites. The largest is Elkmont, near Gatlinburg. All are accessible by car, and most accept trailers and motor homes, though there are usually length limitations. Fees range from $14 to $23 per night. Developed campgrounds have pit or flush toilets, picnic tables, and grills, but none has showers. Larger ones have camp stores. Sites at Elkmont, Smokemont, Cades Cove, and Cosby may be reserved online or by phone from May 15 to October 31. The six other campgrounds are first-come, first-served, and they do fill up, especially on weekends in summer and fall. Back-country camping, requiring a hike of several miles, is free and available at a number of undeveloped campgrounds and shelters all over the park. Even in the backcountry, you must camp only at designated campgrounds or shelters. Advance reservations are required for 17 of the park's backcountry campgrounds and at all shelters. They may be made by telephone only up to one month in advance. The maximum stay at any one backcountry camp is three days and one day at shelters. Free permits for backcountry camping are required.

CLOSE UP

Tips for RVers

All but one of the 10 developed campgrounds in the park accept travel trailers and RVs. Only Big Creek, on the northeastern edge of the park, with just 12 spaces, doesn't permit them. Most campgrounds, however, limit RV or trailer length. Each campground has different length limits, from 12 to 40 feet. The Look Rock camp on the Tennessee side is the only one with no size limit. There are no RV hookups at any campground in the park, and no showers. In summer and fall, sites at Elkmont, Smokemont, Cades Cove, and Cosby may be reserved online or by phone. The main east–west road through the park, U.S. Highway 441, is suitable for RVs of any size, but many of the park's secondary roads, narrow and unpaved, with blind curves and switchbacks, are not. Outside the park, near the three main entrances and elsewhere, are many commercial campgrounds with full RV hookups.

FISHING

Fishing is permitted year-round in the Great Smoky Mountains National Park, and it can be superb, with more than 2,100 mi of rivers, streams, and creeks. While park waters are not stocked, many streams are at their carrying capacity, with as many as 4,000 trout per mile. The native brook trout are in the headwaters of streams above 3,000 feet. As you go downstream, rainbow and brown trout dominate. At the lowest elevations, near the edge of the park, there are smallmouth bass, rock bass, and other fish. A North Carolina or Tennessee fishing license is required to fish in the Smokies. Children under 16 in North Carolina and under 13 in Tennessee do not need a license. Only artificial lures and flies may be used—bait fishing is prohibited to prevent the accidental introduction of exotic species. The daily possession limit is a total of 5 brown, rainbow, and brook trout, and smallmouth bass, plus 20 rock bass.

Where is the best place to fish? There are so many miles of streams, offering very different fishing experiences, that it's impossible to pick just a few. Wherever you find a lot of bugs—food for fish—you're likely to find a lot of trout. However, Abrams Creek on the Tennessee side is sometimes picked as a favorite of seasoned anglers. Hazel Creek and Deep Creek on the North Carolina side are known far and wide. Regardless of where you fish, keep safety in mind.

Standing on wet, slick, and moss- or silt-covered rocks can be treacherous.

GAZING AT THE SCENERY

The Great Smoky Mountains offer fabulous scenery, whether you are on foot or in your car. Along most of the park's roadways, there are many turnouts and overlooks to stop and look at the scenery. The main road through the park, Newfound Gap Road (U.S. 441), rises from under 1,500 feet to almost a mile in elevation; it's like driving from Georgia to Maine in about an hour. On the park's back roads—all roads in the park are either paved or well-maintained gravel, and passable in a regular car—you'll discover something of interest around almost every curve. In the spring, you'll enjoy vistas of wildflowers and flowering shrubs; in summer, endless panoramas of green hills and valleys; in fall, the magnificent display of yellows, reds, purples, and browns of the autumn leaves; in winter, with views unobstructed, the fairyland of rime ice on tree limbs and snow-covered mountaintops.

HIKING

Few if any other parks in the country offer so many and such diverse opportunities for hikers as do the Great Smokies. You can choose among short quiet walks, history trails, nature trails, waterfall trails, old-growth forest walks, riverside rambles, wildflower walks, and birding trails. There are easy hikes, day hikes, strenuous hikes, and weeklong backcountry treks. Altogether, there are some 150 different trails maintained in the park, covering over 800 mi. Among the most popular trails are Abrams Falls, Alum Cave, Chimney Tops, Forney Ridge, Laurel Falls, Little Cataloochee, Rainbow Falls, Ramsay Cascades, Smokemont Loop, and Trillium Gap. The Appalachian Trail itself meanders about 71 mi along the ridge tops of the park, more or less marking the boundary between the North Carolina and Tennessee sides of the park. Some of the more popular paths and trails are described in this book, and detailed information and maps can be obtained from any of the park visitor centers.

MOUNTAIN CULTURE

The Great Smoky Mountains National Park is unusual among national parks in that it has purposefully left in place some of the artifacts of mountain life and culture that existed before the land became a park. There are old houses, mountain cabins, barns, and churches preserved at Cades Cove, Cataloochee, and the Mountain Life Farm at the Oconaluftee Visitor Center. Historic gristmills operate at Cades Cove and near the Oconaluftee entrance to the park on the North Carolina side. A visit to the park is not just a chance to enjoy the wilderness; it is also an opportunity to learn something about the rich culture of the southern Appalachians. Outside the park there are museums, galleries, and crafts studios dedicated to preserving and extending the art, music, crafts, literature, and folk life of the Highlands.

WILDLIFE-WATCHING

With the great diversity in elevation and habitats in the Smokies, and some 400 species of mammals, birds, reptiles, and amphibians calling the park home, you have nearly limitless opportunities for wildlife viewing. Black bears and elk are the two big animals visitors hope to see, and often do. The best place to spot elk is the Cataloochee Valley. The best times to see wildlife are early in the morning and late in the afternoon. Look for out-of-place shapes and motions, keeping in mind that animals occupy all of the layers in a natural habitat. Use binoculars for close-up views. While out and about try to fade into the woodwork by keeping your movements limited and noise at a minimum. Never feed wild animals in the national park. Not only is it dangerous—it's illegal.

FAMILY FUN

The Great Smoky Mountains National Park is an ideal destination for families. Aside from the obvious outdoor fun of hiking and exploring the woods, families can horseback ride, take classes, and even go to camp together.

GREAT SMOKY MOUNTAINS INSTITUTE

The Great Smoky Mountains Institute is a residential environmental education center located in the park at Tremont. Using the park as a classroom, it offers in-depth education courses such as weekend programs, family camping, Elderhostel programs, and 3- to 5-day school group programs. The Institute also has a naturalist certification program, a native landscape certification program, and other professional-level classes.

HAYRIDES

You can take a hayride in the park. Well, sort of. Most hayrides are on a long trailer pulled by a heavy-duty diesel truck, not a horse-drawn wagon, and there's no hay in the trailer. With a convivial crowd it can be fun, however, and some hayrides are narrated by a park ranger. Unguided tours during the day cost $6 per person, leaving from the Cades Cove riding stables. There's a 15-person minimum. Guided hayrides also leave from the Cades Cove riding stables every evening in the summer and fall. The cost for a two-hour guided hayride is $8 per person. Hayrides also are offered occasionally at Smokemont stable. Advance reservations for both guided and unguided tours are required.

HORSEBACK RIDES

About 550 mi of the park's trails are open to horses. In the park are four commercial horse stables—at Cades Cove, Smokemont near Cherokee, Smoky Mountain near Gatlinburg, and Sugarlands also near Gatlinburg. You can rent a horse with riding gear for around $20 an hour. Stables are open mid-March through late November. Various age and weight limits apply. Five horse camps, where you can bring your own horse, are open April to early November. All five—Anthony Creek, Big Creek, Cataloochee, Round Bottom, and Tow String—have hitch racks and water for your horses, plus picnic tables, grills, pit or flush toilets, and space to pitch a tent.

RANGER PROGRAMS

Especially during summer months, the park presents a busy schedule of classes, programs, and walks led by park rangers. Kids ages 5–12 can become Junior Rangers, complete with a Junior Ranger badge.

SMOKY MOUNTAIN FIELD SCHOOL

The Smoky Mountain Field School is a partnership between the Great Smoky Mountains National Park and the University of Tennessee at Knoxville. The Field School offers workshops, classes, hikes, and other activities. For example, you can take a full-day class on orienteering (using a map and compass to find your way), a half-day class, ideal for kids, called Totally Buggy where you catch spiders and insects, or a day class on wildflower photography.

"UN-NATURAL" FUN

There comes a time on a national park vacation when you can't stand to see even one more wildflower or scramble up another nature trail. That's when you may turn to the "un-natural" attractions outside the park—amusement parks, go-kart tracks, miniature golf courses, and the like. For good or ill, around the park, especially on the Tennessee side in Gatlinburg, Sevierville, and Pigeon Forge, you'll find a plethora of these places. Yes, most are incredibly touristy, but kids do love them. Among the larger attractions on the Tennessee side are the inimitable Dollywood in Pigeon Forge, with 130 spic-n-span acres of carnival rides and music shows and Ober Gatlinburg ski resort and amusement park just above Gatlinburg. There are six Ripley's Believe-It-or-Not operations in Gatlinburg, eight go-kart tracks in Pigeon Forge alone, and uncountable mini-golf courses. Things are a little less touristy on the North Carolina side, but you can find plenty of kitsch, too, including Ghost Town in the Sky in Maggie Valley. In Cherokee, the very informative, not-for-profit Museum of the Cherokee Indian and the epic outdoor drama, *Unto These Hills* make for great family stops. The Great Smoky Mountains Railway runs train trips through the mountains, some pulled by real steam engines. The mountain resort city of Asheville offers respite from the kitsch. Intriguing mountain towns such as Brevard, Black Mountain, Highlands, Hendersonville, and Waynesville have many arts and crafts workshops and galleries to explore.

Exploring the Tennessee Side

2

WORD OF MOUTH

"Don't let the image (which is reality) of Pigeon Forge and Gatlinburg as tourist traps put you off the whole region. The Smokies are just an absolutely gorgeous place. There are more places to hike, picnic, and enjoy the mountains than you will have time for. Cade's Cove is gorgeous, you can also take horseback rides there, and we spent a lazy afternoon tubing in Townsend as well."

—Hellion

By Lan
Sluder

THE TENNESSEE SIDE IS THE active side of the Great Smokies. Here, you can shop, visit historical sites, try a different restaurant at every meal, tire the kids out at nearby theme parks, water slides, music theaters, mini-golf courses, and go-kart tracks, and tour the most popular parts of the park.

The so-called Smokies Corridor in Sevier (pronounced se-VERE) County runs through Pigeon Forge and Gatlinburg to the entrances of the western side of the park. Gatlinburg, the main gateway to and the location of the headquarters of the Great Smoky Mountains National Park, is nothing if not bustling. On some days, 35,000 or more visitors stay in Gatlinburg hotels and crowd the main street that's less than a mile long. While you can stay at a big chain motel in Gatlinburg, Pigeon Forge, or Sevierville, you can also camp at a remote backcountry site or, if you're lucky enough to get a reservation, stay at the hike-in LeConte Lodge, a rustic outpost you'll never forget.

Despite some of the downsides of mass tourism, towns at the edge of the park like Gatlinburg and Pigeon Forge serve an important, positive function: imagine if the hundreds of thousands, or even millions, of visitors who now stay in these towns had to be housed and fed within the park itself.

Even inside the park, the Tennessee side gets heavy action. Some 2 million people a year tour Cades Cove, and on a busy fall weekend the traffic on the Cades Cove Loop may remind you of midtown Manhattan. The Tennessee side also has the largest and busiest campgrounds and picnic areas.

If you prefer peace and quiet and natural beauty, all is not lost. With just a little bit of effort, you can find your way to lovely and little-visited parts of the Tennessee side of the park. Greenbrier, for example, is a picnicking paradise that's often virtually deserted. The Roaring Fork Motor Trail, a 5-mi winding road that passes historic buildings, old-growth forests, and waterfalls, is a delight, and the Foothills Parkway, a scenic, unfinished road along the western and southern edges of the park, is an undiscovered gem. Several of the best hiking trails in the park are also in Tennessee.

WHAT TO SEE

Cades Cove is first among sightseeing spots on the Tennessee side of the park. This broad valley with its preserved old buildings—pioneer homesteads and churches and the Cable Mill—is the most popular destination in the park. It's also one of the best places to see wildlife, including black bears.

Roaring Fork Motor Nature Trail (closed in winter) is a drivable tour that delivers both nature and history. The unfinished Foothills Parkway provides great views into the Smokies from its two sections, one on the western end of the park and the other on the northeast edge.

PARK ENTRANCES

Gatlinburg. Of all entrances to the park, this is the most used. The town of Gatlinburg has an unabashedly touristy, almost carnival-like atmosphere, with nearly every business—souvenir stores, fudge shops, Ripley's museums—focusing entirely on the tourist market, but it is redeemed by views of the Smokies in the near distance. To avoid Gatlinburg gridlock, take the Gatlinburg Bypass. This scenic route takes you around Gatlinburg and reconnects with U.S. 441 just inside the park near Sugarlands Visitor Center. If you're coming from North Carolina take the River Road bypass to avoid downtown Gatlinburg. ⚠ **Although Sevierville, Pigeon Forge, and Gatlinburg are all basically just small towns, the traffic, especially during the summer and fall, is definitely big city.** During peak tourist periods, it can take as long as two hours to drive 20 mi. On top of that, directional signs are often small and hard to spot, so it's easy to miss a turn. ✛ *From the north: from I–40 take Exit 407 (Sevierville) to TN 66 South; at the Sevierville intersection, continue straight onto U.S. 441 South; follow U.S. 441 (also known as Parkway) through Sevierville and Pigeon Forge into the park. From the south: from I–40, take Exit 443 to Foothills Parkway, then U.S. 321 to Gatlinburg.*

Townsend. Townsend is the closest park entrance to Cades Cove. More of a lightly developed commercial strip than a real town, you'll find a few gas stations, fast food outlets, independent motels, and private campgrounds. The Little River runs alongside the town from its headwaters in the park. Traffic is rarely a problem in Townsend, even on the busiest weekends. ✛ *From the north: from I–40 in Knoxville take Exit 386B to U.S. 129 South to Alcoa/*

The Tennessee Side

KEY

- 🏛 Ranger Station / Information
- ⛺ Campground
- 🏕 Picnic Area
- 🏇 Horseback Riding
- ✳ Scenic Viewpoint
- •••• Appalachian Trail
- ⋯⋯ Walking / Hiking Trails

TO KNOXVILLE, TN

TO KNOXVILLE & SEVIERVILLE, TN

Foothills Parkway

Pigeon Forge

Gatlinburg Welcome Center

Gatlinburg

Gatlinburg Bypass Rd

Campbell Overlook

441

416

321

Place of a Thousand Drips

Pittman

Greenbrier

Roaring Fork Motor Nature Trail

Cherokee Orchard Rd

Mount LeConte 6,593

LeConte Lodge

Newfound Gap Rd

Chimney Tops 4,755

Chimney Tops Overlook

Visitor Center

Sugarlands

Ober Gatlinburg Ski Resort

Great Smoky Mountains Institute

Little River Rd

Elkmont

441

Little River

Townsend

Cades Cove Loop Rd.

Cades Cove

Don Lawson Cabin

Visitor Center

Cades Cove

Look Rock

Abrams Creek

Spence Field

Thunderhead Mt 5,530

Silers Bald 5,620

Clingmans Dome 6,643

Andrews Bald 5,920

GREAT SMOKY MOUNTAINS NATIONAL PARK

Appalachian Trail

NORTH CAROLINA

TENNESSEE

TO ATLANTA, GA

TO NANTAHALA

Forney Creek

Fontana Lake

Shuckstack

Gregory Bald 4,949

Gregory Ridge Trail

Parson Branch Rd.

Gregory Bald Rd

NORTH CAROLINA

TENNESSEE

Charlies Bunion

Mt Kephart 6,150

Newfound Gap 5,048

Clingmans Dome Rd

Deep Creek

Mingus Mill

Visitor Center

Oconaluftee

Cherokee

CHEROKEE INDIAN RESERVATION

Pioneer Farmstead

441

Tow String

Big Cove Rd

Oconaluftee Overlook

Collins Creek

Smokemont

Oconaluftee River

Straight Fork Rd

Round Bottom

Luftee Knob 6,122

Mount Guyot 6,621

Old Black 6,356

Cosby Knob 5,145

Mount Sterling 5,842

Catalooche

TO ASHEVILLE, NC

CHEROKEE NATIONAL FOREST

Cosby

Cosby

Mt Cammerer 4,928

Big Creek

Cove Creek Rd

276

321

40

Foothills Parkway

Pigeon River

NORTH CAROLINA

TENNESSEE

0   5 km
0   5 mi

Maryville; at Maryville take U.S. 321 North/TN 73 East
through Townsend; continue straight on TN 73 into the
park. From the south: from I–75 take Exit 376 to I–140 E
towards Oak Ridge/Maryville; merge onto I–140 E via Exit
376B towards Maryville. Turn onto U.S. 129 South (Alcoa
Highway) at Exit 11A and go toward Alcoa; turn onto
TN 35 and follow it to U.S. 321 North; follow U.S. 321
North/TN 73 East through Townsend; continue straight
on TN 73 into the park.

VISITOR CENTERS

INSIDE THE PARK

Cades Cove. This visitor center is located about midway on
the 11-mi Cades Cove Loop. Rangers in the information
center will answer your questions and help you plan your
visit. There is also a bookstore, gift shop, restrooms (the
only ones on Cades Cove Loop Road), and a backcountry permit station here. What makes this visitor center
especially worth visiting is the Cable Mill, which operates
spring through fall, and the Becky Cable House, a pioneer
home with farm outbuildings. ✉*Cades Cove Loop Rd.*
☎*865/436–1200* ☉*Dec. and Jan., daily 9–4:30; Feb. and
Nov., daily 9–5; Mar., Sept., and Oct., daily 9–6; Apr.–
Aug., daily 9–7.*

Sugarlands. Sugarlands is the largest of the park visitor
centers (at least until the planned expansion of the Oconaluftee Visitor Center opens in 2011). Here you can watch a
20-minute film about the park and take in extensive exhibits
about park flora and fauna. Rangers are available to answer
questions and lead programs in summer and fall. There's a
large bookshop and gift shop, along with vending machines,
restrooms, and a backcountry permit station. ✉*U.S. 441,
2 mi inside the park* ☎*865/436–1200* ☉*Dec.–Feb., daily
8–4:30; Mar. and Nov., daily 8–5; Apr., May, Sept., and
Oct., daily 8–6; Jun.–Aug., daily 8–7.*

OUTSIDE THE PARK

Gatlinburg Downtown Welcome Center. In downtown Gatlinburg, this small welcome center has information on the
park. Parking is available in a lot behind the building.
✉*U.S. 441 at U.S. 321, Gatlinburg* ☎*800/343–1475 or
865/436–2392* ☉*Daily 10–6.*

Gatlinburg Welcome Center. The main Gatlinburg Department
of Tourism and Convention Center also functions as an
information clearinghouse for the Smokies, with rangers

GREAT ITINERARIES

TENNESSEE SIDE IN 1 DAY

Start early, pack a picnic lunch, and drive to the **Sugarlands Visitor Center** to orient yourself to the park. Head to the **Cades Cove Loop Road** and drive the 11-mi loop, stopping to explore the preserved farmsteads and churches. Spend some time in the **Cable Mill** area, visiting the grist mill, **Gregg-Cable House,** and other outbuildings. Depending on your timing, you can picnic at one of the stops in Cades Cove or Metcalf Bottoms. Take **Newfound Gap Road** up to **Newfound Gap**. Technically, **Clingmans Dome Road** is just over the state line, but if you've come this far you'll want to drive up. Stretch your legs and walk the .5-mi paved, but fairly steep, trail to the observation tower on **Clingmans Dome**. Return down Clingmans Dome and Newfound Gap roads and walk the self-guided trail around the **Noah "Bud" Ogle** farm. Then, proceed on to **Roaring Fork Motor Nature Trail**. Stop to explore the preserved cabins and other sites along the trail. At Auto Tour site number 5, park in the parking lot at the Trillium Gap trailhead and—if you have the time and are up to a moderate 2.6-mi (round-trip) hike—walk to **Grotto Falls**. Have dinner in **Gatlinburg** or **Pigeon Forge.**

TENNESSEE SIDE IN 3 DAYS

Follow the one-day itinerary to **Cades Cove**. Then, drive **Parson Branch Road** near Cable Mill and picnic in the woods. Turn right on U.S. 129 and drive part of the **"Tail of the Dragon,"** beloved of motorcyclists and sports car buffs for its many curves. At Chilhowee, turn right on **Foothills Parkway** and drive the 17.5-mi scenic parkway. Stop at **Look Rock** and take the short hike to the lookout tower. Have dinner in **Townsend**.

On Day 2, follow the one-day itinerary to **Newfound Gap** and **Clingmans Dome.** Have lunch at the **Chimneys** picnic area and walk the easy .75-mi trail. Keep following the itinerary to **Noah "Bud" Ogle** farm, **Roaring Fork Motor Nature Trail,** and **Grotto Falls** and have dinner in **Gatlinburg**.

On Day 3, depending on your interests, spend the day **horseback riding at Cades Cove**, river tubing **in Townsend, biking Cades Cove Loop Road, fishing the Little River,** or **hiking Alum Cave Bluffs**. Alternatively, drive to **Pigeon Forge** and take in **Dollywood**, the go-kart tracks, mini-golf, and other attractions of the town. Have dinner in **Pigeon Forge**.

available to answer questions. There's a large gift shop and bookstore. This is a major terminus for the Gatlinburg trolley system—if you're visiting Gatlinburg you can park here and take the trolley into and around town. ⊠ *811 E. Pkwy/U.S. 441 S., Gatlinburg* ☎ *800/343–1475 or 865/436–2392* ⊙ *Dec.–Mar., daily 8:30–5:30; Apr.–Nov., daily 8:30–7.*

Sevierville. Operated by the Sevierville Chamber of Commerce, this visitor center, with a bookstore and small gift shop, has information on the park as well as Sevierville and surrounding areas. ⊠ *TN 66, Sevierville* ☎ *888/738–4378 or 865/453–6411* ⊙ *Daily 8:30–5:30.*

Townsend. Located in a log building, this visitor center, operated by the Smoky Mountain Convention and Visitors Bureau, has a large gift shop with displays by local artists, along with a park ranger–staffed information desk. ⊠ *7906 E. Lamar Alexander Pkwy./U.S. Hwy. 321, Townsend* ☎ *800/525–6834 or 865/448–6134* ⊙ *Nov.–May, daily 9–5; June–Oct., daily 9–6.*

SCENIC DRIVES

★ **Fodor's Choice Cades Cove Loop Road.** This 11-mi loop through Cades Cove is the most popular route in the park and arguably the most scenic part of the entire Smokies. The one-way, one-lane paved road starts 7.3 mi from the Townsend entrance. Stop at the orientation shelter at the start of the loop and pick up a Cades Cove Tour booklet ($1.50). The drive begins with views over wide pastures to the mountains at the crest of the Smokies. Few other places in the Appalachians offer such views across wide valley bottoms with hayfields and wildflower meadows, framed by split-rail fences and surrounded by tall mountains. Along the way, you'll pass three 19th-century churches and many restored houses, log cabins, and barns. All are open for exploration. A highlight of the loop road, about midway, is the Cable Mill area, with a visitor center, working water-powered grist mill, and a restored farmstead. The Cades Cove Loop Road is also an excellent place to see wildlife, including black bears (especially in the late summer and fall), white-tailed deer, and wild turkeys. The road, open year-round, is closed from sunset to sunrise. ■TIP→**On Wednesday and Saturday mornings until 10 AM the loop is open only to bicyclists and walkers.** On almost any day, you can expect traffic delays, as passing points on the one-way road are few and far between, and if just one vehicle stops, scores of vehicles behind it also have to stop and wait. Allow at least two hours just to drive the loop, longer if you want to stop and explore the historic buildings.

Foothills Parkway. Foothills Parkway is a long-planned 72-mi scenic parkway that parallels the northern and western edges of the Great Smoky Mountains National Park. At this writing, only two sections of the parkway have been completed and opened to the public, a 17.5-mi western section from U.S. 321 near Townsend to U.S. 129 at Chilhowee Lake and a 5.6-mi portion from Cosby (at TN 32) to I–40. Another 9.5-mi section, as yet unpaved, is opened occasionally, for one weekend in the spring and fall. The 17.5-mi western section is particularly scenic, with stunning views of the western edge of the park. ■TIP→**Known as the "Tail of the Dragon" for its 318 curves in 11 mi, U.S. 129 is popular with motorcycle and sports car enthusiasts. It connects with the end of the Foothills Parkway at Chilhowee.**

OUCH. Visitors to the park often fear bears and snakes, but auto accidents and hiking mishaps are much more likely to cause injuries. Annually about 50 people are seriously injured in motor-vehicle accidents and 38 while walking or hiking. Sixteen injuries a year are bicycle-related and nine involve falls on waterfalls. Compare that to the one person on average injured by snake bite and none by bear attacks!

Newfound Gap Road. In a little over 14 mi Newfound Gap Road (U.S. 441) climbs over 3,500 feet from Gatlinburg to the gap through the crest of the Smokies at 5,046 feet. It takes you through Southern cove hardwood, pine-oak, and Northern hardwood forests to the spruce-fir forest at Newfound Gap. Unlike other roads in the park, Newfound Gap Road has mile markers, starting at the park entrance near Gatlinburg. Sugarlands Visitor Center is at MM 1.7. It's worth stopping at Chimneys picnic area (MM 6.2), even if you're not picnicking. A lovely stream, with huge boulders, cuts through the picnic area, and an easy .75-mi hiking trail takes you through a cove hardwood forest. At around mile marker 7, three overlooks provide a good view of Chimney Tops, two rock spires sticking out of the ridge line. Note the hundreds of dead fir trees, killed by the woolly adelgid, on the mountainsides. You'll probably see a lot of cars parked at Alum Cave trailhead (MM 10.4), which follows Alum Cave Creek to Arch Rock, a natural tunnel caused by weathering, and then to Alum Cave Bluffs, a site of a potash alum and epsomite mine briefly operated by Epsom Salts Company before the Civil War. The trail eventually leads to LeConte Lodge on Mt. LeConte. At Newfound Gap (MM 14.7), you can straddle the Tennessee–North Carolina state line and also hike some of the Appalachian Trail. The two-lane, paved Newfound Gap Road has a 45 MPH speed limit, with lower limits in some curvy areas. It is sometimes closed in winter due to ice and snow.

Parson Branch Road. This 8-mi unpaved road follows a wagon track that has been used for over 150 years. Some believe that Parson Branch and the road were named for ministers (parsons) who held religious retreats nearby, but others believe they were named for Joshua Parson, an early settler in the area. The road begins at the southwestern edge of Cades Cove Loop Road just beyond the visitor center at Cable Mill and comes out on U.S. 129. It is one-way from Cades Cove to U.S. 129. Although unpaved, it doesn't require four-wheel drive except after heavy rains, when a few sections may become flooded or muddy. ⚠ **A few areas are rocky, so avoid this road if you have a low-slung car with little ground clearance.** It offers no scenic vistas, but it runs through old-growth forests, with huge poplars and hemlocks along the roadway. To get back to the Townsend area, turn right as you come to U.S. 129, go about 10 mi on 129 and then take the 17.5-mi western portion of the Foothills Parkway back to U.S. 321. Parson Branch Road is closed December–March and sunset to sunrise.

★ **Roaring Fork Motor Nature Trail.** Roaring Fork offers a dramatic counterpoint to Cades Cove Loop Road. Where Cades Cove Loop meanders through a wide open valley, Roaring Fork closes in, with the forest sometimes literally just inches from your car's fender. The one-way, paved road is so narrow in places that RVs, trailers, and buses are not permitted. To get to Roaring Fork, from Parkway (U.S. 441) turn onto Historic Nature Trail at stop light number 8 in Gatlinburg and follow it to the Cherokee Orchard entrance of the park. The 6-mi Roaring Fork Motor Nature Trail starts just beyond the Noah "Bud" Ogle farmstead and the Rainbow Falls trailhead. Stop and pick up a Roaring Fork Auto Tour booklet ($1) at the information shelter. Numbered markers along the route are keyed to 16 stops highlighted in the booklet. Along the road are many opportunities to stop your car and get closer to nature. Among the sites are several old cabins and the Alfred Reagan place, which is painted in the original blue, yellow, and cream, "all three colors that Sears and Roebuck had," according to a story attributed to Mr. Reagan. At one point the roadside is littered with fallen and now decaying chestnut trees that were killed by the chestnut blight in the early part of the 20th century. There are several good hiking trails starting along the road, including Trillium Gap trail that leads to Mt. LeConte. The road follows Roaring Fork Creek a good part of the way, and the finale is a small waterfall called "The Place of a Thousand Drips," right beside the road. Roaring Fork Motor Nature Trail is closed in winter (usually December–March).

HISTORIC SIGHTS

★ Fodor'sChoice **Cades Cove.** The Cherokee name for this 6,800-acre valley is Tsiyahi, place of otters. Its English name may have come from a Cherokee chief called Kade, or possibly from the name of the wife of another chief, Abraham of Chilhowee, whose wife was called Kate. Under the terms of the Calhoun Treaty of 1819, the Cherokee forfeited their rights to Cades Cove, and the first white settlers came in the early 1820s. By the middle of the 19th century, well over 100 families lived in the cove, growing corn, wheat, oats, cane, and vegetables. For a while, when government-licensed distilleries were allowed in Tennessee, corn whisky was the major product of the valley, and even after Tennessee went dry in 1876 illegal moonshine was still produced. After the establishment of the park in the 1930s, many of the nearly 200 buildings were torn down to allow the land to revert to its natural state. However, in 1940 the Park Service decided that the human history of the valley was worth preserving. Since then, the bottomlands in the cove have been maintained as open fields and the remaining farmsteads and other structures have been restored to depict life in Cades Cove as it was from around 1825 to 1900. Today, Cades Cove has more historic buildings than any other area in the park. Driving, hiking, or biking the 11-mi Cades Cove Loop Road, you can see three old churches (Methodist, Primitive Baptist, and Missionary Baptist), a working grist mill (Cable Mill), a number of log cabins and houses in a variety of styles, and many outbuildings, including cantilevered barns, which used balanced beams to support large overhangs. ⊠*Cades Cove Loop Rd.* ☎*865/436–1200.*

Elkmont. What began as a logging town in the early years of the 20th century evolved into a summer colony for wealthy families from Knoxville, Chattanooga, and elsewhere in Tennessee. In 1910, Little River Lumber Company deeded a tract of 50 acres of land to some prominent Knoxvillians who belonged to a fishing and hunting club called the Appalachian Club. Later, exclusive hunting and fishing rights on a 40,000-acre tract above Elkmont were sold to the club. The Appalachian Club erected a clubhouse and many cottages were built as summer getaways. Other prominent east Tennessee families bought land here and built the Wonderland Hotel. In the 1920s, a debate broke out among property owners in Elkmont. Some owners wanted to keep the Elkmont area private, but others wanted the land to become part of the proposed national park. Eventually, the park won out and was established in 1934. The Elkmont community was placed on the National Registry of Historic Places in 1994. Today, Elkmont is primarily a campground, although some of the original 74 cottages remain along Jakes Creek and Little River. Most of the cottages are just south of the campground. The Wonderland Hotel, in disrepair, began to collapse in 2005–06, and the Park Service demolished most of what was left. The remains of the hotel, primarily a chimney, are just northwest of the campground. In recent years, the Park Service has been stabilizing and restoring several homes along Jakes Creek near the Elkmont campground. However, these and other cottages in the Elkmont area are still off-limits to visitors. About 19 cottages, plus the Appalachian Clubhouse, are expected to be restored, at a cost of over $5 million, and opened to the public, but more than 50 other cottages are slated to be torn down. ⊠ *Elkmont Campground, off Little River Rd. 4½ mi west of Gatlinburg entrance to park* ☎ *865/436–1200.*

Roaring Fork. You can visit several preserved mountain cabins and other buildings in the Roaring Fork area near Gatlinburg. Roaring Fork was settled by Europeans in the 1830s and '40s. The land was rocky and steep and not particularly well suited to farming. At its height around the turn of the 20th century, there were about two dozen families in the area. Most lived a simple, even hardscrabble existence, trying to scrape out a living from the rough mountain land. The Noah "Bud" Ogle self-guided nature trail, on Orchard Road just before entering the one-way Roaring Fork Motor Nature Trail, offers a walking tour of an authentic mountain farmstead and surrounding hardwood forest. Highlights include a log cabin, barn, streamside tub mill, and a wooden flume system to bring water to the farm. Among historic structures on the Motor Nature Trail, all open for you to explore, are the Jim Bales cabin, the Ephraim Bales cabin, and the Alfred Reagan house, one of the more "upscale" residences at Roaring Fork. ⊠*Orchard Rd. and Roaring Fork Motor Nature Trail* ☎*865/436–1200.*

SCENIC STOPS

Campbell Overlook. Named for Carlos Campbell, a conservationist who was instrumental in helping to establish the park, Campbell Overlook provides a good view up a valley to Bull Head peak and, farther up, to Balsam Point. An exhibit at the overlook explains the different types of forests within the park. ⊠*MM 3.9, Newfound Gap Rd. (U.S. 441).*

★ **Chimney Tops Overlook.** From any of the three overlooks grouped together on Newfound Gap Road, you'll have a good view of the Chimney Tops—twin peaks that cap 2,000-foot-high cliffs. You also see hundreds of dead fir and spruce trees, along with some dead hemlocks, victims of woolly adelgids and air pollution. ⊠*MM 7.1, Newfound Gap Rd. (U.S. 441).*

★ **Dan Lawson Cabin.** From many points along the 11-mi, one-way Cades Cove Loop Road, you'll enjoy iconic views of the broad Cades Cove valley. The Park Service keeps hayfields and pastures cleared, so you can see how the valley may have looked in the late 19th century when it was farmed by more than 100 families. Typical is the view across the valley from the front porch of the Dan Lawson cabin, the original portion of which was built in 1856. ⊠*6.6 mi from the beginning of Cades Cove Loop Rd.*

Gatlinburg Bypass Overlook. The Gatlinburg Bypass is a 4-mi roadway that connects Newfound Gap Road within the park a little north of Sugarlands Visitor Center and U.S. 441 just north of Gatlinburg going toward Pigeon Forge. It tracks around the side of Mt. Harrison. ■TIP→ **Take the Bypass to avoid the stop-and-go traffic of downtown Gatlinburg when leaving or entering the park.** The second overlook when headed out of the park toward Pigeon Forge has the best views of Gatlinburg and Mt. LeConte beyond. ⊠*Gatlinburg Bypass.*

CLOSE UP

Smokies By Number

9,000,000: Visitors annually to Great Smoky Mountains National Park

8,500,000: Visitors who don't venture into the backcountry

2,000,000: Visitors to Cades Cove annually

1,350,000: Visitors in July (the busiest month)

521,866: Acres of land in the park

300,000: Visitors in January (the least busy month)

200,000: Visitors who hike to waterfalls in the park

100,000: Different species of life forms in the park

90,000: Acres covered by hemlocks subject to infestation by hemlock woolly adelgid

77,000: Backcountry camping nights annually

6,643: Elevation in feet of highest peak in the Smokies, Clingmans Dome

6,000: White-tailed deer in the park

2,115: Miles of rivers, creeks, and streams in the park

1,660: Kinds of wildflowers and other flowering plants in the park

1,500: Black bears in the park

947: Individual campsites in developed campgrounds

784: Picnic tables (not counting group pavilions)

240: Species of birds spotted in the park

150: Hiking trails in the park

95: Elk in the park

85: Average inches of annual precipitation at Clingmans Dome

80: Historic buildings preserved in the park

69: Average inches of snow annually at Newfound Gap

50: Minimum number of yards to stay away from bears and elk

30: Salamander species in the park

2: Bears per square mile in the park

1: Hotels in the park

0: Average number of serious injuries to park visitors from bear attacks annually

Gregory Bald. From almost 5,000 feet on Gregory Bald, you have a breathtaking view of Cades Cove and Rich Mountain to the north, and the Nantahala and Yellow Creek mountains to the south. You can also see Fontana Lake to the southeast. Many hybrid rhododendrons grow on and around the bald. Gregory Bald is one of only two balds in the Smokies that are being kept cleared of tree growth by the Park Service. This is a view that just a few thousand people a year will see, as it's reachable only by a hike of more than 5 mi. ⊹*Hike the Gregory Ridge Trail (5.5 mi) from Cades Cove.*

★ **Look Rock.** The overlooks looking east on the western section of the Foothills Parkway, around Look Rock, have remarkable views. This is also a great spot to enjoy the sunrise over the Smokies. ■TIP→**Star gazers gather at the five overlooks south of the Look Rock exit where light pollution is especially low.** ⊠*Look Rock Overlook, Foothills Parkway West.*

Roaring Fork Motor Nature Trail Site No. 3. While most of the Roaring Fork Motor Nature Trail takes you on a narrow and winding one-way road, through forested areas where the views are limited, at the beginning of the drive the first and second overlooks present good views of the distant mountain ridges. The best scenery is from the second overlook, marked as the number 3 site on the Roaring Fork auto tour. ⊠*Number 3 Tour Stop, Roaring Fork Motor Nature Trail.*

DAY HIKES

The park has more than 800 mi of hiking trails, of which about one-half are on the Tennessee side. The trails range from short nature walks to long, strenuous hikes that gain several thousand feet in elevation. Park trails are maintained, but on many trails maintenance is seasonal. Be prepared for trail erosion and washouts, especially December through May when staffing levels may not permit much trail work.

Although permits are not required for day hikes, **you must have a backcountry permit for overnight or longer trips** (⇨*see Permits in the Travel Smart Great Smoky Mountains chapter at the end of this book*).

Some of the more popular trails on the Tennessee side are listed in this chapter; more detailed information and maps can be obtained from visitor centers at the park. Also, rangers can help design a trip to suit your abilities.

Keep in mind that the park has significant elevation changes and that some summer days, especially at lower elevations, can be hot and humid. Also, high ozone levels are an issue on some days. Together, these can pose problems for people who aren't in good shape or who have heart or respiratory problems. ⚠ **Be realistic about your physical condition. Carry**

CLOSE UP

Temperate Rain Forest

When you think about rainforests, you may picture the lush tropical Amazon. But parts of the Great Smokies are considered rainforests, too—temperate ones. Temperate rainforests are either coniferous or broadleaf forests that occur in the temperate zone and receive high rainfall. Most of the temperate rainforests in North America are in oceanic-moist climates on west-facing mountains near the Pacific coast, from southeastern Alaska through British Columbia, Washington State, and Oregon to central California. However, the highest elevations of the Smokies qualify, too, as these areas get as much as 85 inches of rain a year. The Smokies are hundreds of miles from an ocean, but weather systems coming from the west and the Gulf of Mexico cause orographic precipitation. Orographic precipitation occurs when an air mass is forced from a low elevation to a higher elevation—the western edge of the park is under 2,000 feet in elevation and Clingmans Dome at the crest of the Smokies is over 6,600 feet—as it moves over rising terrain. As the air mass gains elevation it expands and cools. This cooler air cannot hold the moisture as well as warm air, which raises the relative humidity to near 100%, creating clouds and locally heavy precipitation. Some parts of the nearby Pisgah, Nantahala, and Chattahoochee national forests also are considered temperate rainforests.

plenty of water and energy-rich foods like GORP (good old raisins and peanuts), energy bars, and fruit.

Weather in the park is subject to rapid change. A day in spring or fall might start out warm and sunny, but by the time you reach a mile-high elevation the temperature may be near freezing, and it could be snowing heavily. The higher elevations of the park can get up to 85 inches of precipitation annually. ⚠ **Dress in layers, and be prepared for temperature changes, snow in winter, and rain anytime.** Be sure to allow plenty of time to complete your hike before dark. As a rule of thumb, when hiking in the Smokies you'll travel only about 1.5 mi per hour, so a 10-mi hike will take almost 7 hours. Remember, dogs and other pets are not allowed on most park trails.

SPOTLIGHT HIKE: ALUM CAVE BLUFFS

One of the best and most popular hikes, the fairly short 2.3-mi one-way hike (4.6 mi round-trip) to Alum Cave Bluffs contains some of the most interesting geological formations in the Smokies. Arch Rock, a natural arch created by millions of years of freezing and thawing, and Alum Bluffs, a large overhanging rock ledge, are the highlights. This very well-known trail does not offer much solitude, especially on weekends. From the bluffs you can continue on another 2.8 mi and reach Mt. LeConte, passing awe-inspiring mountain vistas. This additional section of the trail is difficult and steep. Alum Cave Bluffs is the shortest of five trail routes to LeConte Lodge, but it is the steepest, with an elevation gain of over 2,700 feet. The elevation gain to Alum Cave is only about 1,125 feet. ✉*Trailhead is well-marked, with a large parking lot on the east side of Newfound Gap Rd. at MM 10.4* ☞*Moderate to Difficult.*

0.1 MI: ALUM CREEK
Cross Alum Cave Creek on a small bridge. The creek floods frequently and the rushing waters clear out the undergrowth and moss found on many other park creeks. The trail takes you through birch and hemlock, many of the latter dying from the woolly adelgid infestation.

1.3 MI: ARCH ROCK
Cross Styx Branch, named for the River Styx, over a footbridge. In Greek mythology, the River Styx was the river dividing the earth and the underworld (make a run for it if you see Charon, the ferryman who transports the souls of the dead into the underworld!). Turn left to Arch Rock which will lead you through the arch. It was formed by the alternate freezing and thawing of water trapped in the rock over long periods.

1.9 MI: INSPIRATION POINT
Almost 2 mi in, you'll cross a small heath bald onto a flat area of outcropping rock called Inspiration Point. There's a good view of Sugarland Mountain to the west.

2.3 MI: ALUM CAVE BLUFFS
Climb the steep steps up to Alum Cave, which is not a cave but a large bluff, about 85 or 90 feet high and 500 feet wide. In winter huge icicles often hang from the top of the bluff. The name comes from deposits of alum, a chemical compound formerly used in a variety of industrial processes including dyeing. Before the Civil War, the Epsom Salts

Manufacturing Co. was formed to mine alum, Epsom salt, saltpeter, magnesia, and copperas at the site, but production never reached a profitable commercial level. Peregrine falcons were reintroduced into the Smokies starting in 1984, and several nesting pairs have been seen on the ridges near Alum Cave. From here you can turn back or continue on to Mt. LeConte.

2.5 MI: GRACIE'S PULPIT

The first .5 mi beyond the bluffs is the single steepest portion of the hike, and included in this section is Gracie's Pulpit. Formerly called Devil's Pulpit, it was renamed for Gracie McNichol, who reportedly hiked the trail on her 92nd birthday. The pulpit roughly marks the halfway point of the Alum Cave Bluff Trail. In clear weather, you can get a good view of the four peaks of Mt. Le Conte (West Point, Cliff Tops, High Top, and Myrtle Point).

4 MI: GRASSY SLIDE

Trout Branch crosses the trail at Grassy Slide, at about 6,000 feet. The grassy area is home to many wildflowers, and there are good views of Newfound Gap and Clingmans Dome.

5.1 MI: LECONTE LODGE

LeConte Lodge, at 6,360 feet, marks the end of the main Alum Cave Bluffs trail. There are three slightly higher peaks beyond the lodge. Cliff Tops is the best peak for sunsets, and Myrtle Point for sunrises. If you are not staying the night at the rustic lodge (advance reservations are essential ⇨ *see Chapter 4: Lodging and Dining*), you can either return the way you came down Alum Cave Bluffs, or take one of the other four trails back down the mountains. Trillium Gap is 6.5 mi, with a 3,000-foot elevation change, and Bull Head is 7.5 mi, with a 4,000-foot elevation change. The Boulevard Trail is 8.8 mi, with only a 1,700-foot elevation change, but it has many steep grades up and down. Rainbow Falls has many loose rocks and is generally not considered a safe way to descend.

SPOTLIGHT HIKE: GREGORY RIDGE TRAIL

In early summer, this hike through old-growth forests to Gregory Bald offers an astounding display of hybrid flame azalea. When there are three or more varieties of rhododendrons in an area, as at Gregory Bald, they crossbreed, creating dozens of hybrid varieties with different colored blossoms. This is a popular hike during peak azalea bloom.

CLOSE UP

Ask a Ranger: Tips for Hiking Safely

Here are some hiking safety tips to keep in mind even on short day hikes:

■ Let a responsible person know your route and return time. Have them contact the park at ☎ 865/436–1230 if you do not return within a reasonable time.

■ Always hike with another person. Keep your hiking party together and stay on officially maintained trails.

■ Keep children in your sight at all times—do not allow them to get ahead of you or fall behind.

■ Carry a current park trail map and know how to read it.

■ Carry two small flashlights or headlamps—even on a day hike. If you have trouble on the trail, darkness may fall before you can finish your hike.

■ Take adequate water—you'll need a minimum 2 quarts per person per day. All water obtained from the backcountry should be treated either by filtering or boiling.

■ Carry a small first aid kit.

■ Check the weather forecast and be prepared for quickly changing conditions. Call ☎

865/436–1200 Ext. 630 for park weather information.

■ Wear shoes or boots that provide good ankle support.

■ Avoid hypothermia by keeping dry. Avoid cotton clothing. Dress in layers that can be easily removed or added as you heat up or cool down. Always carry a wind-resistant jacket and rain gear—even on sunny days.

■ In winter, many trails will be covered in ice. Use crampons or other traction devices on your boots.

■ Don't attempt to cross rain-swollen streams; they will recede rapidly after precipitation stops and the wait may save your life. When crossing any stream more than ankle-deep: unbuckle the waist strap of your pack so you can remove it quickly if you fall into deep water, wear shoes, and use a staff to steady yourself.

■ Be especially careful around waterfalls. Walking on slick rocks can result in a dangerous, even fatal, fall.

■ Be aware of parking lot thieves. Lock your car and take your valuables with you, or leave them at home.

Even if you miss the rhododendron in bloom, Gregory Bald has great views of Cades Cove, Fontana Lake, and the surrounding mountains. Gregory Bald is named for Russell Gregory, a pre–Civil War Cades Cove settler who at one time had a cabin on the bald. Parts of the hike are strenu-

ous because of the elevation gain, about 2,700 fe
total distance round-trip is 11.2 mi. Get an early st
you're doing this as a day hike. A slightly easier approac
to Gregory Bald is via the Gregory Bald trail from Parsons
Branch Road, about 9 mi round-trip with a 2,200-foot
elevation gain. ☒ *Forge Creek Rd.* ✛*From the start of the*
Cades Cove Loop Rd., drive 5.4 mi and turn right on Forge
Creek Rd., immediately past the parking area for Cable
Mill. Follow Forge Creek Rd. 2.2 mi to the Gregory Ridge
trailhead ☞ *Difficult.*

1.4 MI: FORGE CREEK CROSSING
This is the first of three creek crossings you'll make on
footbridges. Nearby is Coalen Ground Ridge, named for
the charcoal that was made here to fuel a forge on Forge
Creek.

1.6 MI: OLD-GROWTH FOREST
Just after you make the second crossing of Forge Creek,
you'll come to a stand of old-growth tulip poplars, some
4 feet or more in diameter. At about 2 mi, after the third
creek crossing, you'll see campsite 12, a pleasant spot,
though a good deal of foot traffic passes by it.

2 MI: CLIMB BEGINS
The next 3 mi is the steep part of the hike, in heavy woods
for the first 2 mi. The altitude gain is almost 800 feet per
mile, from 2,600 feet near campsite 12 to 5,000 feet at
Gregory Bald.

4 MI: VIEWS OPEN UP
At this point, the views begin to open up, and for the next
1 mi there are beautiful views of the backbone of the Smokies. The open meadow in the distance is Spence Field, with
the peak of Thunderhead Mountain above it.

5 MI: JUNCTION WITH GREGORY BALD TRAIL
At 5 mi, you reach the junction with Gregory Bald trail,
coming from Parsons Branch Road. If you turn left onto
Gregory Bald trail, in 2 mi you will reach the Appalachian
Trail. Instead, turn right (west) and go about .7 mi to
Gregory Bald.

5.6 MI: GREGORY BALD
The last .5 mi to Gregory Bald, along a ridge line, is fairly
steep. The bald is carpeted with mountain oat grass, and
there are splashes of color everywhere during the azalea
bloom. In the distance, Cades Cove is to the northeast, the
Joyce Kilmer Wilderness is to the southwest, and Fontana

e south. To return, backtrack on Gregory Ridge
lhead at Forge Creek Road or descend 4 mi on
Bald trail to Sams Gap on Parsons Branch Road.
till have about 4 mi on the Parsons Branch gravel
to your vehicle at Forge Creek.

OTHER HIKES

EASY

Elkmont Nature Trail. This 1-mi loop is good for families, especially if you're camping at Elkmont. Pick up a self-guided
brochure (50¢) at the start of the trail. ⊠*Near Elkmont
campground* ☞*Easy.*

Gatlinburg Trail. This is one of only two trails in the park
(the other one is Oconaluftee River Trail on the North
Carolina side) where dogs are permitted. ■TIP→**Dogs must
be on leashes.** The trail, which starts at Sugarlands Visitor
Center, follows the Little Pigeon River. The first .3 mi of
the 1.9-mi trail is through the park headquarters and on
a service road. The total round-trip distance is 3.8 mi.
⊠*Trailhead at Sugarlands Visitor Center* ☞*Easy.*

Laurel Falls. Mostly paved, this trail is easy except for the
last .75 mi, which is moderate. It takes you past a series of
cascades to a 60-foot waterfall and a stand of old-growth
forest. The trail is extremely popular in summer and on
weekends almost anytime (trolleys from Gatlingburg stop
here), so don't expect solitude. ■TIP→ **The 1.3-mi paved
trail to the falls is wheelchair accessible.** Wooden posts mark
every tenth of a mile and the total round-trip hike is 4.1 mi.
⊠*Trailhead is on the west side of Little River Rd. between
Sugarlands Visitor Center and Elkmont campground, about
3.9 mi west of Sugarlands* ☞*Easy to Moderate.*

★ **Little River.** This 7.5-mi trail (round-trip) offers a little of
everything—historical buildings, fly-fishing, a waterfall,
and wildflowers. The first part of the trail wanders past
remnants of old logging operations and dilapidated cottages that were once the summer homes of wealthy Tennesseans (currently closed to the public). Huskey Branch
Falls appears at about 2 mi. The Little River trail passes the
junction with three other trails, offering the possibility for
even longer hikes—Cucumber Gap at 2.3 mi, Huskey Gap
at 2.7 mi, and Goshen Prong trail at 3.7 mi. At any point
you can try your hand at fly-fishing for trout in the Little
River, one of the best trout streams in the park. ■TIP→**This
is the habitat of the synchronous fireflies, which put on their light**

Tennessee Hikes

KEY

🏠 Ranger Station / Information

⛺ Campground

🏕 Picnic Area

🏇 Horseback Riding

✿ Scenic Viewpoint

••••• Appalachian Trail

······· Walking / Hiking Trails

CHEROKEE NATIONAL FOREST

Foothills Parkway

Cosby

Big Creek

Cataloochee

Mount Sterling 5,842

Cherokee Knob 5,145

Camperer 6,028

Mt.

Cosby

Old Black 6,356

Mount Guyot 6,621

Luftee Knob 6,122

Round Bottom

Straight Fork Rd.

TENNESSEE / NORTH CAROLINA

Tow String

Pioneer Farmstead

CHEROKEE INDIAN RESERVATION

Cherokee

Mingus Mill

Oconaluftee

Visitor Center

Smokemont

Collins Creek

Oconaluftee Overlook

Newfound Gap 5,048

Mt Kephart 6,150

LeConte Lodge

Charlies Bunch

6,593

Mount LeConte 6,593

Alum Cave Bluffs

Alum Cave Bluffs

Grotto Falls

Trillium Gap Trail

Roaring Fork Motor Nature Trail

Greenbrier

Place of a Thousand Drips

Pittman Center

Cherokee Orchard Rd.

Campbell Overlook

Pigeon Forge

Gatlinburg Welcom Center

Gatlinburg

Sugarlands

Visitor Center

Great Smoky Mountains Institute

Ober Gatlinburg Ski Resort

Sugarlands Trail

Gatlinburg Trail

Elkmont

Little River Trail

Little River

Laurel Falls Trail

Chimney Tops

Chimney Tops Trail

Indian Gap

Clingmans Dome Rd.

Newfound Gap Rd.

Chimney Tops Overlook

Clingmans Dome 6,643

Andrews Bald 5,920

Silers Bald 5,620

Spence Field

Thunderhead Mtn 5,530

GREAT SMOKY MOUNTAINS NATIONAL PARK

Appalachian Trail

Cades Cove

Cades Cove Loop Rd.

Dan Lawson Cabin

Cades Cove Visitor Center

Abrams Creek

Abrams Falls Trail

Abrams Falls

Look Rock

Foothills Parkway

Townsend

Little River

Forge Creek Rd.

Parson Bald

Gregory Bald 4,949

Gregory Ridge Trail

Gregory Bald Trail

Shuckstack

TENNESSEE / NORTH CAROLINA

TO KNOXVILLE & SEVIERVILLE, TN

TO KNOXVILLE, TN

TO ASHEVILLE, NC

TO NANTAHALA

TO ATLANTA, GA

Eagle Creek

0   5 mi

0   5 km

show on June evenings. ⊠*Trailhead is near Elkmont camp-ground. Turn left just before entrance to campground and go .6 mi to a fork in the road. The trail is a continuation of the left fork* ☞*Easy to Moderate.*

★ **Noah "Bud" Ogle Nature Trail.** Settlers Noah "Bud" Ogle and
🕑 his wife, Cindy, built a cabin and started farming here in 1879. Although this is more of a nature walk than a hike, it offers a lot in a .75-mi loop. You'll see the Ogle Tub Mill on LeConte Creek, lots of wildflowers, and the Ogle cabin and barn, which you can explore. It's a fine trail for families with kids. ⊠*Cherokee Orchard Rd., just before entering the Roaring Fork Motor Nature Trail* ☞*Easy.*

Sugarlands Trail. The easiest trail in the park, it's only .25-mi long (.5 mi round-trip), virtually level, and paved, so it's suitable for young children, strollers, and wheelchairs. A brochure available at the start of the trail (50¢) explains the numbered exhibits and features of the trail. ⊠*Trailhead is .3 mi south of Sugarlands Visitor Center on Newfound Gap Rd. (U.S. 441)* ☞*Easy.*

MODERATE

★ **Abrams Falls.** This 5-mi round-trip trail is one of the most popular in the Smokies, in part due to the trailhead location at Cades Cove, which gets more than 2 million visitors a year. Beginning at the wooden bridge over Abrams Creek, the trail first goes along a pleasant course through rhododendron. It becomes somewhat steep at a couple of points, especially near Arbutus Ridge. The path then leads above Abrams Falls and down to Wilson Creek. Though only about 20 feet high, the falls are beautiful, with a good volume of water and a broad pool below. ⊠*For trailhead, park in the large parking lot on an unpaved side road between signposts 10 and 11 on Cades Cove Loop Rd.* ☞*Moderate.*

★ **Appalachian Trail at Newfound Gap.** For those who want to say they hiked part of the AT, this section is a great place to start; it's easy to get to and not too steep. From Newfound Gap to Indian Gap the trail goes 1.7 mi through spruce-fir high-elevation forest, and in late spring and summer there are quite a few wildflowers along the trail. The total round-trip distance is 3.4 mi. ⊠*Park at Newfound Gap parking lot and cross Newfound Gap Rd. (U.S. 441) to the AT trailhead* ☞*Moderate.*

Trillium Gap Trail to Grotto Falls. Grotto Falls is the only water-fall in the park that you can walk behind. The Trillium Gap trail, off of the Roaring Fork Motor Nature Trail, which leads to Grotto Falls, is primarily through a hemlock for-est. With an easy slope and only 1.3 mi long, this trail is suitable for novice hikers. The total round-trip distance is 2.6 mi. The Motor Nature Trail is closed in winter. ✉*Take the Roaring Fork Motor Nature Trail to stop number 5 on the auto tour and the trailhead for Trillium Gap trail* ↪*Moderate.*

DIFFICULT

★ **Chimney Tops.** Pant, wheeze, and gasp. This is a steep trail that will take a lot out of you, but it gives back a lot, too. The payoff for the difficult climb is one of the best views in the Smokies, from the top of Chimney Tops. In places the trail has loose rock, and the elevation gain is 1,350 feet. ⚠ **This trail is not recommended for small children.** The total distance round-trip is 4 mi. ✉*Trailhead is about halfway between Sugarlands Visitor Center and Newfound Gap, 6.7 mi south of Sugarlands on Newfound Gap Rd. (U.S. 441)* ↪*Difficult.*

SUMMER SPORTS & ACTIVITIES

BICYCLING

The park has no mountain biking trails, and bicycles are not permitted on most hiking trails, but the Smoky Mountains offer good bicycling on back roads. Tennessee requires that children age 16 and under wear a helmet, and it's strongly recommended that all riders do so, regardless of age.

★ **Cades Cove.** Arguably the best place to bike, the 11-mi loop road is mostly level and being on a bike allows you to get around traffic back-ups. However, traffic can be heavy, especially on weekends in summer and fall, and the road is narrow. ■TIP➔**The best time to bike the Cove is from mid-May to mid-September on Wednesday and Saturday mornings until 10 AM when it is closed to motor vehicles.** Bicycles and helmets can be rented ($20 per day) in summer and fall at an annex behind Cades Cove Campground Store (✉*Cades Cove Campground* ☎*865/448–9034*).

TENNESSEE HIKES

	Grade	Miles (one-way)	Elevation Gain (feet)	Horses	Campground	Open Info	Water	Ranger Station	Toilet	Level	Conditions
Abrams Falls Trail	Level to Moderately Steep	2.5	200	N	Y	Y/R*	Y**	Y	Y	Mod.	Good
Alum Cave Bluffs Trail	Slightly to Very Steep	5.1	2580	N	N	Y/R*	Y**	N	N	Mod to Diff.	Good
Appalachian Trail at Newfound Gap	Somewhat Steep	1.7	1000	N	N	Y/R*	Y	N	N	Mod.	Good
Chimney Tops Trail	Steep	2.0	1350	N	N	Y/R*	Y**	N	N	Diff.	Good
Elkmont Nature Trail	Mostly Level	1.0 Loop	120	N	Y	Y/R	Y	Y	Y	Easy	Good
Gatlinburg Trail	Level	1.9	100	N	N	Y/R	Y	Y	Y	Easy	Good

* access road occasionally closed due to snow and ice in winter

** water should be purified

Y/R=year-round

TENNESSEE HIKES (CONT.)

	Grade	Miles (one-way)	Elevation Gain (feet)	Horses	Camp-ground	Open Info	Water	Ranger Station	Toilet	Level	Conditions
Gregory Ridge Trail	Slightly to Very Steep	5.6	2170	N	Y	Y/R	Y**	Y	Y	Diff.	Good
Laurel Falls Trail	Level to Slightly Steep	2.0	200	N	N	Y/R	Y**	N	N	Easy to Mod.	Good
Little River Trail	Lev el to Moderately Steep	3.7	1000	N	Y	Y/R	Y	Y	Y	Easy to Mod.	Good
Noah "Bud" Ogle Trail	Mostly Level	.75 Loop	160	N	N	Y/R	Y	Y	N	Easy	Good
Sugarlands Trail	Level	.25	100	N	N	Y/R	Y	Y	Y	Easy	Paved
Trillium Gap Trail to Grotto Falls	Slightly Steep	1.3	560	Y	N	Closed Winter	Y**	N	N	Mod.	Good

* access road occasionally closed due to snow and ice in winter
** water should be purified
Y/R=year-round

Foothills Parkway West. The 17.5-mi road has light vehicular traffic and is a scenic and fairly safe place for bicycling. Safe biking also is available on the lightly used access roads to **Greenbrier** picnic area and **Cosby** campground.

MOUNTAIN BIKING

Cherokee National Forest. Mountain biking is available in the nearby Cherokee National Forest, which encompasses 640,000 acres in eastern Tennessee, stretching from Chattanooga to Bristol along the North Carolina border. ⊠*2800 North Ocoee St., Cleveland, TN* ☎*423/476–9700.*

Gatlinburg Trail. This is the only hiking trail on the Tennessee side where bikes are permitted. The trail travels 1.9 mi (one-way) from the Sugarlands Visitor Center to the outskirts of Gatlinburg. Pets on leashes are also allowed on this trail.

Parsons Branch Road. The unpaved, narrow, one-lane back road that twists and dips from near Cable Mill on the Cades Cove Loop Road to U.S. 129, appeals to mountain bikers.

FISHING

There are over 200 mi of wild trout streams on the Tennessee side of the park. Trout streams are open to fishing year-round. Among the best trout streams on the Tennessee side are Little River, Abrams Creek, and Little Pigeon River. Often, the best fishing is in higher elevation streams, in areas that are more difficult to reach. Streams that are easily accessible, such as parts of the Little River, have greater fishing pressure.

FISHING RULES

To fish in the park you must possess a valid fishing license or permit from either Tennessee or North Carolina, but a trout stamp is not required. Children under 13 don't need a license. Fishing licenses are not available in the park, but may be purchased in nearby towns, online, or by telephone.

Only artificial flies or lures with a single hook can be used— no live bait. Fishing is permitted from a half hour before official sunrise to a half hour after official sunset. The limit is five brook, rainbow, or brown trout, smallmouth bass, or a combination of these, each day or in possession, regardless of whether they are fresh, stored in an ice chest, or otherwise preserved. Twenty rock bass may be kept in addition to the above limit.

The minimum size is 7 inches for brook, rainbow, and brown trout and also 7 inches for smallmouth bass. For rock bass there is no minimum size.

LICENSES

Tennessee Wildlife Resources Agency. A Tennessee fishing license is valid throughout the park and also for fishing in other areas of Tennessee. A 3-day non-resident fishing license good for all types of fish including trout is $33.50, a 10-day is $50.50, and an annual non-resident license is $81. An extra fee is charged for paying with a credit card. Licenses for Tennessee residents vary, but cost less.
■TIP→ **For non-residents, North Carolina fishing licenses are significantly cheaper, and since either NC or TN licenses are good anywhere in the park, you'll save by buying a NC license.** ⇨*See Fishing, in Chapter 3: Exploring the North Carolina Side.* ✉*TWRA Sales Office, Box 41729, Nashville, TN 37204* ☎*888/814–8972* ⊕*www.wildlifelicense.com/tn.*

OUTFITTERS

For backcountry trips, you may want to hire a guide. Full-day trips cost about $200–$300 for one angler, $240–$350 for two. Only guides approved by the National Park Service are permitted to take anglers into the park backcountry.

Little River Outfitters (✉*106 Town Square Dr., Townsend, TN* ☎*877/448–3474 or 865/448–9459* ⊕*littleriveroutfitters.com*) is a park-licensed fishing guide that has been in business since 1984 and specializes in teaching beginners to fly-fish.

Rocky Top Outfitters (✉*2611 Ruth Hall Rd., Pigeon Forge, TN* ☎*865/661–3474* ⊕*www.rockytopoutfitter.com*) offers fly or spin trout fishing trips.

Smoky Mountain Angler (✉*466 Brookside Village Way, Suite 8, Gatlinburg, TN* ☎*865/436–8746* ⊕*www.smokymountainangler.com*) offers half-day and full-day trips with up to three people per guide.

HORSEBACK RIDING

Several hundred miles of backcountry trails on the Tennessee side are open to horseback riders. Horses are restricted to trails specifically designated for horse use; check the park trail map ($1) for horse trails and rules and regulations about riding in the backcountry. You can also download a map from ⊕*www.nps.gov/grsm/planyourvisit/ horseriding.htm.*

If you bring a horse to a horse camp or ride a horse in the park, you must have either the original or a copy of an official negative test for equine infectious anemia (called a Coggins test). Pets are permitted in the horse camps but must be on a leash.

Anthony Creek is a drive-in horse camp at Cades Cove campground with three campsites. Three park concession stables are located on the Tennessee side—Cades Cove, Sugarlands, and Smoky Mountain Riding Stables near Gatlinburg—offering guided horseback rides at $20 to $25 an hour. Weight limit for riders is generally 225 pounds. Reservations are not available except for large groups.

HORSE CAMPS

Anthony Creek. Cades Cove has three horse camping sites (tents only), with pit toilets, picnic tables, fire rings, designated parking, refuse containers, and hitch racks. Water is available for horses, and potable water for human consumption is available nearby at Cades Cove campground. Each campsite has a limit of six people and four horses. Reservations are required and can be made as far as six months in advance. ⊠*Cades Cove campground, past the picnic area and through the gate to Anthony Creek trail* ☎877/444–6777 ⊕*www.nps.gov/grsm/planyourvisit/horse-camps.htm* ☜$20 ☉*Apr.–Oct.*

OUTFITTERS

Cades Cove Riding Stables (⊠*Cades Cove Campground* ☎865/448–6286 ☉*Mar.–Oct.*) offers carriage rides and hayrides in addition to horseback riding.

Smoky Mountain Riding Stables (⊠*U.S. 321, Gatlinburg, TN* ☎865/436–5634 ⊕*www.smokymountainridingstables.com* ☉*Mid-Mar.–late Nov.*) has been in business for 20 years and has 40 trained horses.

A mile from the park's Gatlinburg entrance, near Sugarlands Visitor Center, **Sugarlands Riding Stables** (⊠*Sugarlands Visitor Center* ☎865/436–3535 ☉*Mar.–Oct.*) offers horseback rides through the park.

RAFTING & TUBING

Rafting on the Tennessee side of the Smokies isn't as good as on the North Carolina side, but the Upper Pigeon River, about 25 mi northeast of Gatlinburg, has 5 mi of white-water, including Class III and IV rapids. The Lower Pigeon River has tamer waters, with rafting trips suitable even for younger children. The minimum age and weight for the Upper Pigeon trip is usually 8 years old or 70 pounds, and at least 3 years old for the Lower Pigeon float trip. Several outfitters offer guided rafting trips on the Upper Pigeon. Expect to pay around $30–$40 per person for a two-hour rafting trip on the Upper Pigeon and about the same for a two-hour float trip on the Lower Pigeon.

Tubing requires little skill beyond the ability to let yourself float down a river and can be done at almost any age. Little River is the most popular tubing river on the west side of the Smokies. It flows east to west from its headwaters in the park through the town of Townsend. The Little River is mostly flat water (Class I), with a few mild Class II rapids. Although you can tube on the Little River within the park, several outfitters in Townsend rent tubes and life jackets and provide shuttle buses or vans that drop you at an entry point from which you can float a mile or two downriver to the outfitter's store. Expect to pay from $8 to $13 per person, which includes a full day's tube and life jacket rental plus unlimited use of the shuttle. Kayak rentals are also offered by some outfitters. Typically the cost is $15 for the kayak rental and the first shuttle trip, and $5 each for additional shuttle trips. Outfitters are generally open May–September or October.

RAFTING OUTFITTERS

Rafting in the Smokies (⊠ *376 E. Parkway, Gatlinburg, TN* ☎ *800/776-7238 or 865/436-5008* ⊕ *www.raftinginthesmokies.com*) has been around since 1978 and offers whitewater trips on the Upper Pigeon River and float trips on the Lower Pigeon River.

Rapid Expeditions (⊠ *3605 Hartford Rd., Hartford, TN* ☎ *888/504-7238 or 423/487-0160* ⊕ *www.rapidexpeditions.com*) offers Upper and Lower Pigeon River rafting trips as well as kayak instruction.

Smoky Mountain Outdoors (⊠ *Hartford Rd., Hartford, TN* ☎ *800/771-7238* ⊕ *www.smokymountainrafting.com*) offers white-water and float trips as well as inflatable kayak trips down the Pigeon River.

TUBING OUTFITTERS

River Rage (✉8303 Hwy. 73, Townsend, TN ☎865/448–8000 ⊕www.riverragetubing.com) has inner tubes available for rent on the Little River, a go-kart track, and a barbecue restaurant next door.

The River Rat (✉205 Wears Valley Rd., Townsend, TN ☎865/448–8888 ⊕www.smokymtnriverrat.com) offers tubing and kayaking on the Little River and whitewater rafting on the Pigeon River.

WINTER SPORTS & ACTIVITIES

Gatlinburg, Pigeon Forge, and Townsend at the western edge of the park are mostly at elevations under 2,000 feet, with winters generally too mild for snow sports. However, there is one ski resort, Ober Gatlinburg, on a 3,300-foot mountain near Gatlinburg.

SKIING

Ober Gatlinburg Ski Resort. Whenever temperatures fall low enough, the resort makes snow for the eight skiing and snowboarding trails. A single-session chairlift ticket is $30 on weekdays and $45 on weekends. Season lift passes are $209–$249, depending on when purchased. There is also a snow tubing park with 10 lanes and a 50-foot vertical drop. Rates are $20 per person weekdays and $25 weekends for an hour and 45 minutes. Ober Gatlinburg's winter season usually begins in mid-December and ends in early March. (✉1001 Parkway, Gatlinburg, TN ☎865/436–5423, 800/251–9202 snow report line ⊕www. obergatlinburg.com)

EXPLORING THE BACKCOUNTRY

Park statistics show that 94% of park visitors never venture even a few hundred feet into the backcountry, even though the majority of the hiking trails in the park are in backcountry areas.

At Sugarlands, Townsend, or other visitor centers, pick up a copy of the park's brochure, "Backpack Loops" ($1). It describes 12 of the best loop trails in the park—follow these loops, which are typically cobbled together from two or more trails, and you won't have to backtrack on a trail you've already visited. Some of these loop trails are strenuous and as long as 25 mi in length. All are at least overnight, and some are two- or three-night hikes. "Day

CLOSE UP

Backcountry Rules and Regulations

1. You must possess a back-country permit while camping in the backcountry.

2. Camping is permitted only at designated sites and shelters.

3. Use of reserved sites and shelters must be confirmed through the Backcountry Reservation Office.

4. You may stay up to three consecutive nights at a camp-site. You may not stay two nights in a row at a shelter.

5. Maximum camping party size is eight persons.

6. Open fires are prohibited except at designated sites. Use only wood that is dead and on the ground. Use only estab-lished fire rings.

7. The use of tents at shelters is prohibited.

8. Food storage: when not being consumed or transported,

all food and trash must be suspended at least 10 feet off the ground and 4 feet from the nearest limb or trunk, or stored as otherwise designated.

9. Toilet use must be at least 100 feet from a campsite or water source and out of sight of the trail. Human feces must be buried in a 6-inch-deep hole.

10. All trash must be carried out.

11. All plants, wildlife, and natural and historic features are protected by law. Do not carve, deface, or cut any trees or shrubs.

12. Polluting park waters is prohibited. Do not wash dishes or bathe with soap in a stream.

13. Pets, motorized vehicles, and bicycles are not permitted in the backcountry.

Hikes" ($1) is another helpful brochure, which describes easy to difficult hikes that can be done in a day or less.

Permits are required for overnight camping, hiking, or backpacking, but unlike many national parks, backcoun-try permits and campsites are free. It couldn't be easier to get into the backcountry. The only restrictions are that advance reservations are required for all shelters and 17 of the more than 100 backcountry campsites. The majority of backcountry campsites are first-come, first-served.

BACKCOUNTRY PERMITS

Backcountry Permit Stations. On the Tennessee side, back-country permits are available at the following locations: Abrams Creek ranger station, Cades Cove campground office, Cosby campground office, Greenbrier ranger station,

Elkmont campground office, and Tremont Environmental Center. When you arrive in the park, you must complete a permit at one of these self-registration stations. Your permit must designate the campsite or shelter at which you will stay for each night of your trip. You can download a trail map from the park Web site to find the location of backcountry shelters and campsites in the park. Keep the permit with you and drop the top copy in the registration box. ☎865/436–1297 ⊕*www.nps.gov/grsm/planyourvisit/ backcountry-camping.htm* ☖*Free.*

Backcountry Reservation Office. Backcountry shelters and reserved campsites are free, but you must reserve them in advance by calling Backcountry Reservations. Only 17 of the more than 100 backcountry campsites require reservations. Reserved campsites have capacity limitations of from 8 to 20 campers; some also permit horses. You may make reservations up to one month in advance of the first day of your trip and you should be prepared to give your complete trip itinerary. Reservations may *only* be obtained by telephone. ☎865/436–1231 ☖*Free* ☉*Daily 8–6.*

EDUCATIONAL PROGRAMS

Discover the flora and fauna and mountain culture of the Smokies with scheduled ranger programs, nature walks, classes, and residential learning courses.

SMOKY MOUNTAINS INSTITUTE & FIELD SCHOOL

☪ **Great Smoky Mountains Institute at Tremont.** Located within the park at Tremont, this residential environmental education center offers a variety of programs year-round for student groups, adults, and families. The adult programs include photography, crafts, naturalist certification, and three-day backpacking nature trips. Summer camp programs are offered for children 9–17, starting at $435. Family camp weekends for a family of four, including accommodations, meals, and instructional programs cost $365 ($80 for each additional family member), and the week-long program is $1,000 ($200 for each additional family member). Dates vary, but family weekends are usually held in early February and late June. Accommodations at Tremont are in Caylor Lodge, a heated and air-conditioned dormitory that can sleep up to 125 people, and also in tents on platforms. Meals are served family-style in a large dining hall. Some 5,000 students and adults attend programs at the

Institute each year. ⊠*9275 Tremont Rd., Townsend, TN* ☎*865/448–6709* ⊕*www.gsmit.org.*

Smoky Mountain Field School. The University of Tennessee's Smoky Mountain Field School offers workshops, hikes, and outdoor adventures for adults and families. Several dozen programs are presented, including ones on salamanders, animal tracks, birding, wildflowers, orienteering (using a map and compass to get from one place to another), mushrooms, nature photography, and nature sketching. Classes are held at various locations both within the park and on the UT campus in Knoxville. Field School programs are generally held on weekends and last from four hours to two days. Fees vary, with most programs from $29 to $49, and overnight hikes $98 to $155. ⊠*UT Smoky Mountain Field School, 313 Conference Center Bldg., Knoxville, TN* ☎*865/974–0150* ⊕*www.outreach.utk.edu/smoky.*

RANGER PROGRAMS

☙ **Interpretive Ranger Programs.** Ranger programs are available on a variety of subjects, from the danger of invasive plants and alien insects to wildflower identification, and from demonstrations of blacksmithing and basket making to mountain music. On the Tennessee side, most of the programs are held at Sugarlands and Cades Cove visitor centers and at the amphitheaters at Cades Cove, Elkmont, and Cosby campgrounds. Most programs are free and many are suitable for older children and adults. Pick up a copy of *Smokies Guide* at any visitor center or check the schedule online. ☎*865/436–1200* ⊕*www.nps.gov/grsm/planyourvisit/events.htm* ⊠*Free.*

☙ **Junior Ranger Program for Families.** Children ages 5 to 12 can pick up a Junior Ranger booklet ($3) at Sugarlands or at other park visitor centers. After they've completed the activities in the booklet, they can stop by a visitor center to talk to a ranger and receive a Junior Ranger badge. Especially during the summer, the park offers many age-appropriate demonstrations, classes, and programs for Junior Rangers, such as Bear-in the Winter, Life on the Farm, and Critters and Crawlies. ☎*865/436–1200* ⊕*www.nps.gov/grsm/forkids/index.htm* ⊠*$3.*

ARTS & ENTERTAINMENT

There are no restaurants or bars in the park, and only one hotel (the remote LeConte Lodge), so except for a few ranger programs—pick up *Smokies Guide* or check online for schedules—entertainment in the park itself is mostly of the do-it-yourself variety. For more arts and entertainment options, you'll want to visit nearby towns, such as Gatlinburg or Pigeon Forge. Downtown Gatlinburg has many restaurants and Pigeon Forge has musical theater for the entire family. ⇨ *See Chapter 5: Knoxville and Other Tennessee Towns for more information.*

Full Moon Hikes (☎ *865/436–1200* ⊕*www.nps.gov/grsm*) begin around sunset on some full moon nights in summer and fall at the Cades Cove orientation shelter, and last about 2 hours. It's an easy hike into Cades Cove, and since cars are prohibited on the loop road after dark, you don't have to worry about traffic.

Hayrides (☎*865/436–1200* ⊕*www.nps.gov/grsm*) are held Friday and Saturday evenings at 6 PM in summer and fall. A ranger explains the history and talks about wildlife in the cove. Hayrides start at Cades Cove Riding Stables and cost $8.50. They last 1½ to 2 hours.

Join a ranger and the members of the Smoky Mountain Astronomical Society for some **stargazing** (☎ *865/436–1200* ⊕*www.nps.gov/grsm*), where you'll learn about the stars and galaxies. Programs, usually once a month, begin a little after sunset at the Cades Cove orientation shelter, and last about 2 hours. Telescopes are provided.

Traditional Old Tyme Music (☎*865/436–1200* ⊕*www.nps. gov/grsm*) can be heard at the Cable Mill area of the Cades Cove Visitor Center 10:30–4 on many days in the summer and fall.

FESTIVALS & EVENTS

Cosby in the Park Festival (☎*865/436–1291* ⊕*www.nps.gov/ grsm* ✍ *Free*) has old-time music, craft demonstrations, storytelling, and children's games. It's held on a Saturday in mid-May near the Cosby campground.

Festival of Christmas Past (☎*865/436–1291* ⊕*www.nps. gov/grsm* ✍*Free*) is held on a Saturday in early December at Sugarlands Visitor Center. This festival celebrates the culture of the Smokies, with an emphasis on old-time

Christmas traditions, plus a visit from Santa. You can hear storytelling and mountain music and watch demonstrations of quilt making, basket weaving, and apple-butter and lye-soap making.

Visitors are invited to bring lawn chairs and a picnic along to enjoy **Old Timers' Day at Cades Cove** (☎*865/436–1200* ⊕*www.nps.gov/grsm Free*). Held the last weekend in September or first weekend in October at the Cable Mill area of Cades Cove, Old Timers' Day allows former residents of Cades Cove, and their descendants, along with the general public, to reminisce about the old days in the valley. The event usually attracts more than 4,000 people.

★ **Fodor's**Choice Each year in late April, the Great Smoky Mountains National Park hosts the **Spring Wildflower Pilgrimage** (☎*865/436–7318 Ext. 222* ⊕*www.springwildflower-pilgrimage.org* ✉*Registration $25–$40; some events free*). It attracts wildflower enthusiasts from all over the country for five days of wildflower and natural history walks, seminars, classes, photography tours, and other events. Instructors include National Park Service staff, along with outside experts. Most activities are at various locations in the park, both on the North Carolina and Tennessee sides, but some are in Gatlinburg or elsewhere outside the park. Begun in 1951, the Pilgrimage has grown to more than 150 different walks, classes, and events. Upcoming pilgrimages are set for April 22–26, 2009, and April 23–27, 2010. Check the Web site for more details.

The **Townsend in the Smokies Spring Festival** (☎ *800/525–6834 or 865/448–6134* ⊕*www.smokymountainfestivals. org* ✉*Free*) is usually held the last weekend in April and first weekend in May at the Townsend Visitor Center. It features bluegrass bands, antique tractors, craft booths, and mountain craft demonstrations. Townsend also holds a winter festival, usually the first weekend in February, a fall festival and "Old Timers Day," usually the last weekend in September, and a pottery festival in early June.

SHOPPING

The Sugarlands, Townsend, and Cades Cove visitor centers have attractive gift shops and bookstores, with first-rate selections of books and maps on the Smokies and nearby mountain areas, as well as some souvenirs. The Great Smoky Mountains Institute at Tremont also has a small gift shop and bookstore. The main Gatlinburg Welcome Center, which also serves as a park visitor center, has a large gift shop featuring Tennessee-made crafts and foods.

The park also has an official online store for books, maps, park logo items, gift baskets, CDs, DVDs, and local mountain foods (⊕*www.smokiesinformation.org*). It is operated by the nonprofit Great Smoky Mountains Association. Association members get a 15% discount on purchases online and at park visitor center stores. An individual membership costs $30 a year. Proceeds generated by purchases at the Association's online and visitor center stores are donated to educational, scientific, and historical projects in the park. The Association donates almost $2 million annually to fund projects in the park.

There is a small convenience store with some picnic and camping items, along with a snack bar at the Cades Cove campground. Firewood is available at Cades Cove campground and Elkmont. Surrounding communities such as Townsend and Pigeon Forge also have stores with firewood for sale. ⚠ **Note that firewood cannot be brought into the park from the states of Illinois, Indiana, Michigan, Ohio, New Jersey, or New York, due to a quarantine to protect against the spread of destructive insects.**

For groceries, camping supplies, and other shopping items, your best bet is Sevierville. Pigeon Forge, Townsend, and suburban Gatlinburg also have grocery stores, gas stations, and other shopping outlets.

For tourist souvenirs, head to Gatlinburg or Pigeon Forge. For higher-quality crafts and gifts tour the **Great Smoky Arts & Crafts Trail** (⊕*www.gatlinburgcrafts.com*), an 8-mi loop of shops, galleries, and studios that begins in downtown Gatlinburg. **Arrowmont School of Arts and Crafts** (⊕*www. arrowmont.org*), a nationally known contemporary crafts school in Gatlinburg, has five galleries that are open to the public. Knoxville has the widest selection of shopping choices, including large malls. ⇨ *For more information, see Chapter 5: Knoxville and Other Tennessee Towns.*

Exploring the North Carolina Side

WORD OF MOUTH

"We like the North Carolina side [of the Smokies] near Asheville. Great scenic drives, waterfalls, Biltmore House (beautiful gardens in the spring), nice art/craft shops and dining."

—Katie7

By Lan
Sluder

THE GREAT SMOKY MOUNTAINS NATIONAL Park head-quarters is in Gatlinburg, Tennessee, and many people think of the Smokies as being a Tennessee national park. In fact, slightly more of the park is on the eastern, or North Carolina side, than on the Tennessee side—276,000 acres to 246,000 acres to be exact.

It boasts the highest mountain in the park—Clingmans Dome, elevation 6,643 feet—and four more of the 10 highest peaks: Mount Guyot, Mount Chapman, Old Black, and Luftee Knob. North Carolina also claims the biggest body of water—Fontana Lake, which forms much of the southwestern boundary of the park.

The land here is contained within three North Carolina counties—Haywood, which is home to more 6,000-foot or higher peaks than any other county in the eastern United States; Graham, which is over two-thirds national forest and national park land; and Swain, which has the largest portion of the park than any other county. Development in these rural counties generally is at a much lower key than on the Tennessee side. A few small towns, including Robbinsville, Bryson City, Dillsboro, and Sylva, are along the edge of the park. They sometimes bill themselves as "the quiet side of the park," and with good reason.

Only a little more than an hour's drive from the main entrance at Oconaluftee, the city of Asheville (metropolitan population 400,000) is nationally known for its art and craft galleries, hip downtown scene, eclectic restaurants, and varied lodgings, including one of the largest collections of B&Bs in the Southeast.

The eastern side of the park abuts other large expanses of protected forests, including the 531,000-acre Nantahala National Forest and the 510,000-acre Pisgah National Forest. At the Oconaluftee entrance near Cherokee, NC, the Blue Ridge Parkway begins its 469-mi meandering journey north through the North Carolina mountains to the Skyline Drive in Virginia. Also adjoining the eastern side of the park is the Cherokee Indian Reservation, officially known as the Qualla Boundary.

But there's no reason for Carolinians and Tennesseans to get into a bragging match. Within the park itself, both sides are actually quite similar in terms of scenery, activities, flora and fauna, and historical sites.

WHAT TO SEE

The North Carolina side of the park provides you with a great variety of sights and experiences, from high peaks to historical houses. Right at the Oconaluftee Visitor Center at the entrance to the park is the Mountain Farm Museum, one of the best-preserved collections of historic log buildings in the region. If you're interested in seeing wildlife, Cataloochee, like Cades Cove on the Tennessee side, is a beautiful valley where you can spot deer, wild turkeys, and even elk. Even if you never leave your car, Newfound Gap Road offers plenty of scenic views. If, however, you're ready to lace up your hiking boots, there are hundreds of miles of hiking trails to be explored, from the paved trail to the top of Clingmans Dome to the granddaddy of all trails, the Appalachian Trail, which skims 71 mi of the ridges along the North Carolina–Tennessee border.

PARK ENTRANCES

While there are a total of seven vehicular entrances to the park from North Carolina—including two entrances near Bryson City, one on Big Cove Road near Cherokee, one from Heintooga Ridge Road off the Blue Ridge Parkway, one to Cataloochee via Cove Creek Road, and one at Big Creek—most visitors to the park's eastern side enter by car on U.S. 441 at Oconaluftee Visitor Center near Cherokee. Also known as Newfound Gap Road, U.S. 441 between Cherokee and Gatlinburg is the only paved route through the park.

VISITOR CENTER

INSIDE THE PARK

Oconaluftee. The park's only information center on the North Carolina side is 1½ mi from Cherokee. Inside the pleasant old stone-and-wood main building you'll find helpful rangers to answer your questions, bulletin boards describing upcoming park activities, information on current campsite availabilities, and a small shop selling books, maps, and souvenirs. The restrooms are downstairs, around the back. A backcountry permit station is near the restrooms. A planned new visitor center, projected to open in 2010, will expand the center's space seven-fold. The current plans call for a new 6,000-square-foot visitor center, a new information kiosk, and a new restroom and vending building. The existing building will remain as administra-

North Carolina Side

KEY

Ranger Station / Information
Campground
Picnic Area
Horseback Riding
Scenic Viewpoint
Appalachian Trail
Walking / Hiking Trails

GREAT SMOKY MOUNTAINS NATIONAL PARK

TENNESSEE
NORTH CAROLINA

see detail map

Blue Ridge Parkway

Waterrock Knob

Big Creek
Cosby
Mt Cammerer 4,928
Old Black 6,356
Mount Guyot 6,621
Mount Sterling 5,842
Cosby Knob 5,145
Cataloochee
Luftee Knob 6,122
Round Bottom
Heintooga Overlook
Heintooga Ridge Rd.
Mile High Maggie Valley Overlook
Balsam Mountain
Balsam Mountain Rd.
19
Greenbrier
Pittmans Center
Charlies Bunion
Mt Kephart 6,150
Newfound Gap 5,048
Oconaluftee Overlook
Tow String
Smokemont
Collins Creek
Pioneer Farmstead
CHEROKEE INDIAN RESERVATION
Mount LeConte 6,593
LeConte Lodge
Mingus Mill
Visitor Center Oconaluftee
Cherokee
441
Gatlinburg
Gatlinburg Welcom Center
441
Chimney Tops
Elkmont
Clingmans Dome 6,643
Silers Bald 5,620
Appalachian Trail
Andrews Bald 5,920
Deep Creek
Bryson City
TO KNOXVILLE & SEVIERVILLE, TN
321
Sugarlands
Visitor Center Sugarlands
Little River Rd.
River Rd. Townsend
Spence Field
Thunderhead Mtn 5,530
Cades Cove
Abrams Creek
Look Rock
Visitor Center Cades Cove
Foothills Parkway
Shuckstack
Fontana Dam
Fontana Village
Fontana Lake
Eagle Creek
Forney Creek
Lakeview Dr.
TO NANTAHALA
TO ATLANTA, GA
28

Cove Creek Rd.
TO ASHEVILLE, NC
276
40

N

0   5 mi
0   5 km

TRIP PLANNING

The official Great Smoky Mountains National Park Web site (⊕www.nps.gov/grsm) provides a wealth of information on the park. Before you go, download the **Smokies Trip Planner** at ⊕www.nps. gov/grsm/planyourvisit/trip-planner.htm. Several commercial Web sites also are useful for trip planning. Among the best are **My Smoky Mountain Vacation** (⊕www. mysmokymountainvacation. com), **Romantic Asheville** (⊕www.romanticasheville.

com), and **Bryson City & the Great Smokies** (⊕www. greatsmokies.com).

Once you arrive at the park, pick up the *Smokies Guide*, a free tabloid newspaper published once a season with an area map, schedule of free park programs, and information on destinations in the park, birding, wildlife, wildflowers, and hiking. The park visitor centers have shops with large collections of books on every aspect of the park.

tive offices. Adjoining the present visitor center, in a large, level field next to the Oconaluftee River, is the Mountain Farm Museum. You can explore a collection of log buildings, most dating from the late 19th century and assembled from buildings elsewhere in the park, including a chestnut-wood cabin, barn, apple house, springhouse, corncrib, and a blacksmith's shop. In season, there's a garden, and park staff occasionally put on demonstrations of blacksmithing and other pioneer activities. If you want to take an easy hike, the 1.6-mi (3.2 mi round-trip) Oconaluftee River Trail begins nearby. ⊠U.S. 441, 1½ mi from Cherokee ☎865/436-1200 ⊙Nov.–Apr., daily 8–4:30; May, daily 8:30–5:30; June–Aug., daily 8–6; Sept. and Oct., daily 8:30–6 ⚏Free.

SPOTLIGHT DRIVE: BLUE RIDGE PARKWAY

★ **Fodor's**Choice The beautiful Blue Ridge Parkway (or BRP as it's known on local bumper stickers) gently winds through mountains and meadows and crosses mountain streams for more than 469 mi on its way from the north near Waynesboro, Virginia, south to Cherokee, North Carolina, connecting the Great Smoky Mountains and Shenandoah national parks. Beginning at mile 0 at Rockfish Gap, Virginia, the BRP crosses the Virginia–North Carolina border at about mile 217. About 252 mi of the Parkway are in

GREAT ITINERARIES

NORTH CAROLINA SIDE IN 1 DAY

Start early, pack a picnic lunch, and drive to the **Oconaluftee Visitor Center**, to pick up orientation maps and brochures. While you're there, spend an hour or so exploring the **Mountain Farm Museum**. Then, drive ½ mi to **Mingus Mill** and see corn being ground into meal in an authentic working grist mill. Head up **Newfound Gap Road** and **Clingmans Dome Road** to Clingmans Dome. Stretch your legs and walk the .5-mi paved, but fairly steep, trail to the observation tower on Clingmans Dome. Head back down the mountain and stop for a leisurely picnic at **Collins Creek** picnic area. For a moderate afternoon hike, the 4-mi (round-trip) **Kephart Prong** trail is nearby. Alternatively, and especially if it's a hot summer day, take your lunch to the **Heintooga** picnic area at Balsam Springs. At a mile high, this part of the Smokies is usually cool even in mid-July. From here, you can hike all (about 5 mi round-trip) or part of the **Flat Creek Trail**, one of the hidden jewels in the park.

NORTH CAROLINA SIDE IN 3 DAYS

On Day 1, follow the one-day itinerary. On Day 2, drive to **Bryson City** and then 3 mi to **Deep Creek**. If you have children with you, rent inner tubes and spend several hours tubing and swimming in Deep Creek. Have a picnic at Deep Creek picnic area, or drive into Bryson City for lunch. In the afternoon, take one of the nearby loop hikes to see waterfalls. Your hiking options include **Juney Whank Falls** (0.6 mi round-trip), **Three Waterfalls Loop** (2.4 mi), and **Deep Creek–Indian Creek Loop** (4.4 mi). Alternatively, drive U.S. 74 to NC 28, a winding and scenic road, and visit **Fontana Lake** and Fontana Dam. On Day 3, take I–40 (Exit 20) to **Cove Creek Road** and drive to **Cataloochee Cove**. Spend the morning spying elk and exploring the deserted homes, barns, and churches of the Cataloochee community. After a leisurely picnic by Cataloochee Creek, continue on Cove Creek Road toward Big Creek. On the way, stop and hike at least a little of the **Mt. Sterling** trail—it's a strenuous, steep 5.4-mi (round-trip) hike to an old fire tower, so you may not have the time or the energy to hike the entire trail. Reconnect with I–40 (Exit 451) near Big Creek and return home.

North Carolina. With elevations ranging from 649 to 6,047 feet, and with more than 250 scenic lookout points, it is truly one of the most beautiful drives in North America. Admission to the Parkway is free. No commercial vehicles are allowed, and the entire Parkway is free of billboards, although in a few places residential or commercial development encroaches close to the road. The BRP, which has a maximum speed limit of 45 MPH, is generally open year-round but sections of it, or all of it, close during inclement weather. In winter, sections can be closed for weeks at a time due to snow, and even in good weather fog and clouds occasionally make driving difficult. Maps and information are available at information centers along the highway. Mile markers (MMs) identify points of interest and indicate the distance from the Parkway's starting point in Virginia (MM 0). A new park headquarters and visitor center near Asheville at MM 384 opened in late 2007. It has a "green roof" with plants growing on it. ∎TIP→**Remember to fill up your gas tank before you get on the BRP. There are no gas stations on the scenic drive, but you'll find stations at intersecting highways near exits.** *Superintendent, Blue Ridge Pkwy., 199 Hemphill Knob Rd., Asheville 28803 ☎828/298-0398 ⊕www.nps.gov/blri ☜Free.*

Along the Blue Ridge Parkway and up 5,721 feet, you'll find **Mt. Pisgah** (⊠*MM 408.6 ☎828/648-2664 campground*), which is one of the most easily recognized peaks due to the television tower installed here in the 1950s. Mt. Pisgah has walking trails, an amphitheater where nature programs are held most evenings June through October, a campground, inn, picnic area, and small grocery. The nearby area called **Graveyard Fields** is popular for blueberry picking in July. In 1992 a snowstorm in *May* dropped more than 5 feet of snow here.

The **Folk Art Center** (⊠*MM 382 at Asheville ☎828/298-7928 ⊗Jan.–Mar., daily 9–5; Apr.–Dec., daily 9–6*) near Asheville displays and sells authentic mountain crafts made by members of the Southern Highland Craft Guild. Demonstrations are held frequently. ∎TIP→**This is one of the best places in the region to buy high-quality crafts.**

Craggy Gardens (⊠*MM 364.6 ☎828/298-0398 ☜Free*) at 5,500 to 6,000 feet, has some of the Parkway's most colorful displays of rhododendrons, usually in June. You can also hike trails and picnic here.

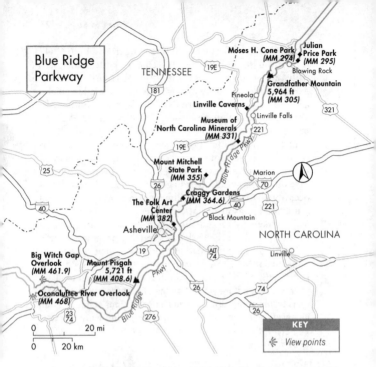

**Blue Ridge
Parkway**

TENNESSEE

Moses H. Cone Park
(MM 294)

Julian
Price Park
(MM 295)

Blowing Rock

Pineola

Grandfather Mountain
5,964 ft
(MM 305)

Linville Caverns

Linville Falls

**Museum of
North Carolina Minerals
(MM 331)**

**Mount Mitchell
State Park
(MM 355)**

Marion

**Craggy Gardens
(MM 364.6)**

**The Folk Art
Center
(MM 382)**

Black Mountain

Asheville

NORTH CAROLINA

Linville

**Big Witch Gap
Overlook
(MM 461.9)**

**Mount Pisgah
5,721 ft
(MM 408.6)**

**Oconaluftee River Overlook
(MM 468)**

0   20 mi

0   20 km

KEY

View points

Mt. Mitchell State Park (✉*2388 NC Hwy. 128, MM 355, Burnsville* ☎*828/675–4611* 💲*Free*) includes the highest mountain peak east of the Rockies, Mt. Mitchell, at 6,684 feet. The summit was named after Elisha Mitchell, who died from a fall while trying to prove the mountain's true height. At the 1,855-acre park, you can climb an observation tower and get food at a restaurant. Keep an eye on the weather here, as high winds and snow can occur at almost any time, occasionally even in summer. The lowest temperature ever recorded in North Carolina was at Mt. Mitchell on January 21, 1985: -34°F. Clouds obscure the views here for at least parts of 8 days out of 10.

🍂 The **Museum of North Carolina Minerals** (✉*MM 331 at U.S. 226* ☎*828/765–2761* 💲*Free* ⊙*Daily 9–5*) has hands-on displays about gold, copper, kaolin, and other minerals found nearby.

🍂 **Linville Caverns** (✉*U.S. 221, between Linville and Marion* ☎*828/756–4171* ⊕*www.linvillecaverns.com* 💲*$6* ⊙*June–early Sept., daily 9–6; Apr., May, and mid-Sept.–Oct., daily 9–5; Nov. and Mar., daily 9–4:30; closed Dec.–Feb.*) are the only caverns in the Carolinas. They go 2,000 feet beneath

Humpback Mountain and have a year-round temperature of 51°F. North of Asheville, exit the Parkway at mile marker 317.4 and turn left onto U.S. 221.

Just off the Parkway at mile marker 305, **Grandfather Mountain** (✉ *Blue Ridge Pkwy. and U.S. 221, Linville* ☎ *828/733–4337 or 800/468–7325* ⊕ *www.grandfather.com* 🎫 *$14* ⊙ *Apr.–mid-Nov., daily 8–dusk; mid-Nov.–Mar., daily 8–5*) soars to 6,000 feet and is famous for its Mile-High Swinging Bridge, a 228-foot-long bridge that sways over a 1,000-foot drop into the Linville Valley. The **Natural History Museum** has exhibits on native minerals, flora and fauna, and pioneer life. The annual **Singing on the Mountain,** in June, is an opportunity to hear old-time gospel music and preaching, and the **Highland Games** in July bring together Scottish clans from all over North America for athletic events and Highland dancing. The owner of Grandfather Mountain, Hugh Morton, was a noted nature photographer; he died in 2006 at age 86. In late 2008, the state of North Carolina announced an agreement to purchase Grandfather Mountain and the surrounding land, a total of more than 3,000 acres, from the Morton family for $12 million. Grandfather Mountain will be preserved as a state park.

Green spaces along the Parkway include **Julian Price Park** (✉ *MM 295–MM 298.1*), which has hiking, canoeing on a mountain lake, trout fishing, and camping.

The **Moses H. Cone Park** (✉ *MM 292.7–MM 295* ☎ *828/295–7938* ⊙ *Mid-Mar.–Nov., daily 9–5*) has a turn-of-the-20th-century manor house that's now the **Parkway Craft Center.** The center sells fine work by area craftspeople.

SCENIC DRIVES

★ **Fodor'sChoice Cove Creek Road.** This drive takes you to one of the most beautiful valleys in the Smokies. From the North Carolina side, take I-40 to Exit 20 at U.S. 276. Go about ¼ mi south and turn on to Cove Creek Road (also known as Old NC 284). The first 7 mi of Cove Creek is a mostly paved, winding two-lane road through a scenic rural valley. Entering the park, the road becomes gravel. ■TIP→**Although in the park this is a two-way road, in places it is wide enough only for one vehicle, so you may have to pull over and let oncoming vehicle pass. At points, the curvy road hugs the mountainside, with steep drop-offs. It is not suitable for large RVs or travel trailers.** As you near the Cataloochee Valley, suddenly you're on a nice, paved road again. Follow the paved road: it's a short cut to the historic old buildings of Cataloochee. (You can also continue on the unpaved Cove Creek Road toward Crosby, Tennessee, and in about 5 mi you can enter Cataloochee from the back.) Follow the signs for a driving tour of the old houses, barns, churches, a school, and other buildings that are all that remain of the once-thriving Cataloochee community, which at its peak in 1910 had about 1,200 residents. You can stop and walk through most of the buildings. Keep a lookout for elk, wild turkeys, deer, and other wildlife here. From Cataloochee continue on the unpaved Cove Creek Road to Big Creek campground near the North Carolina–Tennessee line to reconnect with I–40 at Exit 451 on the Tennessee side.

Heintooga Ridge–Balsam Mountain Roads. Begin this drive near mile marker 458 of the Blue Ridge Parkway, about 11 mi from the entrance to the Parkway at Cherokee. Go about 8 mi on the paved Heintooga Ridge Road to the Balsam Mountain campground and Heintooga picnic area. Heintooga Ridge Road, at about a mile high, is lined with evergreens and makes for a lovely drive. At this elevation, you're often literally in the clouds. The narrow, unpaved 18-mi Balsam Mountain Road, sometimes called Roundbottom Road, begins near the Heintooga picnic area, and it is one-way, although the last 5-mi section, before you get to the paved Big Cove Road, is two-way. Balsam Mountain Road, though only one lane wide and with many sharp curves, is well maintained and four-wheel drive is not required. The roadside scenery changes as you descend from the higher elevations with firs and hemlocks of Balsam Mountain to the lowlands toward Cherokee. There is a profusion of flowers along Balsam Mountain Road especially in the spring. ⚠ **Take it slow: on this narrow, winding gravel road, it's unsafe to go faster than 10 to 15 MPH. Motor homes and travel trailers are prohibited on Balsam Mountain Road, and it is closed November–April.** If you tire of driving, there are plenty of places to pull over and walk around, and several trails intersect this road, including the 11-mi Balsam Mountain Trail and 3.3-mi Palmer Creek Trail. Another 12 mi on Big Cove Road, mostly through rural areas outside the park, gets you back to Cherokee.

Newfound Gap Road. Newfound Gap Road, or U.S. Highway 441, is the busiest road in the park by far, with more than a million vehicles making the 16-mi climb from the 2,000-foot elevation near Cherokee to almost a mile high at Newfound Gap (and then down to Gatlinburg on the

Tennessee side). It's the only road that goes all the way through the center of the park, and the only fully paved road. While it's not a route to escape from the crowds, and especially not on prime weekends in the summer and fall, the scenery is memorable. If you don't have time to explore the back roads or to go hiking, Newfound Gap Road will give you a flavor of the richness and variety of the Smokies. The Park Service compares a drive over the Newfound Gap Road to a drive from Georgia to Maine in terms of the variety of forest ecosystems one experiences. Unlike other roads in the park, Newfound Gap Road has mile markers; however, the markers run "backwards" (as far as North Carolinians are concerned), starting at 0 at the park boundary near Gatlinburg to 31.1 at the border of the park at the entrance to the Blue Ridge Parkway near Cherokee. Along the way you'll find Oconaluftee Visitor Center and Mountain Farm Museum (MM 30.3); Mingus Mill (MM 29.9); Smokemont Campground and Nature Trail (MM 27.2); Web Overlook (MM 17.7), from which there's a good view almost due west of Clingmans Dome; and Newfound Gap (MM 14.7), the start of the 7-mi road to Clingmans Dome, the highest peak in the Smokies.

Road to Nowhere (Lakeview Drive). In the early 1940s, the federal government began construction on a new road to replace an old highway that had been flooded by the filling of Fontana Lake and to provide local Swain County families with access to cemeteries in the park. The road was supposed to follow the north shore of Fontana Lake, running some 30 mi from Bryson City. It was called Lakeview Drive, the Northshore Road, or New Fontana Road, but it soon came to be known unofficially as the Road to Nowhere. Naturalists fought the road, fearing traffic would disturb the sensitive ecosystems of the area. The environmentalists won, and although a viaduct over Noland Creek and a tunnel had already been completed, construction was halted. The Road to Nowhere is now a winding paved road with great views of Fontana Lake, but it goes, well, nowhere. The 6-mi Noland Creek hiking trail intersects the road. To get to the road, from the old Swain County Courthouse in Bryson City turn right onto Everett Street and cross the Tuckasegee River. Follow Everett Street through town (it changes to Lakeview Drive), and continue to the park boundary. Continue about 5 mi until the road abruptly ends at the tunnel. In 2007, Swain County settled its dispute about the road with the federal government. It accepted a cash settlement of $52 million, in lieu of completing the road, which might have cost the government $600 million. Thus, the Road to Nowhere will remain just that.

HISTORIC SIGHTS

★ Fodor$Choice **Cataloochee Valley.** This is one of the eeriest sites in all of the Smokies. At one time Cataloochee was a community of more than 1,200 people, in some 200 buildings. After the land was taken over in 1934 for the national park, the community dispersed. Although many of the original buildings are now gone, more than a dozen houses, cabins, and barns, two churches, and other structures have been kept up. You can visit the Palmer Methodist Chapel, a one-room schoolhouse, Beach Grove School, and the Woody and Messer homesteads. It's much like Cades Cove on the Tennessee side, but much less visited. On a quiet day, you can almost hear the ghosts of the former Cataloochee settlers. You will often spot a few elk here, especially in the evening and early morning. Cataloochee is one of the most remote parts of the Smokies reachable by car, via a narrow, winding, gravel road. ⊠ *Cataloochee Community, via U.S. 276 near Maggie Valley, off Exit 20 of I–40, to Cove Creek Rd.* ☎ *865/436–1200.*

Mingus Mill. In its time, the late 19th century, this was the state of the art in grist mills, with two large grist stones powered by a store-bought turbine rather than a hand-built wheel. You can watch the miller make cornmeal, and even buy a pound of it. ⊠ *U.S. 441, 2 mi north of Cherokee* ☎ *828/497–1904* ⊙ *Mid-Mar.–late Nov.*

★ **Mountain Farm Museum.** This museum at the Oconaluftee
⚬ Visitor Center is perhaps the best re-creation anywhere of a mountain farmstead. The nine farm buildings, all dating from around 1900, were moved here from locations within the park. Besides a furnished two-story log cabin, you'll see a barn, apple house, corncrib, smokehouse, chicken coop, and other outbuildings. In season, corn, tomatoes, pole beans, squash, and other mountain crops are grown in the garden, and park staff sometimes put on demonstrations of pioneer activities, such as making apple butter and molasses. ⊠ *U.S. 441 at Oconaluftee Visitor Center* ☎ *828/497–1904* ⊙ *Mid-Mar.–late Nov.*

Proctor. Once a thriving lumber and copper mining town on Hazel Creek with a railroad spur to carry out the virgin timber, Proctor is now abandoned, with most of its houses and buildings taken over by nature. By the time the main lumber company, W.M. Ritter, pulled out in 1928, some 200 million board feet of lumber had been harvested in the area, enough to build 20,000 homes. Among the structures remaining are the white-frame Calhoun house, probably built in the early 1900s; the foundations of a church and of several other buildings; and bridges over Hazel Creek. About ½ mi away from the remains of the town is the Proctor cemetery. Proctor is best reached by boat across Fontana Lake. After arriving on the north shore of the lake, it's a .25- to .75-mi walk to the site of the old town, depending on the level of the lake (at times, especially in the late summer and fall, the Tennessee Valley Authority, or TVA, draws down the lake). Local historian Lance Holland gives tours of the ghost town. The Proctor tours, limited to 25 people, depart Fontana Marina at 10:30 AM each Wednesday and Saturday during spring and summer months. The trip lasts about 3½ hours. Fontana Marina also offers boat transport across the lake for hikers and campers who want to see Proctor and surrounding areas on their own. ⇨*See Spotlight Hike: Hazel Creek and Bone Valley in this chapter for more information.* ✉*Hazel Creek* ☎*800/849–2258 or 828/498–2129 Fontana Marina, 828/479–6960 Lance Holland for group tours* 🎫*$15 tour.*

Smokemont Baptist Church. Also known as the Oconaluftee Baptist Church, Smokemont Baptist Church is all that remains of the once-thriving lumbering community of Smokemont. Founded in 1832, and rebuilt in 1916, the church was added to the National Register of Historic Places in 1976. The graceful, white-frame church has been restored. To get to it, turn off Newfound Gap Road at the Smokemont campground (MM 17.2), cross the Oconaluftee, and park in the area just past the bridge. The church is across the road and up the hill. An old cemetery, the Bradley Cemetery, is nearby. ✉*Smokemont, Newfound Gap Rd. (U.S. 441), MM 17.2* ☎*865/426–1200.*

SCENIC STOPS

★ **Andrews Bald.** Getting to Andrews Bald isn't easy. You have to walk the rocky Forney Ridge trail some 1.8 mi one-way, with an elevation gain of almost 600 feet, the equivalent of a 60-story skyscraper. The payoff is several acres of grassy bald at over 5,800 feet, with stunning views of Lake Fontana and the southeastern Smokies. This is one of only two balds in the Smokies (the other is Gregory Bald on the

Tennessee side) that the park service keeps clear. ✉ *1.8 mi from the Forney Ridge trailhead parking lot, at the end of Clingmans Dome Rd.*

BALD IS BEAUTIFUL. If you've ever wondered why some mountains are called balds, you've probably guessed right at the answer—they're missing trees at the top, giving them the appearance of "going bald." This open meadow at a high elevation usually translates into spectacular views unobstructed by trees. The origin of balds is an ecological mystery. Some biologists think balds formed thousands of years ago as a result of frost heaving and soil erosion, with fire, drought, and wind keeping the bald areas clear; others think that natural chemicals in grasses and low shrubs kept trees from sinking their roots into the balds. The balds in the park probably took on their present form after settlers used high fields for summer pasture for their cattle. After livestock were removed with the coming of the park shrubs and trees grew and the balds shrank in size.

Big Witch Gap Overlook. The 2-mi drive on the Blue Ridge Parkway between Big Witch Gap Overlook and Noland Divide Overlook offers fine views into the eastern side of the Smokies, and in May and June the roadsides are heavily abloom with rhododendron. ✉ *MM 461.9 on the BRP.*

★ **Cataloochee Overlook.** Coming from Cove Creek Road onto the paved section of Cataloochee Road, this is your first opportunity to stop and see the broad expanse of Cataloochee Cove. Cataloochee is taken from a Cherokee word meaning "row upon row" or "standing in rows," and indeed you'll see rows of mountain ridges here. The overlook is well-marked and has a split-rail fence. ✉ *Cataloochee Rd.*

★ **Fodor's**Choice **Clingmans Dome.** At an elevation of more than 6,600 feet, this is the third-highest peak east of the Rockies, only a few feet shorter than the highest, Mt. Mitchell. Walk up a paved, but steep, .5-mi trail to an observation tower offering 360-degree views from the "top of Old Smoky." Temperatures here are usually 10°F lower than at the entrance to the park near Cherokee. Clingmans Dome Road is closed to vehicular traffic in winter (December–March), but if there's snow on the ground you can put on your skis or snow shoes and go up to the peak. ✉ *At the end of Clingmans Dome Rd., 7 mi from U.S. 441.*

AVOID THE CROWDS

The Great Smokies gets twice as many visitors as any other national park. It's hard to commune with nature while you're searching for a parking place, dodging video cameras, and stepping out of the way of strollers. However, this scenario is likely to occur only during the peak fall color season (usually October to early November) and on weekends in July and August. Your best bet to beat the crowds is to visit during the off-peak spring, late summer, and even winter seasons. Any time of year, weekday crowds will be smaller than weekend ones.

Another trick is to avoid Newfound Gap Road, the main road through the park. Even if you want to stay in your car, back roads such as Balsam Mountain Road and Cove Creek Road have almost no traffic, even at peak times. In fact, you can usually drive for miles and not see another vehicle. Note that these back roads are generally unpaved, may be one-way, and some are closed in winter. Also, anytime you step out of your car and onto a hiking trail, solitude is almost guaranteed.

★ **Heintooga Overlook.** This is one of the best spots to watch the sunset, with a sweeping view westward of the crest of the Great Smokies. ⊠*Off Heintooga Ridge Rd., at the picnic area, 7 mi from the BRP—the entrance to Heintooga Ridge Rd. is at MM 458.2.*

Lakeview Drive Fontana Lake Overlook. This is the first scenic overlook you come to after entering the park on Lakeview Drive, better known as the Road to Nowhere. It's a little over 3 mi from the Lakeview entrance to the park. You can see parts of Fontana Lake, which marks the southwestern boundary of the park. The lake, part of the Tennessee Valley Authority system, is drawn down at times, especially in the fall, so the water level and the shoreline change significantly depending on whether the gates on Fontana Dam, the tallest dam in the East, are open or closed. ⊠*First scenic overlook on Lakeview Dr., 3.1 mi from Lakeview Dr. park entrance near Bryson City.*

Mile High Overlook. This overlook has a panoramic view of much of the eastern side of the Smokies. ⊠*Heintooga Ridge Rd., 1.3 mi from the BRP—the entrance to Heintooga Ridge Rd. is at MM 458.2.*

Oconaluftee River Overlook. From this spot on the Blue Ridge Parkway you have a good aerial view of the Mountain

Farm Museum at Oconaluftee Visitor Center. ⊠*MM 468 on the BRP, about 1 mi from the entrance to the Parkway near Cherokee.*

Oconaluftee Valley Overlook. From atop the Thomas Divide, just a little below the crest of the Smokies, you can look down and see the winding Newfound Gap Road. This is also a good spot to view sunrise in the Smokies. ⊠*Newfound Gap Rd. (U.S. 441) at MM 15.4.*

RIDE THE RAILS
Great Smoky Mountains Railroad. While it doesn't actually go into the Great Smoky Mountains National Park, the railroad's excursions from Bryson City on a train pulled by a diesel-electric or, on occasion, steam locomotive offer views of the Great Smokies in the distance, as you go southwest along the edge of the park and into the Nantahala National Forest. The 4½-hour, 44-mi (round-trip) excursion travels along the Tuckasegee River, crosses the Fontana Lake Trestle, and goes into the Nantahala Gorge. Open-sided cars or standard coaches are ideal for picture taking as the mountain scenery glides by. There are also mystery dinner theater and gourmet dinner rides. The train has been featured in several movies, including *The Fugitive* (1993), *My Fellow Americans* (1996), and *Forces of Nature* (1998). ⊠*225 Everett St., Suites G and H, Bryson City* ☎*800/872–4681* ⊕*www.gsmr.com* ☜*Standard seating $34 Jan.–Mar.; $49 Apr.–Sept., Nov., and Dec.; $53 Oct. Upgraded seating $12–$20 additional; most tickets include admission to the Smoky Mountain Model Railroad Museum (associated with a model train store) in Bryson City.*

DAY HIKES

The Great Smoky Mountains National Park has more than 800 mi of hiking trails, of which about half are on the North Carolina side. The trails range from short nature walks to long, strenuous hikes that gain several thousand feet in elevation. Park trails are maintained, but on many trails maintenance is seasonal. Be prepared for trail erosion and washouts, especially December through May when staffing levels may not permit much trail work.

Although permits are not required for day hikes, **you must have a backcountry permit for overnight or longer trips** (⇨*see Permits under Essentials in the Travel Smart Great*

3

THE AT

Each spring about 1,500 hikers set out to conquer the Appalachian Trail (AT), the 2,175-mi granddaddy of all hikes. Most hike north from Springer Mountain, Georgia, to Mt. Katahdin, Maine. By the time they get to the Great Smokies, where the AT reaches its highest elevation (6,625 feet) near Clingmans Dome, 160 mi from the trailhead in Georgia, about one-half of the hikers will already have dropped out. Typically, only about 400 hikers per year complete the entire AT. Of course, you don't have to hike the entire thing to experience the wonders of the trail. About 71 mi of the AT falls within the park. One of the easiest places to get on the trail for a short hike is at Newfound Gap, on U.S. 441 (Newfound Gap Road) at the North Carolina–Tennessee line.

Smoky Mountains National Park chapter at the end of this book).

Some of the more popular trails on the North Carolina side are listed in this chapter; more detailed information and maps can be obtained from visitor centers at the park. Also, rangers can help design a trip to suit your abilities.

Keep in mind that the park has significant elevation changes and that some summer days, especially at lower elevations, can be hot and humid. Also, high ozone levels are an issue on some days. Together, these can pose problems for people who aren't in good shape or who have heart or respiratory problems. △ **Be realistic about your physical condition and abilities. Carry plenty of water and energy-rich foods, like GORP (good old raisins and peanuts), energy bars, and fruit.**

Weather in the park is subject to rapid change. A day in March or April might start out warm and sunny, but by the time you reach a mile-high elevation the temperature may be near freezing, and it could be snowing heavily. The higher elevations of the park can get up to 80 inches of precipitation annually. ■**TIP→ Dress in layers and be prepared for temperature changes and snow in winter. Carry raingear and expect rain at any time.** Be sure to allow plenty of time to complete your hike before dark. As a rule of thumb, when hiking in the Smokies you'll travel only about 1½ mi per hour, so a 10-mi hike will take almost 7 hours. Remember, dogs and other pets are not allowed on park trails.

What's in a Name?

The Smoky Mountains have more than their fair share of odd and funny place names. Here are a few on the North Carolina side:

Bee Gum Branch, Noland Creek. A bee gum is a home-made bee hive, usually made from a hollowed-out black gum tree.

Big Butt, Luftee Knob. A butt, in local vernacular, is a hillock or a broken off end of a ridge. This one is pretty big.

Bone Valley, Hazel Creek. Named after the bones of cattle that froze to death in a spring snow storm in 1888.

Boogerman Trail, Cata-loochee. Named after Robert Palmer, who was nicknamed "Boogerman." The story goes that on his first day of school, little Robert was asked his name by the teacher to which he replied, "the boogerman" (or bogeyman), and the name stuck.

Fodderstack Rock, Thunder-head Mountain. Named after the rock's resemblance to a

stack of chopped cornstalks or hay, called livestock fodder.

Hell Ridge, Luftee Knob. The ridge was logged, burned, and badly eroded.

Killpecker Ridge, Thunder-head Mountain. Named after the nickname given to the newest man on a logging crew, who tended to tire himself out chopping (or peckering) before he learned to pace himself.

Maggot Spring Branch, Bunches Bald. Named for small white worms that live in some cold mountain springs (they're not actually maggots).

Paw Paw Creek, Thunder-head Mountain. Named for the American pawpaw (*Asimina triloba*), a small tree that produces a large yellow-green berry.

Sweet Heifer Creek, Cling-mans Dome. This refers to the young cows driven up these steep trails to summer pasture.

Twentymile, Fontana. Named because it was 20 mi from the town of Bushnell, now under the waters of Fontana Lake.

SPOTLIGHT HIKE: HAZEL CREEK AND BONE VALLEY

This hike begins with a boat ride across Fontana Lake, takes you to the old lumber and mining town of Proctor on the Hazel Creek trail (known on some park maps as Lakeshore trail), and provides access to Bone Valley and to the Hazel Creek wilderness. It is an easy hike (as hikes go in the Smokies), with an elevation gain of less than 500 feet. Most of the hike is on an old road and railroad bed. However, it is a long hike, 7.8 mi one-way and nearly 16 mi round-trip, not including the boat rides, if you do the entire route suggested here. Of course, you could do a shorter section. You could also add other trails and turn this into an overnight or multi-night backpacking and camping trip. Hazel Creeks offers good trout fishing, too.

■TIP→ **Arrange in advance with Fontana Marina (☎ 800/849–2258 or 828/498–2211) at Fontana Village on Highway 28 North to take you across the lake on a boat.** The shuttle boat will drop you (and pick you up) near Proctor on Hazel Creek. Due to changing lake levels, the exact drop-off/pick-up point may vary. ⌧*The Hazel Creek trailhead begins near backcountry campsite 86* ⌘*Easy.*

0.5 MI: PROCTOR AND CALHOUN HOUSE
Your boat captain will give you directions to get from the Fontana docking point to the trailhead, depending on where you're dropped off. Changing lake levels due to opening and closing of the TVA dam gates can mean the drop-off (and pick-up) points vary by several hundred yards. For the first few hundred feet of the hike you'll be on the Lakeshore trail, which intersects Hazel Creek trail. Before starting the Hazel Creek hike, look around. You're in what was the booming town of Proctor. For a short time in the late 1800s, Proctor was the site of a copper mine. Then, in 1902, the W.M. Ritter Lumber Co. opened. The company built a spur railway line, roads, bridges, a lumber mill, and other infrastructure. Logging along Hazel Creek began in 1910. By the time the company pulled out in 1928, it had cut and milled 201 million board feet of lumber, enough to build 20,000 houses. Horace Kephart, author of the classic *Our Southern Highlanders* and one of the people most responsible for the establishment of the park, lived in a small cabin (now gone) near Proctor, in 1904. While in Proctor explore the Calhoun House, an attractive white frame house that has been restored and preserved. The owner of the house, Granville Calhoun, knew Kephart well. Next, follow the Hazel Creek trail upstream.

3.5 MI: SAWDUST PILE HORSE CAMP
As you stroll up the old road bed along Hazel Creek, which is a noted trout stream, you'll pass the remains of several brick and concrete structures used by the W.M. Ritter Co. The first, a large one, is an old drying kiln, and another is a water gauge station. You'll cross Hazel Creek three times on old bridges before getting to a popular horse camp, Sawdust Pile Campsite 85.

5.1 MI: JENKINS RIDGE TRAIL

Cross two more bridges, and you'll come to the junction with Jenkins Ridge Trail (formerly Lakeshore trail). Bear right, staying on Hazel Creek trail and crossing Haw Gap Branch on a small bridge. Campsite 84 is nearby, in an attractive location among white pines.

5.9 MI: BONE VALLEY TRAIL

About 0.8 mi farther, you'll come to the junction with Bone Valley trail. Campsite 83, one of the few backcountry campsites that must be reserved in advance, is nearby. Bear left on Bone Valley. The trail runs along beside Bone Valley Creek. Somewhere in this area a herd of cattle, moved here for summer pasture in 1888, died in a spring snowstorm. The valley gets its name from the bones which remained on the ground for many years.

7.8 MI: HALL CABIN

Follow Bone Valley trail. After crossing Bone Valley Creek four times you'll come to a field with Hall cabin. ⚠ **Don't attempt to cross the creek following heavy rains if the water is high. You could get swept away by the current; turn back instead.** The cabin is open and you can look around inside. Nearby was the site of a large lodge built by the owner of the Kress department store, but it burned down in 1960. North of the Hall cabin is a path that leads to the Hall cemetery. Turn around and head back to your pick-up point at Fontana Lake.

SPOTLIGHT HIKE: LITTLE CATALOOCHEE

★ **Fodors**Choice No other hike in the Smokies offers a cultural and historic experience like this one. In the early 20th century, Cataloochee Cove had the largest population of any place in the Smokies, around 1,200 people. Most of the original structures have been torn down or succumbed to the elements, but a few historical frame buildings remain, preserved by park staff. You'll see several of these, along with rock walls and other artifacts, on the Little Cataloochee trail. The trail is 5.9 mi (one-way) including about 0.8 mi at the beginning on Pretty Hollow Gap trail. If you can, hike it with a two-car shuttle, parking one vehicle at the Pretty Hollow Gap trailhead in Cataloochee Valley and the other at the Little Cataloochee trailhead at Cove Creek Road (Old Highway 284). Including the time it takes to explore the historical buildings and cemeteries, you should allow at least six hours for this hike. ✉ *The*

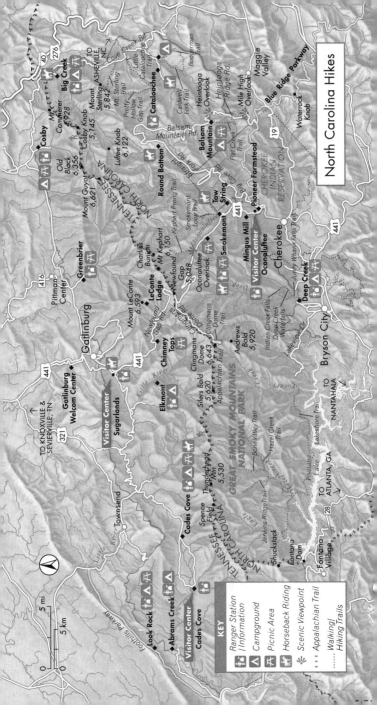

North Carolina Hikes

CLOSE UP

Cataloochee, the Novel

Asheville native Wayne Caldwell's 2007 novel, *Cataloochee*, tells the story of three generations of mountain families in Cataloochee Cove. They came to this distant, beautiful valley in search of a hard-scrabble version of Eden. Some may have found it, but the idyll was not to last. As the government took steps to relocate the settlers out of Cataloochee to make room for the Great Smoky Mountain National Park, a tragic act of violence touches the families.

Toward the end of the novel, a preacher at the Baptist church in Little Cataloochee says:

"I heard Brother Smith over in Big Cataloochee preached about this land being Eden. I hope you see fit to forgive him, even if he is a Methodist. Because, Lord, this is pretty country right enough, but mankind tamed this forest and grubbed out these pastures, and that don't make it Paradise. You made Eden oncet and that's it."

Pretty Hollow Gap trailhead is near Beech Grove School in the Cataloochee Valley ☞ Moderate.

0 MI: BEECH GROVE SCHOOLHOUSE

Near the beginning of the Pretty Hollow Gap trail (which will lead you to the Little Cataloochee trail) is Beech Grove School, a one-room schoolhouse built in 1907. The graffiti on the chalkboards and desks, however, is mostly modern. Before starting this hike, you may also want to explore the old houses, barns, and other buildings of Cataloochee. Several are on or near Cataloochee Creek. When you're ready to hit the trail, walk around the gate at the Pretty Hollow trailhead, following an old dirt road. At 0.2 mi, you'll pass the Cataloochee horse camp. (Note that parts of Pretty Hollow Gap and Little Cataloochee trails have horse traffic, and from time to time the trail is temporarily closed to repair damage from the horses.) Continue along Palmer Creek. At 0.8 mi, you will reach the beginning of Little Cataloochee trail, which goes to the right and up an incline. This part of the trail can be muddy, and you'll cross small streams.

2.6 MI: DAVIDSON GAP

Just before you reach Davidson Gap, the shoulder of Noland Mountain, which divides Little Cataloochee from Big Cataloochee, you may spot the ruins of an old cabin, with a rock wall and a few remains of chestnut logs. When Cataloochee was a thriving community, most of this area was cleared, and you would have a view of the Cataloochee Valley from here. About 0.2 mi along an easy descent from the gap, you'll see the remains of an old homestead, owned by the Messer family, and a little farther, the remains of a rock wall and an old fence line.

3.3 MI: COOK CABIN AND APPLE HOUSE

At one time, Cataloochee was one of the prime apple growing areas of the North Carolina mountains. Many old apple trees continue to bear fruit. Here, you'll spot the remains of an old apple house where apples were stored. Across from the apple house is a fine cabin that dates from 1856. It once belonged to settlers named Dan and Harriet Cook. The cabin was damaged by vandals in the 1970s, but it was rebuilt in 1999, partly from wood saved from the original cabin.

4.0 MI: LITTLE CATALOOCHEE BAPTIST CHURCH

This 1889 church is one of six churches that remain in the park. It has some "frills" not seen on the other churches, such as scalloped facing on the roof and a large church bell. There are about 60 graves in the cemetery down the hill from the church. The names on the stones—Palmer, Hannah, Messer, Cook—are those of the original settlers of Little Cataloochee. On cemetery "decoration days," descendants of the Cataloochee settlers come back to decorate the graves, have a service in the old church, and picnic.

4.8 MI: HANNAH CABIN

Cross Cataloochee Creek on a footbridge and begin a moderate ascent. A short side path to the right leads to the John Jackson Hannah cabin. You'll soon come to a junction with Long Bunk trail on the left. If you want to take a short side trip, about 0.2 mi on Long Bunk is the remains of another old cabin, and 0.2 mi farther is the Hannah cemetery.

5.9 MI: TRAIL'S END AT COVE CREEK ROAD

From Long Bunk, Little Cataloochee trail continues about 1.1 mi on a level and then moderate downhill grade to the trail's end at Cove Creek Road.

CLOSE UP

Follow that Path

Most trails in the Smokies, especially the day-hike trails, are well maintained and marked. Trails are generally signposted, wide, and easy to follow. You'll see wooden signs with trail information at nearly every junction. However, you should carry a trail map, preferably a topographical one, and pay attention to where you are going so you can retrace your route if necessary. With the exception of the Appalachian Trail and the new Mountains to Sea trail, trails in the Smokies are *not* blazed with paint, the way they are in many other parks and hiking areas. (A blaze is a painted marking of a consistent shape—usually rectangular or circular—dimension, and color along the trail route.) The standard blaze for the Appalachian Trail is a white rectangle 2 by 6 inches, usually at eye level. Some trails that intersect with the AT and lead to overlooks, shelters, or parking areas are blazed in blue. The new Mountains to Sea trail, which begins at Clingsmans Dome, connects with the Appalachian Trail, and runs 27 mi in the Smokies to the Blue Ridge Parkway near Cherokee, is also blazed in white. When eventually completed—it is about 40% completed now—it will run some 900 mi to Jockey's Ridge on the Outer Banks of the North Carolina coast.

OTHER HIKES

EASY

Deep Creek Waterfalls. For the effort of a 2.4-mi hike, this trail will reward you with three pretty waterfalls, Tom Branch, Indian Creek, and Juney Whank. Deep Creek also has a picnic area and campground. Tubing on Deep Creek is fun, too. ⊠*Trailhead at end of Deep Creek Rd., near Bryson City entrance to park* ⚐*Easy.*

MODERATE

Boogerman Loop. This 7.4-mi loop is much nicer than its name suggests. Highlights are old-growth forest, including some huge yellow poplars, and wildflowers in the spring. Plus, it is a loop trail, so you don't have to cover the same ground twice. You'll have to cross streams several times on this hike, but unless a heavy rain has washed them away, the streams have footbridges across them. On weekends in summer and fall, the trail is fairly busy. ⊠*From Cataloochee campground, walk to the Caldwell Fork trailhead and follow to Boogerman trail; stay on Boogerman until* *it intersects again with Caldwell Fork and take it back to the trailhead ☞Moderate.*

★ **Fodor'sChoice Clingmans Dome Trail.** The .5-mi (1 mi round-trip) path from the parking lot to the observation tower at the top of Clingmans Dome is short and paved, but fairly steep. At well over 6,000 feet you'll probably be gasping for air. Also, high ozone levels, which can occur 30 to 50 days a year at this elevation, can cause problems for those with respiratory problems. The view, however, is worth it. ⊠*Trail begins at the Clingmans Dome parking lot* ☉*Clingmans Dome Rd. is closed in winter* ☞*Moderate.*

Flat Creek. This is one of the hidden gems among Smokies trails. It's little known, but it's a delightful hike, especially in the summer when the high elevation means respite from stifling temperatures. The path stretches through a pretty woodland, with evergreens, birch, rhododendron, and wildflowers. The elevation gain is about 570 feet. The trail is only 2.6 mi if you use a two-car shuttle, one at the trailhead at mile 5.4 of Heintooga Ridge Road, and the other at the Heintooga picnic area; if you don't do a two-car shuttle, you'll have to walk 3.6 mi along Heintooga Ridge Road to your car, but even this is pleasant, with spruce and fir lining the road and little traffic. ⊠*Trail begins at Flat Creek trailhead at mile 5.4 of Heintooga Ridge Rd.; alternatively, you can begin at the trailhead at Heintooga picnic area, 3.6 mi away* ☉*Heintooga Ridge Rd. is closed in winter* ☞*Moderate.*

Kephart Prong. A 4-mi (round-trip) woodland trail wanders beside a stream to the remains of a Civilian Conservation Corps camp. ⊠*Trailhead is 5 mi north of Smokemont Campground on Newfound Gap Rd. (U.S. 441)* ☞*Moderate.*

Smokemont Loop. A 6.1-mi (round-trip) loop takes you by streams and, in the spring and summer, lots of wildflowers, including trailing arbutus. The trail also passes a field with old chestnut trees killed by the chestnut blight decades ago. With access off Newfound Gap Road (U.S. 441) this is an easy trail to get to. ⊠ *Bradley Fork trailhead is at D loop of Smokemont campground, follow Bradley Fork trail to Smokemont Loop trail* ☞ *Moderate.*

Civilian Conservation Corps

The Civilian Conservation Corps, or CCC, was established in 1933 by President Franklin Delano Roosevelt during the Great Depression. It gave young men a job, a roof over their heads, and something to eat. The law stipulated that the CCC was for men 18–26 who were unmarried and out of work. Enrollment was for a minimum of six months, but most CCC participants reenlisted. They were paid about a dollar a day and they were required to send $25 of their monthly $30 paycheck home to their family. In the Smokies, as many as 4,000 enrollees were assigned to 22 CCC camps at various times from 1933 to 1942, building roads, bridges, trails, and fire towers, and planting trees. The legacy of the CCC—especially hiking trails and back roads—can still be seen in the park. Remains of CCC camps can be found on several trails in the Smokies, including Forney Creek (building foundations) and Kephart Prong (foundations and part of a cistern used as a CCC fish hatchery).

DIFFICULT

Mt. Sterling. A 5.4-mi (round-trip) hike takes you to an old fire watchtower, which you can climb. The route is steep, with an elevation gain of almost 2,000 feet, so you should consider this a strenuous, difficult hike. ⊠*Trailhead on Cove Creek Rd. (Old Hwy. 284), midway between Cataloochee and Deep Creek campground* ☞*Difficult.*

SUMMER SPORTS & ACTIVITIES

BICYCLING

The North Carolina side of the Smokies offers excellent cycling, and bicycles are permitted on most roads. However, you have to be selective about where you bike. △**Vehicular traffic on the main roads, especially Newfound Gap Road (U.S. 441), can be very heavy. Steep terrain, and curvy, narrow back roads with narrow shoulders and blind spots make biking difficult or unsafe in some areas.**

NORTH CAROLINA HIKES

	Grade	Miles (one-way)	Eleva-tion Gain (feet)	Horses	Camp-ground	Open Info	Water	Ranger Station	Toilet	Level	Conditions
Boogerman Loop	Slightly Steep	7.4 Loop	1300	Y***	N	Y/R	Y**	Y	Y	Mod.	Good
Clingmans Dome	Steep	0.5	400	N	N	Closed Winter	N	N	N	Mod.	Paved
Deep Creek Waterfalls	Level to Slightly Steep	2.4 Loop	200	N	N	Y/R	Y**	Y	Y	Easy	Good
Flat Creek	Slightly Steep	2.6*	570	N	Y	Closed Winter	Y**	N	Y	Mod.	Good
Hazel Creek & Bone Valley	Level to Slightly Steep	7.8	500	Y***	B/C Only	Y/R	Y**	N	N	Easy	Old Roadbed
Kephart Prong	Steep	2.0	750	N	Y	Y/R	Y**	N	N	Mod.	Good
Little Cataloochee	Level to Steep	5.9*	1000	Y***	Y	Y/R	Y**	Y	Y	Mod.	Good
Mt. Sterling	Very Steep	2.7	1960	N	Y	Y/R	Y**	N	N	Diff.	Fair
Smokemont Loop	Slightly Steep	6.1 Loop	1000	Y***	N	Y/R	Y**	Y	Y	Mod.	Good

* 2-car shuttle recommended, ** water must be purified, *** horses permitted on part of trail only, B/C = back country, Y/R = year-round

Two good places for biking on (mostly) paved roads are Lakeview Drive—the so-called Road to Nowhere near Bryson City—and Cataloochee Cove. Also, Balsam Mountain Road and Cove Creek Road offer pleasant biking with very little auto traffic. Since these roads are unpaved, with mostly gravel surfaces, you should use a mountain bike or an all-terrain hybrid. Helmets are not required by law but are strongly recommended.

MOUNTAIN BIKING

There are no mountain biking trails in the Smokies. On the North Carolina side, only two hiking trails, the Oconaluftee River trail, which begins near the Oconaluftee Visitor Center, and the lower Deep Creek trail near Bryson City, formerly a road, allow bikes.

Near the Smokies, the **Tsali Recreation Area** in the Nantahala National Forest, about 15 mi west of Bryson City, is a popular area for biking. With about 40 mi of trails with four excellent loops, it has been rated one of the top places for mountain biking in the country. ✛ *Tsali is on a hilly peninsula reaching into Fontana Lake, at the base of the Smokies. From Bryson City, follow U.S. 19/74 to the intersection with NC 28. Follow NC 28 north about 3 mi. Look for a sign for the Tsali Recreation Area; turn right. Follow the paved road to the campground and trailhead parking lot; park in the lot with the sign* BIKERS PARK AND PAY HERE. ⊙*April to October.*

The Pisgah National Forest also offers many opportunities for cycling.

BIKE RENTALS

Nantahala Outdoor Center Bike Shop. Watch river rafters swoosh by on the Nantahala River as you get your bike tuned up or rent a bike at this friendly outfitter. Avid bikers on staff will give you tips on the best biking spots. Mountain bikes rent for $40 to $60 a day, and road bikes for $40. Off-season discounts are sometimes available. All bike rentals include a helmet and a bike rack to transport the bike on your car. ✉*13077 Hwy. 19 W, Bryson City* ☎*828/488–2176* ⊕*www.noc.com.*

FISHING

The North Carolina side of the Smokies has one of the best wild trout fisheries in the East. Deep Creek, Little Cataloochee, and Hazel Creek are streams known to serious anglers all over the country. The North Carolina side has more than 1,000 mi of streams (not all contain trout), and all are open to fishing year-round, except Bear Creek at its junction with Forney Creek, and upstream from there.

Among the best trout streams on this side of the park are Big Creek, Cataloochee Creek, Palmer Creek, Raven Fork, Deep Creek, Hazel Creek, and Noland Creek. Often, the best fishing is in higher elevation streams, in areas that are more difficult to reach. Streams that are easily accessible, such as the Pigeon River, have greater fishing pressure.

Another option for fishing is Lake Fontana. Its cold, deep waters provide an ideal habitat for muskie, walleye, and smallmouth bass.

FISHING RULES

To fish in the park you must possess a valid fishing license or permit from either Tennessee or North Carolina. Either state license is valid throughout the park, and no trout stamp is required. Children under 16 don't need a license. Fishing licenses are not available in the park, but may be purchased in nearby towns or online.

Only artificial flies or lures with a single hook can be used— no live bait. Fishing is permitted from a half hour before official sunrise to a half hour after official sunset. The limit for the combined total of brook, rainbow, or brown trout, or smallmouth bass, must not exceed five fish each day. You may not have more than five fish in your possession, regardless of whether they are fresh, stored in an ice chest, or otherwise preserved. Twenty rock bass may be kept in addition to the above limit.

The size limit is 7 inches for brook, rainbow, and brown trout and also 7 inches for smallmouth bass. For rock bass there is no minimum size.

LICENSES

North Carolina Wildlife Resources Commission. You can order a North Carolina inland fishing license, valid throughout the park, online. A 10-day non-resident fishing license is $10, and an annual non-resident license is $30. Licenses for North Carolina residents cost half the non-resident fee. To fish for trout outside the park, you'll also need a trout stamp, which costs an extra $10. ✉*1751 Varsity Dr., Raleigh, NC* ☎*919/707–0010* ⊕*www.ncwildlife.org.*

OUTFITTERS

For backcountry trips, you may want to hire a licensed guide. Full-day trips cost around $225–$300 for one angler, $300–$400 for two. Only guides approved by the National Park Service are permitted to take anglers into the backcountry.

Lowe Fly Shop (✉*15 Woodland Dr., Waynesville, NC* ☎*828/ 452–0039* ⊕*www.loweguideservice.com*) offers guided angling trips in the Smokies for all skill levels.

Smoky Mountain Fly Fishing (✉*626 Tsali Blvd., Cherokee, NC* ☎*828/497–1555* ⊕*www.smokymountainflyfishing. net*) is a park-licensed guide that conducts guided fly-fishing trips in the park.

HORSEBACK RIDING

Get back to nature and away from the crowds with a horseback ride through the forest. Guided horseback rides are offered by one park concessionaire stable on the North Carolina side, at Smokemont near Cherokee. Rides are at a walking pace, so they are suitable for even inexperienced riders.

Another option is to bring your own horse. The Smoky Mountains National Park is one of the best places to ride in the Southeast. About 550 mi of the park's hiking trails are open to horses. Horses are restricted to trails specifically designated for horse use. Five drive-in horse camps, open April through October, allow you easy access to the park's horse trails and cost from $20 to $25 a night. Four of these are on the North Carolina side—Big Creek, Cataloochee Cove, Tow String, and Roundbottom.

If you bring a horse to any park horse camp or ride a horse in the park, you must have either the original or a copy of an official negative test for equine infectious anemia (called a Coggins test). Pets are permitted in the horse camps but must be on a leash.

HORSE CAMPS

Big Creek Horse Camp. Big Creek has six tent-only horse camping sites, with flush toilets, potable water, picnic tables, grills, designated parking, refuse containers, horse stalls, and hitch racks. ✉*Exit 451, I-40, 16 mi southeast of Crosby, TN* ☎*877/444-6777* ⊕*www.recreation.gov* ⊗*Apr.–early Nov.*

Cataloochee. Cataloochee has seven tent-only horse camping sites, pit toilets, picnic tables, grills, designated parking, refuse containers, horse stalls, and hitch racks. The horse camp has a creek-side setting in the beautiful Cataloochee Valley; elk may wander into the camp. ✉*I-40, Exit 20, 25 mi northwest of Asheville, NC; turn on Cove Creek Rd. and go 11 mi to horse camp* ☎*877/444-6777* ⊕*www. recreation.gov* ⊗*Apr.–early Nov.*

Roundbottom. Roundbottom has five tent-only horse camping sites, pit toilets, picnic tables, grills, designated parking, refuse containers, horse stalls, and hitch racks. ✉*From Cherokee: take U.S. 441 south. Just after entering the park, turn right to Big Cove Rd. Go .2 mi to stop sign and turn left onto Big Cove Rd. Go 8.8 mi to a T. Turn right and go .9 mi to the end of the pavement. Take the gravel Straight Fork–Round Bottom Rd., adjacent to a trout rearing facility, 3.5 mi to the horse camp* ☎*877/444-6777* ⊕*www. recreation.gov* ⊗*Apr.–early Nov.*

Tow String. Tow String has only two tent-only horse camping sites, pit toilets, picnic tables, grills, designated parking, refuse containers, horse stalls, and hitch racks. ✉*4 mi north of Cherokee off Newfound Gap Rd. (U.S. 441). Turn right at sign for Tow String. Turn left after crossing bridge* ☎*877/444-6777* ⊕*www.recreation.gov* ⊗*Apr.– early Nov.*

OUTFITTERS

Smokemont Riding Stable. The emphasis here is on a family-friendly horseback-riding experience, suitable even for novice riders. Choose either the one-hour trail ride or a 2.5-hour waterfall ride (departing daily at 9 and noon). Riders must be at least 5 years old and weigh no more than 225 pounds. Smokemont also occasionally offers wagon rides. Check with the stables for dates and times. ✉*135 Smokemont Riding Stable Rd. (near MM 27.2), Cherokee* ☎*828/497-2373* ⊕*www.smokemontridingstable.com* 🖃*$20–$48* ⊗*Late May–Oct., daily 9–5.*

BOATING, RAFTING & TUBING

For lake boating near the Smokies, your best bet is Fontana Lake. This 29-mi-long, 11,700-acre TVA lake offers great views of the southwestern side of the Smokies. Canoes, kayaks, and other boats are available to rent at several marinas on the lake. You can even rent a houseboat. If you're towing your own boat, there are several boat ramps, including two near Bryson City. The Old 288 ramp is west of town; turn off Everett Street and continue on Lakeview Drive, following the Tuckasegee River, to the boat ramp signs. The Lemons Branch ramp is also west of Bryson City. Follow U.S. 74, then turn north on Highway 28; look for the Tsali Recreation Area on your right and follow signs to the boat launch.

For a serious water experience, go rafting on the Nantahala River or one of the other rivers near the Smokies. The Nantahala, near Bryson City, is the closest to the Smokies. It has mild but still exciting Class II and III rapids. ■TIP→ **Serious rafters and kayakers looking for a challenge on a Class IV/IV+ river should consider the Cheoah near Robbinsville, North Carolina.** The Cheoah River has reopened for rafting and kayaking after being dammed and closed for years, but only for about 17 days a year, mostly in the summer and fall. The French Broad near Asheville is another option. However, as of this writing most rafting trips on the French Broad have been discontinued due to a regional drought that has reduced water levels to lows not seen in more than 100 years.

On a hot summer's day, there's nothing like tubing. You can swim or go tubing on Deep Creek near Bryson City. The upper section is a little wild and woolly, with white-water flowing from cold mountain springs. The put-in is at the convergence of Indian Creek and Deep Creek where the sign says NO TUBING BEYOND THIS POINT. The lower section of Deep Creek is more suitable for kids. Put-in for this section is at the swimming hole just above the first bridge on the Deep Creek trail. There are several tubing outfitters near the entrance of the park at Deep Creek. Some have changing rooms and showers. Tubes rent for less than $5 a day. Wear a swim suit and bring towels and dry clothes to change into which you can leave in your car. Most tubing outfitters are open April–October. Note that the National Park Service warns against tubing and swimming in the park, due to the risk of water-related injuries and even drowning; however, many thousands of visitors to the park enjoy the experience every summer.

BOATING OUTFITTERS

To rent a small power boat—a 15-foot boat with 15 horse-power motor is $50 a day, and a 24-foot pontoon boat with 90 horsepower motor is $165 a day—check with **Alarka Boat Dock** (✉️*7230 Grassy Branch Rd., Bryson City* ☎️*828/488–3841*).

Boat rentals on Fontana Lake, including kayaks, canoes, pontoon boats, small powerboats, houseboats (around $500 a day), and jet skis, are available at **Fontana Village Marina** (✉️*Fontana Village, Hwy. 28 N, Fontana Dam* ☎️*800/849–2258 or 828/498–2211*), open April–October.

For a fast boating experience, try **Smoky Mountain Jet Boats** (✉️*22 Needmore Rd., Bryson City 28713* ☎️*828/488–0522 or 888/900–9091*), offering half-hour rides on Fontana Lake for $28 a person.

RAFTING OUTFITTERS

Nantahala Outdoor Center (*NOC* ✉️*13077 U.S. Hwy. 19 W, Bryson City* ☎️*800/232–7238 or 828/488–2176* ⊕*www.noc.com*) guides more than 30,000 rafters every year on the Nantahala and eight other rivers in North Carolina, Tennessee, Georgia, and West Virginia. ⇨*For more information, see Bryson City in Chapter 6.*

TUBING OUTFITTERS

Deep Creek Store & Tubes (✉️*1840 W. Deep Creek Rd., Bryson City* ☎️*828/488–9665* ⊕*www.smokymtncampground.com*) rents tubes and sells camping supplies.

Deep Creek Tube Center (✉️*1090 Deep Creek Rd., Bryson City* ☎️*882/488–6055* ⊕*www.deepcreekcamping.com/Tubing.html*) rents inner tubes and sells creek shoes and other tubing accessories in its camp store.

WINTER SPORTS & ACTIVITIES

SKIING

It doesn't snow much at the lower elevations of the Smokies, but in winter the higher elevations of the park frequently get heavy snow. Newfound Gap, at nearly a mile high, gets almost 5 feet of snow in the average year. You can check on the amount of snow on the ground at the higher elevations by visiting the park's webcam at Purchase Knob, on the

North Carolina side at about 5,000 feet (⊕*www.nature. nps.gov/air/webcams/parks/grsmpkcam/grsmpkcam.cfm*). Some roads, including Clingmans Dome Road and Balsam Mountain Road, are closed in winter, and even the main road through the park, Newfound Gap Road, closes when there's snow and ice, cutting off access to snowy areas. If Newfound Gap Road is not closed, you can enjoy cross-country skiing and hiking in the snow along Clingmans Dome Road, which is closed to vehicles in winter. For weather information, call ☎*865/436–1200 Ext. 630*, and for road closings, call ☎*865/436–1200 Ext. 631*.

EXPLORING THE BACKCOUNTRY

Of the 9 million people visiting the Great Smoky Mountains National Park each year, only a tiny fraction explore its secrets on an overnight trip. The park has more than 800 mi of hiking trails. Most of these trails, including 71 mi of the Appalachian Trail, are in backcountry areas.

At Oconaluftee Visitor Center, pick up a copy of the brochure "Backpack Loops" ($1) which describes 12 of the best overnight backpacking loops.

Free permits are required for overnight camping, hiking, or backpacking, and advance reservations are required for all shelters and 17 of the backcountry campsites. ⇨*See Exploring the Backcountry in Chapter 2 for information on backcountry rules and regulations.*

BACKCOUNTRY PERMITS

Backcountry Permit Stations. On the North Carolina side, backcountry permits are available at the following locations: Oconaluftee Visitor Center, Twentymile Ranger Station, Fontana Marina, Fontana Dam Visitor Center, Deep Creek Campground Office, Smokemont Campground Office, Big Creek Ranger Station, and Cataloochee Valley near the campground. When you arrive in the park, you must complete a permit at one of these self-registration stations. Your permit must designate the campsite or shelter at which you will stay for each night of your trip. You can download a trail map from the park Web site to find the location of backcountry shelters and campsites in the park. Keep the permit with you and drop the top copy in the registration box. ☎*865/436–1297* ⊕*www.nps.gov/grsm/ planyourvisit/backcountrycamping.htm* ⊠*Free.*

CLOSE UP

Freebies in the Smokies

The Great Smoky Mountains National Park is one of the biggest bargains in the country. Freebies include:

■ Admission to the park, no matter where you enter or how many times you visit.

■ All hiking trails.

■ All backcountry camping, both at campsites and at shelters.

■ All picnic sites.

■ All historic sites, including admission to Mingus Mill, Cable Mill, Cataloochee Cove, Cades Cove, and Roaring Fork Motor Nature Trail.

■ Ranger-led programs, offered year-round.

■ Junior Ranger programs for kids 5–12, with ever-changing activities including hikes and hands-on experiments.

Backcountry Reservation Office. Reserve backcountry shelters and campsites in advance by calling Backcountry Reservations. ☎865/436–1231 ⬚Free ⊙Daily 8–6.

EDUCATIONAL PROGRAMS

Discover the flora, fauna, and mountain culture of the Smokies with scheduled ranger programs and nature walks.

SCIENCE LEARNING CENTER

Appalachian Highlands Science Learning Center. Established in 2000, and located at Purchase Knob in Haywood County on the North Carolina side of the Smokies, the Appalachian Highlands Science Learning Center is one of what eventually will be 32 research learning centers in the national park system. While not open to individuals, the Center runs teacher workshops, provides research grants, and offers field trips for middle-school, high-school, and college students. It also has a limited number of summer internships for high-school students. ⬚Purchase Knob ☎828/926–6251 ⬚www.nps.gov/grsm/naturescience/pk-homepage.htm.

RANGER PROGRAMS

☼ **Interpretive Ranger Programs.** The National Park Service sponsors all sorts of orientation activities, such as daily guided hikes and talks. The focus of the programs varies widely, from Earthcaching (like geocaching—a high-tech treasure hunt played with GPS devices—but with an education component) using GPS units loaned by the park to talks on mountain culture to old-time fiddle and banjo music. For schedules, go to the Oconaluftee Visitor Center and pick up a free copy of *Smokies Guide*, or check online. ☎865/436–1200 ⊕*www.nps.gov/grsm/planyourvisit/ events.htm* ☒*Free.*

☼ **Junior Ranger Program for Families.** Children ages 5 to 12 can take part in these hands-on educational programs. Kids should pick up a Junior Ranger booklet ($3) at Oconaluftee or at other park visitor centers. After they've completed the activities in the booklet, they can stop by a visitor center to talk to a ranger and receive a Junior Ranger badge. Especially during the summer, the park offers many age-appropriate demonstrations, classes, and programs for Junior Rangers, such as Blacksmithing, Stream Splashin', Geology, Cherokee Pottery for Kids, and—our favorite— Whose Poop's on Our Boots? ☎865/436–1200 ⊕*www. nps.gov/grsm/forkids/index.htm* ☒*$3.*

ARTS & ENTERTAINMENT

For more arts and entertainment options on the North Carolina side, you'll want to visit nearby towns, such as Cherokee (keep in mind that no alcohol is sold on the Cherokee reservation), Bryson City, or Waynesville. Asheville, a little over an hour away, is known for its theater, art galleries, restaurants, and clubs. ⇨ *See Chapter 6: Asheville and Other North Carolina Towns for more information.*

Ranger-led **Full Moon on Top of the Smokies** (☎865/436– 1200 ⊕*www.nps.gov/grsm*) hikes begin at 8 PM at the Clingmans Dome trailhead, and last about 1½ hours. Only offered during the full moon, usually on a Thursday, you'll enjoy a spectacular sunset and a full moon view. If the moon is waxing or waning, there's often a sunset hike up the Clingmans Dome trail. For schedules, go to the Oconaluftee Visitor Center and pick up a free copy of *Smokies Guide*, or check online.

Bring a blanket or lawn chair to Smokemont Campground to hear local musicians at the one-hour **Music Nights** (☎865/436–1200 ⊕www.nps.gov/grsm). You might hear gospel, bluegrass, or old-time mountain music. Usually these are held on Saturday nights at 7.

If you like mystery, humor, and tall tales, check out the **Smokemont Players Story Hour** (☎865/436–1200 ⊕www.nps.gov/grsm) for an hour of mountain storytelling. Story hours are held in an open field at the Smokemont Campground, between C and D loops, usually on Fridays at 7 PM in the summer.

FESTIVALS & EVENTS

Many of the festivals in the park are held on the Tennessee side. These include Old Timers' Day at Cades Cove in the fall, Festival of Christmas Past in December at Sugarlands Visitor Center, and Cosby in the Park at Cosby Picnic Area in the spring. ⇨*See Chapter 2: Exploring the Tennessee Side for more information.*

The **Mountain Life Festival** (☎865/436–1200 ⊠*Free*) is held on a Saturday in late September at the Mountain Farm Museum at Oconaluftee. At the festival, you'll see demonstrations of traditional mountain activities and crafts, such as hearth cooking, hominy making, apple butter, apple cider, and soap making. The highlight is traditional sorghum syrup making, using a horse-powered cane mill and wood-fired cooker.

★ **Fodor's**Choice The **Spring Wildflower Pilgrimage** (☎865/436–7318 Ext. 222 ⊕ *www.springwildflowerpilgrimage.org* ⊠*Registration $25–$40; some events free*), held in late April attracts wildflower enthusiasts from all over the country for five days of wildflower and natural history walks, seminars, classes, photography tours, and other events. Upcoming pilgrimages are set for April 22–26, 2009, and April 23–27, 2010. Check the Web site for more details.

SHOPPING

On the North Carolina side, Oconaluftee Visitor Center has an attractive gift shop and bookstore, with a first-rate selection of books and maps on the Smokies and nearby mountain areas, as well as T-shirts. While there's a camp store on the Tennessee side at Cades Cove campground, there isn't one on the North Carolina side. You can buy firewood at Smokemont Riding Stable. (Note that firewood cannot be brought into the park from the states of Illinois, Indiana, Michigan, Ohio, New Jersey, or New York, due to a quarantine to protect against the spread of destructive insects.)

For groceries, camping supplies, souvenirs, and other shopping items, visit one of the small towns near the park entrances, including Cherokee, Bryson City, Robbinsville, and Waynesville. Asheville, a little more than an hour away, has the widest selection of shopping choices, including many galleries selling high-quality mountain crafts.

The park also has an official online store for books, maps, park logo items, gift baskets, CDs, DVDs, and local mountain foods (⊛*www.smokiesinformation.org*). It is operated by the nonprofit Great Smoky Mountains Association and proceeds generated by purchases at the store are donated to educational, scientific, and historical projects in the park.

Lodging & Dining in the Park

WORD OF MOUTH

"We have done the hike many times and stayed at LeConte Lodge—we love it. The cabins are rustic and have the bunks / beds and little else. There is a main lodge where the family-style meals are served. Short hikes from the lodge area take you to the sunset and sunrise lookouts. It is simple, peaceful, and full of great memories for our family. Reservations can be difficult to come by."

—sprin2

By Lan
Sluder

TOURISM IN THE MOUNTAINS HAS a fairly long history. In the early 19th century, wealthy planters from the South Carolina and Georgia Low Country began to spend summers in the western North Carolina mountains to escape the heat and diseases of the coast. Later in the century, the mountains became known as a place to recover from consumption (Tuberculosis) and other diseases. Several large hotels and health resorts were constructed in Asheville and elsewhere, and a few small hunting lodges sprang up to serve intrepid travelers to the southern Appalachians. Then, in 1890, George Vanderbilt began construction on his 250-room home, Biltmore, on 125,000 acres around Asheville. This, combined with the development of railroads in the region, made Asheville's name as a mountain resort town full of fine hotels and restaurants, and Asheville's fame trickled out to other parts of the region, including towns around what is now the Great Smoky Mountains National Park.

Over on the Tennessee side, Knoxville took advantage of its central location, and its river and railroad transport, to establish itself as a major distribution and lumbering center. Business leaders in Knoxville were prominent among those working to set up a large new national park in the Tennessee–North Carolina mountains.

Although the advent of the Great Depression in 1929 essentially stopped tourism development in western North Carolina and eastern Tennessee, there were a sufficient number of hotels and other accommodations in the region so that when the Great Smoky Mountains National Park was officially established in 1934 there was no need—and indeed during the Depression no funds—to build hotels in the park, as had been done in some of the remote western national parks, such as Yellowstone and the Grand Canyon.

Thus, today, there is no lodging in the park except for one small hike-in lodge on the Tennessee side. Likewise, the park has no dining establishments, save for a small snack bar at Cades Cove. However, there are tens of thousands of hotel rooms around the edges of the park, in every lodging category from B&Bs to mom 'n pop motor courts to chain motels and large mountain resorts. Here also, within a short drive of the park, are thousands of restaurants in all price ranges.

WHERE TO EAT

The closest thing to fine dining you can find in the park is a hot dog at the snack bar in Cades Cove or a Coke from a vending machine at a visitor center. You'll have to make your own fine dining with an alfresco picnic at one of the park's 11 attractive picnic areas, which together have almost 800 picnic tables. Most have raised grills for cooking. You can dine beside a stream or in a shaded woodland area. All picnic areas have restrooms, some with pit toilets and some with flush toilets but not all have running water in the bathrooms (bring hand sanitizer) or potable drinking water. Six of the picnic sites have pavilions for group picnics, which can be reserved in advance for a small fee; all other picnic sites are free. Unless otherwise noted, picnic areas are open 24 hours year-round. Of course, you can also just plop down on a moss-covered rock, a fallen tree trunk, or in a grassy field and make your own picnic area. Do-it-yourself picnicking is permitted anywhere in the park, but keep an eye out for bears and pack out any trash or leftovers.

WHAT IT COSTS				
¢	$	$$	$$$	$$$$
RESTAURANT				
under $10	$10–$14	$15–$19	$20–$24	over $24

Restaurant prices are per person for a main course at dinner and do not include any service charges or taxes.

TENNESSEE SIDE

¢ ✕**Cades Cove Camp Store Snack Bar.** *American.* The only eating establishment in the park is a little snack bar inside the Cades Cove camp store. Here, you can buy hot dogs, pizza, sandwiches, soup, soft serve ice cream, and other snacks. Breakfast items include coffee and bagels. The camp store, about the size of a small convenience store, also sells canned pork 'n beans, s'more fixings, soft drinks, chips, and other junk food. Firewood is also sold here and you can rent bicycles. ⊠*Cades Cove Campground* ☎*865/436–1200* ⊕*www.nps.gov/grsm* ⊟*MC, V.*

PICNIC AREAS

Cades Cove Picnic Area. This picnic area, near the beginning of the Cades Cove loop, has 81 picnic tables. Its big advantage is that you're near the beautiful Cades Cove valley; the disadvantage is that as many as 2 million people come through this area each year. At only 1,800 feet high, it can be hot and humid here in the summer. Potable water and flush toilets are available. Bears are fairly common here, so closely observe food storage precautions. Spence Field, Anthony Creek, and Thunderhead trailheads are at the picnic area. ⊠*9 mi east of Townsend, near the entrance to Cades Cove Loop and near the Cades Cove campground* ☉*Sept.–Apr., daily dawn–dusk; May–Aug., daily dawn–8.*

★ Fodor'sChoice **Chimneys Picnic Area.** Chimneys, just off Newfound Gap Road and a little over 6 mi from the Sugarlands Visitor Center, may be the most popular picnic area in the park. Along both sides of a well-shaded loop road through the area are 89 picnic tables with grills. Some are wheelchair accessible. The prime spots along the stream that runs through the site fill up first. Huge boulders in the stream make for a striking view from your table. Potable water and flush toilets are available. ⊠*Newfound Gap Rd. (U.S. 441), MM 6.2* ☉*Sept.–Apr., daily dawn–dusk; May–Aug., daily dawn–8.*

Cosby Picnic Area. On the northeast edge of the park, this picnic area has 95 tables in well-tended grassy areas under large poplar trees. Cosby Creek runs through the grounds. A wheelchair-accessible pavilion seats 55 and can be reserved for $20. There's a ranger station, restrooms, trailheads, and horse trails. Cosby has easy access from I–40 via the Foothills Parkway and TN 32. ⊠*Off Exit 443 of I–40 via the eastern section of the Foothills Pkwy. and TN 32.*

★ **Greenbrier Picnic Area.** Greenbrier is the second-smallest picnic area in the park, with only 12 spaces near a shady, boulder-strewn creek. Its large pavilion seats 70 and can be reserved for $10. This picnic area off U.S. 321 is rarely busy. The Greenbrier access road is partly unpaved and is partly one-way. There is a ranger station here and restrooms with pit toilets but no running water. The Ramsey Cascades trail is nearby, leading to the Ramsey waterfalls about 4 mi away. ⊠*Off U.S. 321 northeast of Sugarlands Visitor Center.*

Look Rock Picnic Area. Access the picnic area via the western section of the beautiful Foothills Parkway. Foothills

Getting Groceries

Other than a small convenience store at Cades Cove campground, there is no place to buy picnic supplies and groceries in the park. However, near the park entrances in North Carolina and Tennessee, you'll find good-sized supermarkets. **Food City** (⊠*Newfound Gap Rd., Pigeon Forge, TN* ☎*865/453–4977* ⊠*741 Dolly Parton Pkwy., Sevierville, TN* ☎*865/908–3710* ⊠ *1219 East Pkwy./U.S. 321, Gatlinburg, TN* ☎*865/430–3116*) has outlets in Pigeon Forge, Sevierville, and Gatlinburg. There's a **Wal-Mart Supercenter** (⊠*1414 Parkway, Sevierville, TN* ☎*865/429–0029* ⊠*210 Wal-Mart Plaza, Sylva, NC* ☎*828/586–0211*) in Sevierville and Sylva. In North Carolina, **Ingles** (⊠*U.S. 19/23 at Hughes Branch Rd., Bryson City, NC* ☎*828/488–6600* ⊠*201 Barber Blvd., Waynesville, NC* ☎*828/456–7599* ⊠*251 Welch Rd., Waynesville, NC* ☎*828/456–8776* ⊠*2 Sweetwater Rd., Robbinsville, NC* ☎*828/479–6748*) is the dominant supermarket chain, with stores in Bryson City, Waynesville, and Robbinsville, among other towns near the park. **Bi-Lo** (⊠*404 Russ Ave., Waynesville, NC* ☎*828/456–8222*) has a location in Waynesville.

In Asheville and Knoxville you have an even larger selection of supermarkets, including a number of gourmet and upscale organic markets.

Parkway is lightly traveled, so there are usually few people here. A ½-mi hike takes you to the observation tower at Look Rock, which offers panoramic views into the Smokies. There are 51 picnic tables, restrooms with flush toilets, potable water, and a ranger station. ⊠ *Off Foothills Pkwy. 11 mi southeast of U.S. 321 entrance to Pkwy.* ☉*Early May–Oct.*

Metcalf Bottoms Picnic Area. This large, 165-table picnic area is midway between Sugarlands Visitor Center and Cades Cove. The Little River is nearby, where you can fish or take a cooling dip. Metcalf Bottoms has restrooms with flush toilets, potable water, and a 70-seat pavilion (open March–October) that can be reserved in advance for $20. Two easy hiking trails, Metcalf Bottoms and Little Brier, begin at the picnic area. ⊠*Off Little River Rd. about 11 mi west of Gatlinburg.*

NORTH CAROLINA SIDE

PICNIC AREAS

Big Creek Picnic Area. This is the smallest picnic area in the park, with only 10 picnic tables. It's accessible via Exit 451 off I–40, or the unpaved Cove Creek Road from Cataloochee. There's a small campground here and restrooms. Several good hiking trails can be reached from the picnic area, and Big Creek has some Class IV rapids nearby. ⊠ *Off I–40 at exit 451 (Waterville). Follow the road past the Walters Power Generating Station to a 4-way intersection; continue straight through and follow signs.*

Collins Creek Picnic Area. The largest developed picnic area in the park, Collins Creek has 182 picnic tables. Collins Creek, which runs near the picnic area, is a small stream with above-average trout fishing. The site has restrooms with flush toilets, potable water, and a 70-seat pavilion that can be reserved in advance for $20. ⊠ *Newfound Gap Rd. (U.S. 441) at MM 25.4, about 8 mi from Cherokee* ⊙ *Early Mar.–Apr. and Sept.–Oct., daily dawn–dusk; May–Aug., daily dawn–8.*

★ **Deep Creek Picnic Area.** Deep Creek offers more than picnicking. You can go tubing, hike to three waterfalls, go trout fishing, and even mountain bike here. The picnic area, open year-round, has 58 picnic tables, plus a pavilion that seats up to 70. ⊠ *1912 East Deep Creek Rd., Bryson City, NC* ✛ *From downtown Bryson City, follow signs for 3 mi to Deep Creek.*

★ Fodor'sChoice **Heintooga Picnic Area.** Located at over a mile high and set in a stand of spruce and fir, this 41-table picnic area is the best in the park. Nearby is Mile High Overlook, which offers one of the most scenic views of the Smokies and is a great place to enjoy the sunset. For birders, this is a good spot to see golden-crowned kinglets, red-breasted nuthatches, and other species that prefer higher elevations. You're almost certain to see the common raven here. Nearby is a campground and trailheads for several good hiking trails including Flat Creek. You can return to Cherokee via an unpaved back road, Balsam Mountain Road, which is one-way, to Big Cove Road. ⊠ *Near end of Heintooga Ridge Rd. From Cherokee, take the BRP 11 mi to the turnoff for Heintooga Ridge Rd.; follow Heintooga Ridge Rd. about 9 mi to picnic area* ⊙ *Early May–Oct.*

WHERE TO STAY

The only accommodations actually in the park, besides camping, are at LeConte Lodge. Outside the park, you have a gargantuan selection of hotels of every ilk. On the Tennessee side, in Gatlinburg you'll see a street sign that says "2000 Hotel Rooms" and points up the hill, and that's just in one section of town. From overlooks near the park, you can look down on Gatlinburg and see high-rise hotels that rise up like modern megaliths on the mountainsides. In nearby Pigeon Forge you'll find nearly every chain motel you can think of. More hotels and RV parks await in Sevierville, Townsend, and, 40 mi away, in Knoxville. On the North Carolina side, lodging is more low-key, but you can choose from old mountain inns, B&Bs, and motels in the small towns of Bryson City, Waynesville, Robbinsville, and Dillsboro. A seemingly ever-expanding number of hotel towers are connected to the giant Harrah's casino in Cherokee, soon to have 1,000 rooms. About 50 mi away, in and around Asheville, you can choose from among one of the largest collections of B&Bs in the Southeast, along with hip urban hotels and classic mountain resorts. ⇨*See chapters 5 and 6 for lodging outside the park.*

WHAT IT COSTS				
¢	$	$$	$$$	$$$$
HOTEL				
under $100	$100– $150	$151– $200	$201– $250	over $250

Hotel prices are for a double room in high season and do not include taxes, service charges, or resort fees.

TENNESSEE SIDE

★ **Fodor's**Choice ⛰ **LeConte Lodge.** Set at 6,360 feet near the summit of Mt. LeConte, this hike-in lodge is remote, rustic, and remarkable. It is not, however, luxurious. Seven small, rough-hewn wood cabins and three group sleeping rooms have double bunk beds and propane heaters. There is no electricity; lighting is by kerosene lamps. There is also no running water; you bathe in a washbasin or with a bucket (bring your own washcloth and hand towel). Shared bathrooms do have flush toilets. The appeal of LeConte Lodge is in the mountaintop setting, taking in the views from your deck rocking chair and star gazing at night—you can see the Milky Way, meteor showers, and, starting in the early fall, the northern lights. At this elevation, the temperature has never reached 80°F, mornings can be frosty even in June, and spring and fall snows are not uncommon. A hearty breakfast and dinner are included in the $110 per person rate, served family-style in a rustic dining room. Wine with dinner—a bottomless glass—is available for $9 per person. There is no road access to the lodge; the only way in is by foot, up one of five trails, none of which is short or easy. The 6.5-mi Trillium Gap trail is probably the easiest trail to the lodge as it is not as steep as the other trails. The Alum Cave Bluffs trail is the shortest trail to the lodge, but it is fairly steep. If you're in good condition, you may be able to do the Alum Cave Bluffs trail in four hours. Other trails take up to six hours or longer, so get an early start. You can prove you've been to the lodge by purchasing a LeConte Lodge T-shirt, sold only at the lodge. Lodge supplies are brought in by llama, up the Trillium Gap trail, and once a year by helicopter. Pack your backpack lightly and remember a flashlight, rain gear, layered clothing, sturdy shoes, snacks, water for your hike, and personal items. ■TIP→ **Bring cash for purchases and tips, as credit cards are not accepted at the lodge itself (though they are accepted for room reservations).** The lodge typically begins booking reservations for the following year's season (late March to late November) on October 1 of the year before. **Pros:** unique setting high on Mt. LeConte; a true escape from civilization; a special experience available only to a few. **Cons:** books up far in advance; hike-in access only; simplest of accommodations with few modern conveniences. ⊠*Mt. LeConte* ☎*250 Apple Valley Rd., Sevierville, TN* ☎*865/429–5704* ☎*865/774–0045* ⊕*www.lecontelodge. com* ⟿*7 cabins, 3 group sleeping rooms, all with shared bath* ⬧*In-room: no phone, no TV, no a/c. In-hotel: restaurant, no-smoking rooms* ⊟*AE, D, MC, V* ⧖*MAP* ⊙*Open late Mar.–late Nov.*

WHERE TO CAMP

Camping in the park is abundant and reasonably priced. The park has 947 tent and RV camping spaces at 10 developed campgrounds, in addition to more than 100 backcountry campsites and shelters. The cost ranges from free (backcountry sites and shelters) to $23 per night. Big Creek is the only campground that doesn't accept RVs and trailers, and most others have size limits.

Campgrounds at Cades Cove, Cosby, Elkmont, and Smokemont accept reservations for May 15–October 31 which can be made up to six months in advance. Horse camps also can be reserved up to six months in advance. Others are first-come, first-served. Frontcountry stays are limited to 14 consecutive days at any one campground.

Backcountry camping requires a permit (free), which you must complete at the park. Your permit must designate the campsite or shelter at which you will stay for each night of your trip—you can only camp in a designated campsite. ⇨*For permit stations, see Exploring the Backcountry in Chapters 2 and 3.* Campsites 9, 10, 13, 23, 24, 29, 36, 37, 38, 47, 50, 55, 57, 61, 71, 83, and 113 and all shelters require advance reservation. Download a park trail map at ⊕*www.nps.gov/grsm/planyourvisit/backcountry-camping. htm* to get the locations of all backcountry campsites and shelters. The maximum stay at any backcountry campsite is three consecutive nights and one night at any individual shelter.

Be prepared for a considerable hike to most backcountry sites. For questions about backcountry camping, call the Backcountry Information Office at ☎*865/436–1297,* daily from 9 until noon.

Outside the park, there are many commercial campgrounds at entrances to the park. Nearly all have 30 or 50 amp electrical, sewer, and water hookups, restrooms, showers, and dump stations. Many have cable TV and Internet connections. Some have swimming pools. On the North Carolina side, there are numerous campgrounds in Cherokee, Bryson City, and elsewhere. On the Tennessee side, there are at least 50 campgrounds around Pigeon Forge, Gatlinburg, Sevierville, and Townsend.

WHAT IT COSTS				
¢	$	$$	$$$	$$$$
CAMPING				
under $10	$10–$14	$15–$19	$20–$24	over $24

Camping prices are for standard campsite per night.

TENNESSEE SIDE

$ ⚠**Abrams Creek Campground.** At Abrams Creek, you're in Happy Valley. That's the name of the nearby community and of the road you take to get there. This campground is on the extreme western edge of the park, way off the beaten path. Campsites 1–9 are next to Abrams Creek, a good trout stream. At an elevation of only 1,125 feet, the lowest of any campground in the park, it can be hot and humid here in summer. Several trails, including Gold Mine, Cane Creek, Rabbit Creek, and Little Bottoms begin at or near the campground. ■TIP→For a fun drive, head to the 11-mi stretch of U.S. Highway 129 nearby known as the "Tail of the Dragon" for its many curves. **Pros:** small, little-known creekside campground; good spot for motorcyclists; trout fishing. **Cons:** long drive for supplies; hot and humid. ✉ *Off Happy Valley Rd.* ✛ *On the western section of the Foothills Pkwy., turn southeast on Happy Valley Rd. and follow approx. 2 mi to sign at access road to Abrams Creek Campground* ☎*877/444–6777* ⊕*www.recreation.gov* ⏎*16 tent or small trailer (up to 12 feet) sites* ♿*Reservations not accepted* ⚹*Flush toilets, drinking water, fire grates, fire pits, grills, picnic tables, creek* ☉*Early Mar.–Oct.*

$$–$$$ ⚠**Cades Cove Campground.** This is one of the largest camp- ☾ grounds in the Smokies, the one with the most services on-site, and the only one in the park open year-round. It has a small general store with a snack bar, bike rentals, horse stables, hayrides, a small amphitheater, picnic area, and an RV dump station. Located near the entrance to the Cades Cove loop, the most visited destination in the park, this is a popular campground and often fills up in summer and fall. It is one of only three (the others are Smokemont and Elkmont) that offers wheelchair-accessible campsites and restrooms. **Pros:** convenient to beautiful Cades Cove; plenty of services and amenities on-site. **Cons:** overrun at peak times; you'll see (and perhaps hear) your neighbors; hot and humid in summer. ✉*10042 Campground Dr., approx. 9 mi from Townsend* ☎*877/444–6777* ⊕*www.recreation. gov* ⏎*159 tent or RV/trailer (up to 40 feet) sites* ♿*Reservations essential* ⚹*Flush toilets, drinking water, bear boxes, fire pits, grills, picnic tables, food service, general store, public telephone, creek* ☉*Year-round.*

$ ⚠**Cosby Campground.** This large campground is shadily set ☾ among poplars, hemlocks, and rhododendrons, near Cosby and Rock creeks. More than 150 of the campsites are for tents only, and RVs/trailers are limited to just 25 feet. Of the 165 total sites, 20 can be reserved in advance by telephone or online. Bears are in the area, and several campsites may be closed temporarily due to aggressive bear activity. The campground has a small amphitheater, picnic area, horse trails, and an RV dump station. Nearby are many opportunities for hiking, with trailheads for Snake Den Ridge and Gabes Mountain trails. The self-guided nature trail (pick up a booklet at the trailhead, 50¢) winds down into a green ravine. This campground is rarely very busy and nearly always has sites available even when others are full. **Pros:** predominantly tent campsites; plenty of opportunities for hiking and fishing; rarely full. **Cons:** pleasant, rather than spectacular, setting. ⊠*127 Cosby Park Rd, off TN 32 ⊹From Cosby, go south on TN 32 about 1½ mi south of the junction with U.S. 321; turn right at Cosby sign; campground is another 2 mi* ☎877/444–6777 ⊕*www.recreation. gov* ⟁*165 tent and RV/trailer (up to 25 feet) sites* ⚹*Flush toilets, drinking water, bear boxes, fire pits, grills, picnic tables, public telephone, creek* ☉*Early Mar.–Oct.*

\$\$–\$\$\$ ⚠ **Elkmont Campground.** Elkmont is the best place to see the ★ synchronous fireflies *(Photinus carolinus)* blink in unison ☙ in early June. Little River trail is a good viewing spot, but you may not be alone as Gatlinburg runs shuttle trolleys to Elkmont during this time. Easy hiking trails and the ability to wade, tube (bring your own inner tubes), fish, and swim in Little River, which runs through the campground, make it ideal for kids. Also near the campground are a number of old summer cottages formerly owned by wealthy Tennessee families. This resort community was placed on the National Registry of Historic Places in 1994. The Park Service has been stabilizing and restoring several of these homes, but they currently are not open to visitors. ∎TIP→ **The best campsites are along the stream, especially B2–10 and C1–3, D1, 3, 4, and 6, and E1, 3, 5, 7, and 9. Loops C, D, E, F, G, H, J, and K all have a lot of RV sites.** The camp store sells ice, firewood, and a few camping supplies. Even though it is the largest campground in the Smokies, it is often fully booked during peak summer, fall color, and firefly weekends. There are wheelchair-accessible campsites and restrooms. **Pros:** attractive riverside setting; nice spot for families; great place to see the fireflies. **Cons:** a large campground overrun with RVs at times; best spots by river book up early. ⊠*434 Elkmont Rd., 8 mi from Gatlinburg ⊹From Gatlinburg, take Newfound Gap Rd. (U.S. 441) South into the park; turn*

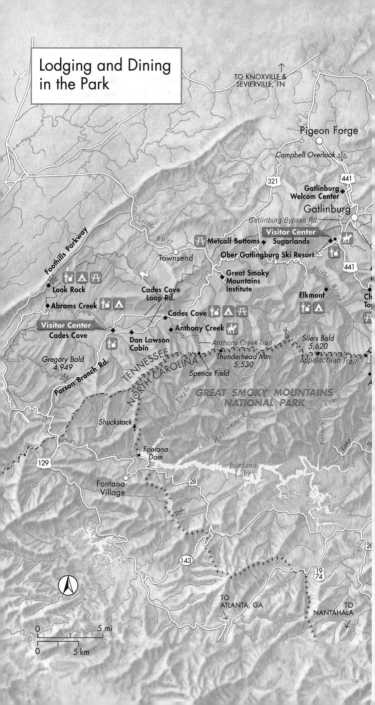

Lodging and Dining in the Park

TO KNOXVILLE & SEVIERVILLE, TN

Pigeon Forge

Campbell Overlook

321

441

Gatlinburg Welcom Center

Gatlinburg

Gatlinburg Bypass Rd.

Visitor Center
Sugarlands

Metcalf Bottoms

Ober Gatlinburg Ski Resort

Little River

Townsend

Great Smoky Mountains Institute

441

Elkmont

Ch
To

Foothills Parkway

Look Rock

Abrams Creek

Cades Cove Loop Rd.

Cades Cove

Anthony Creek

Visitor Center
Cades Cove

Dan Lawson Cabin

Anthony Creek Trail

Silers Bald
5,620

Appalachian Trail

Gregory Bald
4,949

TENNESSEE
NORTH CAROLINA

Thunderhead Mtn
5,530

Spence Field

Parson Branch Rd.

GREAT SMOKY MOUNTAINS
NATIONAL PARK

Eagle Creek

Forney Creek

Hazel Creek

Shuckstack

Fontana Dam

Fontana Lake

129

28

Fontana Village

143

19
74

TO ATLANTA, GA

TO NANTAHALA

0   5 mi

0   5 km

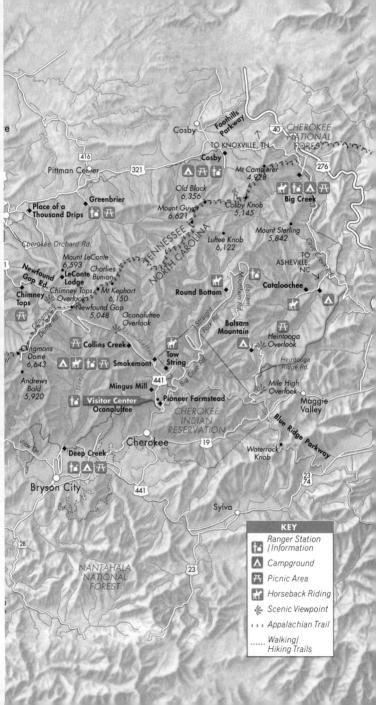

Cosby

Foothills
Parkway

CHEROKEE
NATIONAL
FOREST

40

276

TO KNOXVILLE, TN

416

Pittman Center

321

Cosby

Mt Cammerer
4,928

Old Black
6,356

Mount Guyot
6,621

Cosby Knob
5,145

Big Creek

Place of a
Thousand Drips

Greenbrier

Cherokee Orchard Rd.

Mount LeConte
6,593

LeConte
Lodge

Charlies
Bunion

Mount LeConte
6,593

Chimney Tops
Overlook

Mt Kephart
6,150

Newfound Gap
5,048

Newfound
Gap Rd.

Chimney
Tops

Clingmans
Dome Rd.

Oconaluftee
Overlook

Clingmans
Dome
6,643

Andrews
Bald
5,920

Collins Creek

Smokemont

Tow
String

Mingus Mill

Pioneer Farmstead

Visitor Center
Oconaluftee

Deep
Creek Rd.

View Dr.

Deep Creek

Bryson City

441

28

NANTAHALA
NATIONAL
FOREST

23

TENNESSEE
NORTH CAROLINA

Luftee Knob
6,122

Mount Sterling
5,842

TO
ASHEVILLE,
NC

Cataloochee

Round Bottom

Balsam Mountain Rd.

Balsam
Mountain

Heintooga
Overlook

Straight Fork Rd.

Heintooga
Ridge Rd.

Mile High
Overlook

Big Cove Rd.

Maggie
Valley

CHEROKEE
INDIAN
RESERVATION

Blue Ridge Parkway

Cherokee

19

Waterrock
Knob

23
74

441

Sylva

Cove Creek Rd.

Oconaluftee R.

Deep Creek

KEY

Ranger Station / Information

Campground

Picnic Area

Horseback Riding

Scenic Viewpoint

Appalachian Trail

Walking / Hiking Trails

Kid-Friendly Campgrounds

CLOSE UP

All of the campgrounds in the Smokies are suitable for children, but kids will especially love these.

Deep Creek Campground has tubing, swimming holes, and easy and safe trails that lead to three nearby waterfalls.

You can rent bicycles at **Cades Cove Campground**, take a horseback ride, go for a hayride, listen to a ranger-led talk, and splash in the nearby creek. There's a snack bar that sells ice cream, hot dogs, and pizza and it's an easy drive to the mini-golf courses, go-kart tracks, fudge shops, and amusement parks of Pigeon

Forge and Gatlinburg.

Elkmont Campground has easy hiking trails nearby and tubing, swimming, and fishing in Little River. It's also an easy drive to Dollywood and the other attractions of Pigeon Forge and Gatlinburg.

From **Smokemont Campground**, you can go horseback riding at the nearby Smokemont Stable or tube, play, or fish in the Bradley Fork River. In summer and fall there are mountain music and storytelling programs, and occasional hayrides. It's a short drive to Cherokee, where kids can learn about Native American culture.

---

right at Sugarlands Visitor Center; go 4½ mi to the Elkmont entrance and turn left at the Elkmont Campground sign; go 1.5 mi to the campground office ☎877/444–6777 ⌂Reservations essential ⊕www.recreation.gov ♲220 tent, RV (up to 35 feet), and trailer (up to 32 feet) sites ⌂Flush toilets, drinking water, bear boxes, fire pits, grills, picnic tables, general store, public telephone, dump station, swimming (creek) ⊙Early Mar.–Oct.

$ ⛺**Look Rock Campground.** At the western edge of the park off Foothills Parkway this is the only campground in the park with no length limit for RVs and trailers. Set in oak and pine woods, there's not much to do here except hike. Several trails can be accessed from the campground, including Cane Creek, Little Bottoms, and Rabbit Creek. You can walk to the Look Rock observation tower for a great view of the western side of the Smokies. **Pros:** rarely full; accepts RVs and trailers of all sizes; not far from "Tail of the Dragon" road. **Cons:** doesn't offer the setting or amenities of some other campgrounds in park; somewhat remote and a long drive to groceries and other stores. ⊠*Off Flats Rd.* ✛*From the western portion of Foothills Pkwy., turn east on Happy Valley Rd. to Flats Rd.; go 1 mi and follow signs to camp-*

ground ☎877/444–6777 ⊕www.recreation.gov ♲ 68 tent and RV/trailer sites ₺Flush toilets, drinking water, fire pits, grills, picnic tables, creek ☉Mid-May–Oct.

NORTH CAROLINA SIDE

★ Fodor'sChoice ⚠**Balsam Mountain Campground.** If you like a
$ high, cool campground, with a beautiful setting in ever-greens, Balsam Mountain will be your favorite campground in the park. Nights are chilly at over 5,300 feet and you may want a campfire even in summer. Due to its somewhat remote location off the Blue Ridge Parkway, it is rarely full even on peak summer and fall weekends. Several good hiking trails are nearby, and you can drive or bike the one-way unpaved Balsam Mountain Road and Big Cove Road to Cherokee. The 46 campsites—first-come, first served—are best for tents. Most of the 10- by 10-foot tent pads and the picnic tables have been recently replaced. Bears are rarely a problem in this area. ■TIP➔ **For the Smokies' best sunset, go to the nearby Heintooga picnic area and hike a short way to Mile High overlook.** Pros: appealing high-elevation campground, where it's cool even in summer; rarely busy; good hiking and great scenic vistas nearby. Cons: a little remote and a moderate drive for supplies and groceries; most campsites don't have views and are a little closer together than you'd like. ⊠Near end of Heintooga Ridge Rd. ✛From Cherokee, take the BRP 11 mi to the turnoff for Heintooga Ridge Rd.; follow Heintooga Ridge Rd. about 9 mi to campground, which is just beyond the picnic area ☎877/444–6777 ⊕www.recreation.gov ♲46 tent and RV/trailer (up to 30 feet) sites ₺Flush toilets, drinking water, bear boxes, fire pits, grills, picnic tables ☉Early May–Oct.

$ ⚠**Big Creek Campground.** With just 12 campsites, Big Creek is the smallest campground in the park, and the only one that is for tents only. This is a walk-in, not hike-in, campground. While you can't park your vehicle right beside your tent, you only have to tote your supplies 100 or 200 feet. Five of the 12 first-come, first-served sites (unnumbered) are beside Big Creek, which offers good swimming and fishing. Although it's not far from an I–40 exit, the campground is more remote than it looks on a map, and it's a 30-minute drive to the nearest grocery store, in Newport, Tennessee. There is a small convenience store closer by. Carefully observe bear protection rules, as there have been a number of human–bear interactions nearby. Pros: small secluded spot by a river; tents only, no RVs. Cons: about a

CLOSE UP

Best of the Backcountry

The appeal of backcountry campsites (reached by hiking and requiring a backcountry permit) is at least partly in the eye of the beholder. A dedicated angler may enjoy a site next to a good trout stream, even if it lacks knockout scenery, while a photographer may prefer a mountaintop site with million-dollar views. Of the more than 100 backcountry campsites, the sites listed below are especially prized for their beauty, special location, or unique attributes. All of these sites can be reserved in advance, and all are free. To get to these sites, download a trail map from ⊕www.nps.gov/grsm/planyourvisit/maps.htm.

Campsite #13: This site, in a grassy area banked by birch trees on Gregory Bald trail, is near the spectacular Gregory Bald with its breathtaking views. It is reachable from the Cades Cove and Parson Cove Road area via Gregory Bald and Gregory Ridge trails, in the northwest section of the park on the Tennessee side.

Campsite #38: Located near Mt. Sterling on Baxter Creek trail, at 5,800 feet this is the highest unsheltered backcountry campsite in the park. It is reachable from Big Creek campground in the northeast section of the park, on the North Carolina side.

Campsite #83: The appeal of this site, on Hazel Creek trail off Lakeshore trail, is its location on Hazel Creek, an excellent trout stream, near the historical remains of the Proctor lumber camp. Nearby are several other popular backcountry campsites, including #82, #84, and #85, none of which can be reserved in advance. Access to the Hazel Creek trail is by boat across Fontana Lake in the southwest section of the park, on the North Carolina side.

Tricorner Knob Shelter: For an Appalachian Trail experience without the months of toil, you can hike to this shelter along the AT. Tricorner Knob is one of 12 AT shelters in the Smokies. It's a long hike out to it so it's less likely to be packed with backpackers. The shelter has a stone fireplace, an open front, and sleeps 12 people. Situated at about 5,920 feet, the shelter is near several "sixers"—mountain peaks over 6,000 feet—including Mt. Chapman, Mt. Sequoyah, Mt. Guyot, Old Black, Mt. Hardison, Mt. Yonaguska, and Tricorner Knob itself.

30-minute drive to the nearest grocery. ⊠*Cove Creek Rd. (Old U.S. Hwy. 284)* ✛*Take I–40 to the Waterville (TN) Exit 451; cross the Pigeon River and turn left to follow the Pigeon River upstream; go 2.3 mi to an intersection;*

Best Bets for Camping

CLOSE UP

- **Best to Stay Cool:** Balsam Mountain
- **Best for RVs:** Elkmont, Smokemont
- **Best for Tents:** Balsam Mountain, Big Creek, Cosby
- **Best Fishing:** Abrams Creek, Big Creek, Cataloochee
- **Best for Spotting Elk:** Cataloochee
- **Best for Spotting Bears:** Cades Cove
- **Best for Seeing Synchro-nous Fireflies:** Elkmont
- **Best for Biking:** Cades Cove, Cataloochee
- **Best for Escaping Crowds:** Abrams Creek, Balsam Mountain, Big Creek, Cataloochee, Cosby, Look Rock
- **Best for History:** Cades Cove, Cataloochee, Elkmont
- **Best for Families:** Cades Cove, Deep Creek, Elkmont, Smokemont
- **Best for Winter Camping:** Cades Cove, Smokemont

4

go through the intersection and enter the park; pass the Big Creek Ranger Station and go about 3.5 mi to the end of the gravel road and the campground. An alternate route is on the unpaved Cove Creek Rd. (Old U.S. Hwy. 284) from the Cataloochee valley ☎877/444–6777 ⊕www.recreation.gov ⇆12 tent sites ♿Flush toilets, drinking water, bear boxes, fire pits, grills, picnic tables, swimming (creek) ☉Early Mar.–Oct.

$$ ⚠**Cataloochee Campground.** The appeal of this small camp-
★ ground is its location in the beautiful and historical Cataloochee valley. You can tour the old homesteads and churches, maintained much as they were before the coming of the park, when this valley supported some 1,200 people. You're also virtually guaranteed to see elk, along with white-tailed deer and wild turkeys. Bears are a little less common, but they do come into the campground, so follow bear-proof food storage rules and use bear boxes. The six campsites beside Cataloochee Creek fill up quickly at this first-come, first-served campground. ⚠ **Although the campground allows RVs and trailers up to 31 feet, you may want to think twice before driving anything other than a car or truck into the valley—the unpaved Cove Creek Road is narrow, with sharp curves, and in some places you hug the mountainside with a steep drop just a few feet away.** There's a horse camp here, and nearby you'll find excellent hiking on several trails including Little Cataloochee and Boogerman. **Pros:**

provides access to beautiful, historic Cataloochee valley; small campground with spacious, nicely spaced sites; pleasant creek-side setting. **Cons:** difficult, even scary, drive in a large RV to the campground; long drive for groceries and supplies. ✉*Cataloochee valley* ✛*On I–40, take North Carolina Exit 20 and go 0.2 mi on Hwy. 276; turn right onto Cove Creek Rd. and follow signs 11 mi to the Cataloochee valley and campground* ☎*877/444–6777* ⊕*www. recreation.gov* ⌂*27 tent and RV/trailer (up to 31 feet) sites* ♿*Flush toilets, drinking water, bear boxes, fire pits, grills, picnic tables, creek* ✆*Early Mar.–Oct.*

$$ ⚠**Deep Creek Campground.** Near the most popular tubing ☾ spot in the Smokies, this campground will have you rollin' down the river. ➡*For information on inner tube rentals, see Summer Sports & Activities in Chapter 3: Exploring the North Carolina Side.* There's also swimming in several swimming holes. Of the 92 first-come, first-served sites here, sites 1–42 are for tents only. Nearby are several easy to moderate hiking trails, including a 2-mi loop that takes you to three waterfalls. ⚠**Don't confuse this park campground with a similarly named commercial campground just outside the Deep Creek entrance of the park.** **Pros:** lots of family tubing and swimming fun on the creek; convenient to the pleasant small town of Bryson City. **Cons:** with several private campgrounds and tube rental businesses, the entrance to the park has a commercial feel. ✉*1912 East Deep Creek Rd., Bryson City, NC* ☎*877/444–6777* ⊕*www.recreation.gov* ⌂*92 tent and RV/trailer (up to 26 feet) sites* ♿*Flush toilets, drinking water, bear boxes, fire pits, grills, picnic tables, public telephone, swimming (creek)* ✆*Early Apr.–Oct.*

$$–$$$ ⚠**Smokemont Campground.** With 142 sites, Smokemont is ☾ the largest campground on the North Carolina side of the park. There's fishing and tubing (bring your own tubes) in the Bradley Fork River which runs through the campground. The Bradley Fork Trail, located at the top of D loop, leads to a number of other hiking trails. In summer and fall, rangers offer interpretive talks at the campground, and there are mountain music and storytelling programs. The nearby Smokemont Stable offers horseback rides and sells firewood and ice. Some of the campsites are a little close together, but the individual sites are spacious. Tent sites have a 13- by 13-foot tent pad, fire ring with cooking grill, and a picnic table with lantern pole. ▪TIP➡**Sites in F loop, open to RVs only, are wooded and more private—sites F2, 4, 6, 8, 34, 36, 38, 40, 42, 44, and 46 are on the river.** Generator

use is restricted to 8 AM–8 PM and prohibited in loops A, B, and C mid-May–October. This campground stays open most of the year, closing only from January through the first few days of March. **Pros:** pleasant, large campground; lots for families and kids to do; easy access to Cherokee and to sites such as Mingus Mill and Mountain Farm Museum. **Cons:** with so many RVs, you're not exactly in the wilderness. ✉*Off Newfound Gap Rd. (U.S. 441) 6 mi north of Cherokee* ☎*877/444–6777* ⊕ *www.recreation.gov* ⬎*142 tent, RV (up to 40 feet), and trailer (up to 35 feet) sites* ⚿*Flush toilets, drinking water, bear boxes, pit fires, grills, picnic tables, public telephone, creek* ⊙*Early Mar.–Dec.*

4

CAMPGROUNDS

	Total # of sites	# of tent only sites	# of sites for RVs only (no hookups)	Drive-to sites	Walk-to sites	Flush toilets	Horse Camp	Drinking water	Fire grates/pits	Swimming	Fishing	Tubing	Dump station	Ranger station	Public telephone	Reservations possible	Daily fee per site	Dates open
Abrams Creek	16	0	0	Y	N	Y	Y	Y	Y	N	Y	N	N	Y	N	N	$14	Early Mar.–Oct.
Balsam Mountain	46	6	0	Y	N	Y	N	Y	N	N	Y	N	N	Y	N	N	$14	Early May–Oct.
Big Creek	12	12	0	N	Y	Y	Y	Y	Y	Y	Y	N	Y	Y	Y	N	$14	Early Mar.–Oct.
Cades Cove	159	0	0	Y	N	Y	Y	Y	Y	N	N	N	Y	Y	Y	Y	$17–$20	Y/R
Cataloochee	27	0	0	Y	N	Y	Y	Y	Y	N	Y	Y	N	Y	N	N	$17	Early Mar.–Oct.
Cosby	165	152	13	Y	N	Y	N	Y	Y	N	Y	N	N	Y	Y	Y	$14	Early Mar.–Oct.
Deep Creek	92	42	0	Y	N	Y	N	Y	Y	Y	Y	Y	Y	Y	Y	N	$17	Early Apr.–Oct.
Elkmont	220	0	90	Y	N	Y	N	Y	Y	Y	Y	Y	Y	Y	Y	Y	$17–$23	Early Mar.–Oct.
Look Rock	68	0	0	Y	N	Y	N	Y	Y	N	N	N	Y	Y	N	N	$14	Early May–Oct.
Smokemont	142	0	47	Y	N	Y	N	Y	Y	Y	Y	Y	Y	Y	Y	Y	$17–$20	Early Mar.–Dec.

Y/R = year-round

Knoxville and Other Tennessee Towns

WORD OF MOUTH

"The towns of Pigeon Forge and Gatlinburg most definitely cater to tourists, but that's not always a horrible thing. I'd probably stay in Gatlinburg if you choose to stay in one of those two. Pigeon Forge is much more car-oriented. The activities in PF are more along the lines of outlet shopping (lots), laser tag, mini golf, etc., plus there's Dollywood. In Gatlinburg, you can park the car, walk the Parkway and stop in at shops whenever you like."

—jent103

Updated by Michael Ream

TWO MID-SIZE CITIES, KNOXVILLE AND Asheville, one on each side of the Smokies, plus a host of small towns, offer plenty of places to stay and dine near the park, not to mention adding jazzier activities and entertainment to the natural pleasures found in the mountains.

Knoxville, set in the foothills of the Great Smokies, one to two hours (depending on traffic) from the western entrances to the park, is a college town with numerous museums and a thriving dining scene and nightlife district. The University of Tennessee campus, with over 26,000 students, is just west of downtown, and includes Neyland Stadium, with a capacity of over 100,000, making it one of the largest college football stadiums in the United States. If you're in Knoxville on a fall weekend when the Volunteers have a home game, the city will be a sea of bright UT orange.

The city was the site of the 1982 World's Fair, and its icon, the Sunsphere, a 266-foot steel tower topped with a five-story gold globe, remains a symbol of the city. Knoxville has over 7,500 hotel and motel rooms clustered along I–40 downtown, so if hotels closer to the park are full, you can find a place to lay your head here. Bring your golf clubs, as there are about three dozen golf courses within an hour or so of Knoxville.

Closer to the park, Gatlinburg is a compact chunk of everything you'd expect in a town built on tourism, with a panoply of candy shops, gift stores, and flashy restaurants lining the walkable main street, which has great views of the surrounding mountains. A chair lift and tramway take visitors to the tops of nearby peaks, including one set up for skiing. Millions visit Gatlinburg each year, and some 600,000 of them are here to get married (no blood test or waiting period required, and the 15 wedding chapels accept walk-ins), making the Gatlinburg area the "Wedding Capital of the South."

Pigeon Forge, 5 mi north and thus farther out of the mountains, sprawls along a five-lane parkway lined with motels, go-kart tracks, videogame arcades, fudge shops, country music and comedy entertainment theaters, and Las Vegas–inspired architecture (but without the gambling). In the summer and fall tourist season, Pigeon Forge's population of around 6,000 can swell tenfold, to over 60,000.

Sevierville, the next town down the valley, is more of a bedroom community for the tourist meccas, with its own ever-growing roadside development. The entire area is constantly adding new tourist attractions and taking down old ones. Townsend, several miles west of the tourist areas, feels like a throwback to a quieter age of American vacations—it's much smaller and less developed, and calls itself the "peaceful side of the Smokies."

All told, the Smokies Corridor with its hustle-and-bustle towns covers less than about one-tenth of the geographic area adjoining the Tennessee side of the park. The rest is rural and filled with small homesteads and farms.

ABOUT THE RESTAURANTS

Although restaurants in Gatlinburg and Pigeon Forge put the emphasis on inexpensive meals that appeal to middle-of-the-road tastes, some cooks in eastern Tennessee are offering more sophisticated fare. You can find nearly every world cuisine somewhere in the region, from Thai to Jamaican to northern Indian, and you can still find plenty of places offering authentic mountain food like Smoky Mountains trout, often served family-style.

ABOUT THE HOTELS

Around the mountains, at least in the larger cities and towns such as Knoxville, Gatlinburg, and Pigeon Forge, you can find the usual chain motels and hotels. For more of a local flavor, look at the many mountain lodges and country inns, some with just a few rooms with simple comforts, others with upmarket amenities like tennis courts, golf courses, and spas.

WHAT IT COSTS				
¢	$	$$	$$$	$$$$
RESTAURANTS				
under $10	$10–$14	$15–$19	$20–$24	over $24
HOTELS				
under $100	$100–$150	$151–$200	$201–$250	over $250
CAMPING				
under $10	$10–$14	$15–$19	$20–$24	over $24

Restaurant prices are for a main course at dinner. Hotel prices are for two people in a standard double room in high season. Camping prices are for a standard campsite per night.

KNOXVILLE

45 mi northwest of the Gatlinburg entrance to the Great Smoky Mountains National Park.

In 1786 patriot general James White and a few pioneer settlers built a fort beside the Tennessee River. A few years later, territorial governor William Blount selected White's fort as capital of the newly formed Territory of the United States South of the River Ohio and renamed the settlement Knoxville after his longtime friend, Secretary of War Henry Knox. It flourished from its beginning as the gateway to the frontier and became the state capital when Tennessee was admitted to the Union in 1796.

Throughout the 20th century, and into the 21st, Knoxville has been synonymous with energy: the headquarters of the Tennessee Valley Authority (TVA), with its hydroelectric dams and recreational lakes, is here, and during World War II, atomic energy was secretly developed at nearby Oak Ridge. Today the University of Tennessee adds its own energy—both intellectual and cultural—to this dynamic city. Along the Tennessee River, Volunteer Landing is a series of concrete walkways that includes restaurants and residential town houses. Downtown, Market Square has several restaurants, and the nearby Old City district is a neighborhood of former warehouses converted to hip nightlife spots.

Knoxville is surrounded by three national parks—Great Smoky Mountains National Park, Cumberland Gap National Historic Park nearby in Kentucky, and Big South Fork National River and Recreation Area.

GETTING HERE & AROUND
Knoxville sits at the intersection of I–40, which runs east–west through miles of franchised commercial development on the west side of the city, and I–75, which runs north–south. To get to Great Smoky Mountains National Park and the adjacent tourist towns, take exit 407 off I–40, by the Tennessee Smokies baseball stadium, where there are tourist information centers.

ESSENTIALS
Knoxville Visitor Center (✉ *301 S. Gay St., Knoxville* ☎ *865/523-7263 or 800/727-8045* ⊕ *www.knoxville.org*).

EXPLORING KNOXVILLE

Downtown Knoxville is fairly easy to explore on foot, with Gay Street stretching downhill from the visitor center, passing by restaurant-rich Market Square before ending at the Tennessee River and Volunteer Landing. The Old City, an industrial neighborhood reborn as a hip nightlife spot, lies just north of downtown. The sprawling campus of the University of Tennessee is just west of downtown, right off Cumberland Avenue. The free Knoxville Trolley runs several lines through downtown, stopping at downtown hotels.

The rest of Knoxville sprawls along I–40 west of downtown, a jumble of malls, franchise restaurants, and hotels. The Knoxville Zoo and Creative Discovery Museum are just off I–40 east of downtown, in Chilhowee Park.

❹ **Beck Cultural Exchange Center.** The center commemorates Knoxville's African-American history with photographs, art, and a large archive of books and newspapers. It is located in the former home of one of Knoxville's prominent African-American families. In nearby Morningside Park is a **statue of Alex Haley,** Knoxville resident and author of the book *Roots.* ✉*1927 Dandridge Ave., Morningside* ☎*865/524–8461* ⊕*www.discoveret.org/beckcec* ✎*Free* ☉*Tues.–Sat. 10–6.*

❾ **Crescent Bend House & Gardens.** This historic home, built in 1834, is just past the western edge of the University of Tennessee campus. Its nine formal Italian gardens overlook the Tennessee River. The home includes the Armstrong-Lockett House Museum, with 18th century American and English furniture and a large collection of English silver dating from 1610 to 1830. ✉*2728 Kingston Pike, University* ☎*865/637–3163* ☉*Tue.–Sat. 10–4, Sun. 1–4*

❻ **East Tennessee Discovery Center and Akima Planetarium.** The Discover Center contains pioneer tools and clothes, mounted animals, and fresh- and saltwater aquariums. Children love the hands-on and audiovisual exhibits, which explain concepts including light and sound and the working of simple machines. ✉*516 N. Beaman St., Chilhowee Park* ☎*865/594–1480* ⊕*www.etdiscovery.org* ✎*$4* ☉*Weekdays 9–5, Sat. 10–5; no admission after 4; planetarium show times vary.*

❿ **Frank H. McClung Museum.** Located on the University of Tennessee campus, the museum has diverse collections in

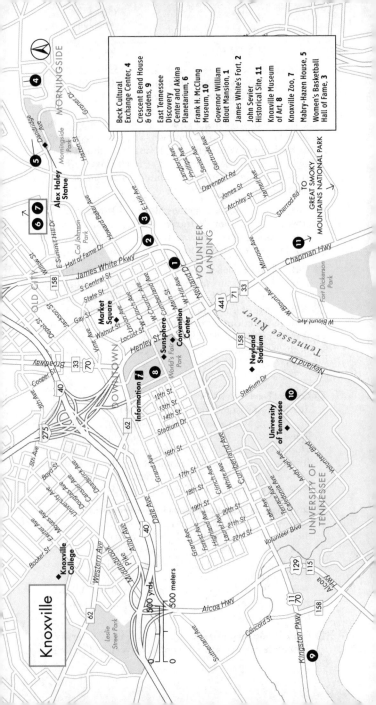

Knoxville

Index (boxed legend)

Beck Cultural Exchange Center, **4**

Crescent Bend House & Gardens, **9**

East Tennessee Discovery Center and Akima Planetarium, **6**

Frank H. McClung Museum, **10**

Governor William Blount Mansion, **1**

James White's Fort, **2**

John Sevier Historical Site, **11**

Knoxville Museum of Art, **8**

Knoxville Zoo, **7**

Mabry-Hazen House, **5**

Women's Basketball Hall of Fame, **3**

MORNINGSIDE

Alex Haley Statue

Morningside Park

Cal Johnson Park

OLD CITY

James White Pkwy

S Central St

State St

Market Square

Gay St

Vine Ave

Walnut St

Union Ave

Locust St

W Clinch Ave

W Church Ave

W Cumberland Ave

Main St

W Hill Ave

Henley

DOWNTOWN

Information

Sunsphere

Convention Center

World's Fair Park

Broadway

12th St

13th St

14th St

Stadium Dr

16th St

17th St

18th St

19th St

20th St

21th St

22nd St

Grand Ave

Forest Ave

Highland Ave

Laurel Ave

Clinch Ave

White Ave

Cumberland Ave

5th Ave

Cooper St

Boyd St

Deaderick Ave

Castle Ave

Douglas Ave

University Ave

Moses Ave

Exeter Ave

Booker St

Knoxville College

Western Ave

Middlebrook

Alcoa Pike

Date Ave

Leslie Street Park

Neyland Stadium

VOLUNTEER LANDING

Tennessee River

University of Tennessee

Andy Holt Ave

Lake Ave

Terrace Ave

Caledonia Ave

Volunteer Blvd

UNIVERSITY OF TENNESSEE

Stadium Dr

Neyland Dr

W Blount Ave

Mimosa Ave

Sherrod Rd

Chapman Hwy

Fort Dickerson Park

TO GREAT SMOKY MOUNTAINS NATIONAL PARK

Atchley St

Jones St

Davenport Rd

Sevier Ave

Phillips Ave

Langford Ave

Gertrude Ave

Yarnell Ave

Alcoa Hwy

Concord St

Kingston Pkwy

Volunteer Blvd

500 yds

500 meters

anthropology, natural history, geology, science, and fine arts. Of special note is the room devoted to ancient Egyptian artifacts. ✉*1327 Circle Park Dr., University* ☎*865/974–2144* ⊕*mcclungmuseum.utk.edu* ☖*Free* ⊙*Mon.–Sat. 9–5, Sun. 1–5.*

➊ **Governor William Blount Mansion.** In this modest white-frame structure dating from 1792, the governor and his associates planned the admission of Tennessee as the 16th state in the Union. The home is furnished with original and period antiques, along with memorabilia of Blount's checkered career. A **visitor center** adjacent to the 1818 **Craighead-Jackson House** presents an introductory slide program, museum exhibits, and a glass collection. ✉*200 W. Hill Ave. at Gay St., Volunteer Landing* ☎*865/525–2375 or 888/654–0016* ⊕*www.blountmansion.org* ☖*$4.95* ⊙*Feb.–late Dec., Tues.–Sat. 9:30–5.*

➋ **James White's Fort.** Different eras of Knoxville history are celebrated at James White's Fort, a series of seven log cabins with authentic furnishings and pioneer artifacts that was once part of White's 1,000-acre estate bequeathed to him after his service as a captain in the American Revolutionary War. ✉*205 E. Hill Ave., Downtown* ☎*865/525–6514* ⊕*www.jameswhitesfort.org* ☖*$5* ⊙*Apr.–Dec., weekdays 9:30–4:30, Sat. 9:30–3:30; Jan.–Mar., weekdays 9–4. Closed during home university football games.*

⓫ **John Sevier Historical Site.** On the outskirts of Knoxville, this historic site includes **Marble Springs**, the summer home of John Sevier, Tennessee's first governor. You can take a tour of the home and watch a craft demonstration at the site. ✉*1220 John Sevier Hwy., Outskirts* ☎*865/573–5508* ☖*$5* ⊙*Tues.–Sun. 10–5.*

➑ **Knoxville Museum of Art.** Designed by renowned museum architect Edward Larrabee Barnes, the four-level concrete-and-steel building is faced in Tennessee pink marble. It devotes plenty of space to regional artists and includes four exhibition galleries, an exploratory gallery for children, a great hall, an auditorium, a museum store, and outdoor sculpture and educational program gardens. ✉*1050 World's Fair Park Dr., World's Fair Park* ☎*865/525–6101* ⊕*www.knoxart.org* ☖*$5* ⊙*Tues.–Thurs. and Sat. 10–5, Fri. 10–8, Sun. 1–5.*

➐ **Knoxville Zoological Park.** You can spend a full day at the ☘ zoo famous for breeding large-cat species and African elephants. Among the 1,100 animals are rare red pandas, wild creatures native to the African plains, polar bears, seals, and penguins. The working miniature steam train, elephant rides, and petting zoo will keep kids occupied for hours. Gorilla Valley, Cheetah Savanna, and Chimpanzee Ridge are among the best exhibits, and the zoo also offers bird shows and camel rides. ⊠*3500 Knoxville Zoo Park, in Chilhowee Park on Rutledge Pike S, 4½ mi east of I–40 Exit 392, Chilhowee Park* ☎*865/637–5331* ⊕*www.knox-ville-zoo.org* ☞*$16.95* ⊙*Memorial Day–Labor Day, daily 9:30–6; Labor Day–Memorial Day, daily 10–4:30.*

❺ **Mabry-Hazen House.** The house served as headquarters for both Confederate and Union forces during the Civil War. It was built by prominent Knoxvillian Joseph A. Mabry Jr. in 1858 and is now on the National Historic Register. ⊠*1711 Dandridge Ave., Morningside* ☎*865/522–8661* ⊕*www.mabryhazen.com* ☞*$5* ⊙*Wed.–Fri. 11–5, Sat. 10–3.*

❸ **Women's Basketball Hall of Fame.** Near Volunteer Landing, the Women's Basketball Hall of Fame is easy to spot—just look for the 30-foot-wide basketball sitting atop a metal cage. Exhibits inside include a collection of 23 jerseys from the WNBA's inaugural all-star game, a modern locker room where you can listen to halftime talks by some of the country's top coaches, and play courts where you can test your skills against those of the game's top players. Several videos feature legends of the game. ⊠*700 Hall of Fame Dr., Downtown* ☎*865/633–9000* ⊕*www.wbhof.com* ☞*$7.95* ⊙*May–Labor Day, weekdays 10–5, Sat. 10–6, Sun. 1–5; Labor Day–Apr., Tues.–Fri. 11–5, Sat. 10–6, Sun. 1–5.*

WHERE TO EAT

$–$$ ✕**Calhoun's on the River.** *Barbecue.* Delicious barbecued ribs are served riverside at this sprawling rib house with an outdoor patio and its own boat dock. Calhoun's ribs are famous throughout the South. ⊠*400 Neyland Dr., Volunteer Landing* ☎*865/673–3335* ⚲*Reservations not accepted* ⊟*AE, D, DC, MC, V.*

$$$ ✕**Copper Cellar.** *American.* This intimate restaurant is a favorite with the college crowd and young professionals. Entrées such as pan-blackened Florida grouper, chicken Oscar, steamed lobster tails, and a full slate of steaks are available. There is also an impressive wine list and microbrews on-tap. ⊠*1807 Cumberland Ave., University*

☎*865/673–3411* ⊕*www.coppercellar.com* ▭*AE, D, DC, MC, V.*

$$ ✕**Cumberland Grill.** *American.* Located in the same building as the Copper Cellar, this brass rail bar and grill has a laid back feel. The pub grub includes burgers and famous chicken wings, as well as steaks and salads. Several microbrews are on-tap. ✉*1807 Cumberland Ave., University* ☎*865/673–3411* ⊕*www.cumberlandgrill.com* ▭*AE, D, MC, V.*

$$–$$$ ✕**Regas Restaurant.** *American.* This cozy, old world–style
★ Knoxville classic, with fireplaces and original art, has been around since 1919. The specialty, prime rib, is baked very slowly all day, then sliced to order and served with creamy horseradish sauce. There is a good selection of steaks and seafood as well. If you're there for lunch, look for hostess Hazel Smith, who's been working at the restaurant since 1954. ✉*318 N. Gay St., Old City* ☎*865/637–3427* ▭*AE, D, DC, MC, V* ⊙*Closed Sun. No lunch Sat.*

$–$$ ✕**Sunspot.** *American.* This low-key off-campus hangout has a healthy mix of salads, sandwiches, and entrees like chili-crusted salmon, Portobello empanadas, and blackened crab quesadillas. It also has several tasty pasta dishes, and is a popular brunch spot. ✉*1909 Cumberland Ave., University* ☎*865/637–4663* ⊕*www.aubreysrestaurant.com* ▭*D, DC, MC,V.*

¢–$ ✕**Tomato Head.** *Vegetarian.* This perennially popular and affordable spot on restaurant-lined Market Square features organic comfort food with a vegetarian twist. The extensive menu of pizzas (with an option of soy cheese) and sandwiches has selections like goat cheese, pesto and herbed tomato, as well as meat choices like Tuscan chicken and lamb sausage. There are good burritos and quesadillas here too. It gets noisy during the lunch and dinner rush. ✉*12 Market Sq., Market Square* ☎*865/637–4067* ⊕*www. thetomatohead.com* ▭*AE, MC, V.*

WHERE TO STAY

$–$$ 🏨**Crowne Plaza Knoxville.** Just north of downtown, this standard business hotel has comfortable rooms and a well-lit lobby. **Pros:** executive floor; convenient for walking to downtown restaurants and Old City nightlife; free Wi-Fi. **Cons:** rather standard rooms; no airport shuttle. ✉*401 W. Summit Hill Dr., Downtown* ☎*865/522–2600* ⊕*www.*

crowneplaza.com ⍦*195 rooms, 2 suites* ⚬*In-room: Wi-Fi. In-hotel: restaurant, room service, bar, pool, gym, laundry service, Wi-Fi, parking (paid), some pets allowed, no-smoking rooms* ⊟*AE, D, DC, MC, V.*

$$ ⌧**Hilton Knoxville.** Originally built for the 1982 World's Fair, this high-rise hotel has since gone through several renovations and is now a modern upscale hotel. Some rooms have views of the mountains and Neyland Stadium. **Pros:** good restaurant; convenient for strolling downtown; free Wi-Fi. **Cons:** no on-site parking; outdoor pool is seasonal only; no airport shuttle. ⌧*501 W. Church Ave., Downtown* ☎*865/523–2300* ⊕*www.hilton.com* ⍦*312 rooms, 5 suites* ⚬*In-room: Wi-Fi. In-hotel: restaurant, room service, bar, pool, gym, laundry service, Wi-Fi , some pets allowed, no-smoking rooms* ⊟*AE, D, MC, V.*

$–$$ ⌧**Knoxville Marriott.** Adjacent to the Women's Basketball Hall of Fame, this white ziggurat sits atop a hill overlooking the Tennessee River and Knoxville's downtown. The eight-story skylighted atrium lobby has modern furnishings and art. Glass elevators take guests to rooms that look out on the surrounding mountains. **Pros:** some rooms a bit larger; lots of amenities on-site. **Cons:** outdoor pool is seasonal only; no airport shuttle; you pay for Wi-Fi. ⌧*500 Hill Ave. SE, Downtown* ☎*865/637–1234 or 800/228–9290* ⊕*www. hyatt.com* ⍦*354 rooms, 24 suites* ⚬*In-room: refrigerator (some), Wi-Fi. In-hotel: restaurant, room service, bar, pool, laundry service, Wi-Fi, parking (free), no-smoking rooms* ⊟*AE, D, DC, MC, V.*

SPORTS & THE OUTDOORS

Whittle Springs Municipal Golf Course (⌧*3113 Valley View Dr., Whittle Springs* ☎*865/525–1022* ⊕*golfwhittlesprings.com*) is an 18-hole, par-70 golf course open to the public.

NIGHTLIFE & THE ARTS

The **Knoxville Opera Company** (☎*865/524–0795* ⊕*www. knoxvilleopera.com*) presents operatic performances as well as other musical events.

The **Knoxville Symphony Orchestra** (☎*865/523–1178* ⊕*www. knoxvillesymphony.com*) offers many concerts a year throughout the Knoxville area, often with esteemed guest artists.

The Knoxville Opera Company and the Knoxville Symphony Orchestra both perform at the **Bijou Theatre** (⊠*803 S. Gay St.* ☎*865/522–0832*), which also hosts a variety of touring pop music acts.

The **Tennessee Theatre** (⊠*803 S. Gay St., Downtown* ☎*865/522–0832* ⊕*www.tennesseetheatre.com*), a grand, ornate former movie house, serves as the city's performing arts center.

The Old City, a historic warehouse district a few blocks north of downtown, is the site of Knoxville's most varied nightlife, with several restaurants and clubs.

Barley's Taproom (⊠*200 E. Jackson Ave., Old City* ☎*865/521–0092*) has a restaurant, patio, pool tables, darts, and 40 brews on tap. The **Crown and Goose** (⊠*100 N. Central St., Old City* ☎*865/637–4255*) is an authentic English pub.

Patrick Sullivan's Steakhouse (⊠*100 N. Central Ave., Old City* ☎*865/637–4255*) is popular both for dining and for its bar.

SEVIERVILLE

27 mi southeast of Knoxville.

Named for John Sevier, Tennessee's first governor, Sevierville (SEVERE-ville) is gradually undergoing the same tourist development that has engulfed Pigeon Forge and Gatlinburg. Franchise restaurants, motels, and outlet malls have sprung up along the main drag, including the massive Tanger Five Oaks Outlet Mall at the southern end of town, where the road winds south into the mountains.

GETTING HERE & AROUND
Sevierville is the first town after leaving I–40, Exit 407, on the road to Great Smoky Mountains National Park, which is about 16 mi south of Sevierville. Like the other towns on the way to the park, Sevierville is laid out along one strip of parkway.

ESSENTIALS
Visitor Information **Sevierville Chamber of Commerce Visitors Center** (⊠3099 Winfield Dunn Pkwy., Kodak, TN ☎865/453-6411 or 888/738-4378 ⊕www.visitsevierville.com).

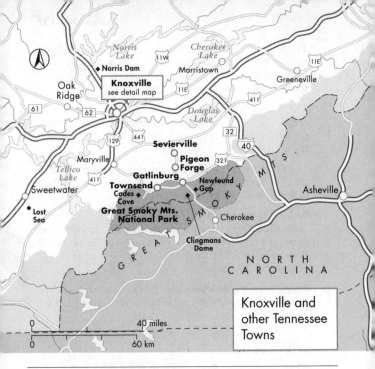

Knoxville and
other Tennessee
Towns

EXPLORING SEVIERVILLE

Forbidden Caverns features guided tours of numerous impressive formations, with plenty of grottoes, breathtaking waterfalls, and a crystal-clear stream. The cave plays a role in Indian legends and its dark passages were once used as clandestine sites for brewing moonshine. A stereophonic sound system adds to the experience. ✉*455 Blowing Cave Rd., about 14 mi northeast of Winfield Dunn Pkwy. on U.S. 411* ☎*865/453–5972* ⊕*www.forbiddencavern.com* ✇*$13* ☾*Apr.–Nov., daily 10–6.*

For a break from outlet shopping and the more frenetic tourist spots in Sevierville, check out **Smoky Mountain Deer Farm Exotic Petting Zoo**, which has a wide assortment of animals, including camels, reindeer, sheep, peacocks, and zebras. An adjacent stable offers horse and pony rides for an additional fee. ✉*478 Happy Hollow La., about 7½ mi northeast of Winfield Dunn Pkwy. (TN 66) on U.S. 411* ☎*865/428–3337* ⊕*www.deerfarmzoo.com* ✇*$10.95* ☾*Daily 10–5:30.*

About 2 mi east of the parkway, next to Gatlinburg/Pigeon Forge Airport, you'll find the **Tennessee Museum of Aviation**, which showcases aviation history and includes a hangar stocked with vintage warplanes as well as numerous displays of artifacts relating to flight. ✉ *135 Air Museum Way* ☎*865/908–0171 or 866/286–8738* ⊕*www.tnairmuseum. org* 🎟*$12.75* ☉*Jan. and Feb., Mon.–Sat. 10–5, Sun. 1–5; Mar.–Dec., Mon.–Sat. 10–6, Sun. 1–6.*

WHERE TO EAT

$–$$ ✕**Applewood Farmhouse Restaurant.** *Southern.* Down-home country cooking is served without pretense at this rambling restaurant just off the main drag at the south end of Sevierville. The menu features chicken, ribs, and fish, including Smoky Mountain trout. ✉ *240 Apple Valley Rd.* ☎*865/428–1222* ⊕*www.applewoodfarmhouserestaurant. com* ▤*AE, D, MC, V.*

¢–$ ✕**The Diner.** *American.* This is an authentic '50s diner, down to the quilted aluminum walls, curbside umbrella tables, and hot rods in the parking lot. The large selection of all-American favorites includes burgers (buffalo and elk), steaks (sirloin and rib eye), chicken and dumplings, meat loaf, and spaghetti and meatballs. The milkshakes are thick and creamy and breakfast is served all day. ✉ *550 Winfield Dunn Pkwy. (TN 66)* ☎*865/908–1904* ⊕*www.thediner.biz* ⊲*Reservations not accepted* ▤*AE, D, MC, V.*

¢ ✕ **Mountain Edge Grill.** *American.* Casual fare, including pizzas and salads, are the mainstays at this restaurant popular with families. Sandwiches include char-grilled chicken and half-pound buffalo burgers. Both locations in Sevierville and Gatlinburg feature numerous big-screen televisions showing a variety of sporting events. ✉ *1645 Pkwy., #975, in Tanger Five Oaks Outlet Mall, Sevierville* ☎*865/453–2939* ⊕*www.mtnedge.com* ▤ *D, MC, V* ✉*631 Pkwy., in Baskins Square Mall, Gatlinburg* ☎*865/436–0013* ⊕*www. mtnedge.com* ▤*D, MC, V.*

WHERE TO STAY

¢–$ ▣**Hampton Inn Sevierville.** You'll find standard rooms with plenty of amenities at this national chain, on the main road through town. **Pros:** convenient to tourist attractions and outlet shopping; complimentary breakfast; free Wi-Fi. **Cons:** on a crowded stretch of road; no restaurant. ✉*681 Winfield Dunn Pkwy.* ☎*865/429–2005* ⊕*www.*

hamptoninn.com ♺*68 rooms, 6 suites* ♿*In-room: refrigerator, Wi-Fi. In-hotel: pool, gym, Wi-Fi, parking (free), no-smoking rooms* ▤*AE, D, DC, MC, V.*

$$$–$$$$ ▦**Wilderness at the Smokies.** This sprawling, family-friendly resort opened in late 2008 and features a 60,000-square-foot indoor water park (included in the room rate) with a wave pool, surf rider, and several water slides. There's also a smaller water park at the six-story main hotel. Standard hotel rooms and suites are located in separate buildings; some suites can sleep up to 15 guests. Plans are in the works for even more accommodations and water parks on-site. **Pros:** concierge; lots of shops and amenities; free Wi-Fi. **Cons:** no airport shuttle; a bit raucous—not the place for travelers seeking peace and quiet. ✉*1425 Old Knoxville Hwy., just west of TN 66 (Pkwy.)* ☎*865/428–5770 or 877/325–9453* ⊕*www.wildernessatthesmokies.com* ♺*232 rooms, 400 suites* ♿*In-room: safe, kitchen (some), refrigerator, DVD, Wi-Fi. In-hotel: 2 restaurants, room service, golf course, fitness center, coin laundry, public Wi-Fi, parking (free), no-smoking rooms* ▤*AE, D, MC, V*

SHOPPING

Tanger Five Oaks Outlet Mall (✉*1645 Pkwy., Sevierville* ☎*865/453–1053* ⊕*www.tangeroutlet.com* ⊙*Mar.–Dec., Mon.–Sat. 9–9, Sun. 10–7; Jan. and Feb., Sun.–Thurs. 10–6, Fri. and Sat. 10–9*) is a massive outlet mall on the southern end of Sevierville by Pigeon Forge. It includes factory stores from numerous national brands, like Polo Ralph Lauren, Tommy Hilfiger, Calvin Klein, and Nautica.

PIGEON FORGE

25 mi southeast of Knoxville; 5 mi south of Sevierville via U.S. 441.

Pigeon Forge, is best known as the home of mountain native Dolly Parton's namesake theme park, Dollywood. In recent years, it has exploded with enough heavy-duty outlet shopping and kids' entertainment—from indoor skydiving simulators to laser tag—to keep families busy for a few days. But the intentionally cornpone image can become wearing, and it fails to reflect the quiet folksiness of the Appalachian communities scattered throughout these parts. Pigeon Forge has more than 200 outlet specialty stores, crafts shops, country hoedown emporiums, and kid-friendly attractions that line the main thoroughfare for several miles.

GETTING HERE & AROUND

Pigeon Forge begins at the southern border of Sevierville and stretches for about 5 mi along U.S. 441, a five-lane parkway that is an endless row of tourist attractions, franchise restaurants, and motels before abruptly ending and narrowing back into a wooded road running alongside the Little Pigeon River. The entrance to Great Smoky Mountains National Park is about 8 mi south of the southern limits of Pigeon Forge.

ESSENTIALS

Visitor Information **Pigeon Forge Information Center** (✉ *3107 Pkwy., Pigeon Forge, TN*). **Pigeon Forge Department of Tourism** (✉ *2450 Pkwy., Pigeon Forge, TN*). **Pigeon Forge Welcome Center** (✉ *1950 Pkwy., Pigeon Forge, TN* ☎ *865/453-8574 or 800/251-9100* 🌐 *www.mypigeonforge.com*).

EXPLORING PIGEON FORGE

The 1830s-era **Old Mill,** beside the Little Pigeon River, still grinds corn, wheat, and rye on water-powered stone wheels. A 20-minute tour explains the process. Flour, meal, grits, and buckwheat are for sale as are other items in the numerous shops around the mill. ✉ *160 Old Mill Ave.* ☎ *865/453-4628 or 888/453-6455* 🌐 *www.old-mill.com* *$3 mill tours* ⏲ *Daily 9–8; mill tours weekdays 9–2.*

★ **Dollywood,** singer Dolly Parton's popular theme park, embodies the country superstar's own flamboyance—plenty of Hollywood flash mixed with simple country charm that you either love or hate. This endeavor brings to life the folklore, fun, food, and music of the Great Smokies, which inspired many of Parton's early songs. In a re-created 1880 mountain village, scores of talented and friendly craftspeople demonstrate their artistry. Museum exhibits trace Parton's rise to stardom from her backwoods upbringing. There are many rides including River Battle, a water adventure, and Thunderhead, a wooden roller coaster. Music, however, is the unifying theme of the park, with live shows on the park's many stages. Dolly occasionally makes a surprise appearance. Nearby is Dollywood's Splash Country, a water park that includes nearly 30 water slides, a 25,000-square-foot wave pool and children's play areas. ✉ *1020 Dollywood La.* ☎ *865/428-9488 or 800/365-5996*

⊕*www.dollywood.com* ▣*$53.50* ⊙*Late Mar.–early Jan.,
days and hours vary.*

WHERE TO EAT

$$ ✕**Bullfish Grill.** *American.* This popular spot on the main drag
offers lots of hearty entrées including meatloaf, fish 'n chips,
and chicken Florentine. There's a full selection of steaks and
numerous grilled fresh fish, including salmon, swordfish,
and Ahi tuna. Finish off your meal with a decadent dessert
such as New York cheesecake or two-layer Key lime pie.
▣*2441 Pkwy.* ☎*865/868–1000* ⊕*www.bullfishgrill.com*
⌂*Reservations not accepted* ▭*AE, D, MC, V.*

¢–$ ✕**The Old Mill.** *American.* This rambling, raucous family-
friendly restaurant just east of the main drag dishes up all-
American specialties like fried chicken, country ham, and
pot roast. Lines start early and spill out the door. Across
the street, the less crowded Old Mill's café and grill serves
sandwiches, salads, steaks, and seafood. The main restau-
rant is open seven days, including breakfast. The café and
grill is open for lunch and dinner only. ▣*164 Old Mill Ave.*
☎*865/429–3463* ⊕*www.old-mill.com* ▭*AE, D, MC, V.*

WHERE TO STAY

¢–$ ▥**Holiday Inn Pigeon Forge.** This hotel is in the middle of the
🕗 action. Its indoor pool includes a waterfall and adjacent
game room, which is sure to please the kids. **Pros:** conve-
nient location; nice pool; free Wi-Fi. **Cons:** uninspiring
surroundings; lots of traffic on road outside. ▣*3230 Pkwy.,*
☎*865/428–2700 or 800/782–3119* ⊕*www.4lodging.com/
PGFTN* ⇗*200 rooms, 6 suites* ⌂*In-room: refrigerator,
Wi-Fi. In-hotel: restaurant, room service, pool, gym, laun-
dry service, Wi-Fi, parking (free), some pets allowed, no-
smoking rooms* ▭*AE, D, DC, MC, V.*

¢ ▥**Best Western Plaza Inn.** Convenient to shops, restaurants,
🕗 and attractions, the Best Western is a good choice for fami-
lies. It has three swimming pools (one indoor and two
outdoor) and some rooms overlook mountain scenery.
Pros: adjacent to Dixieland Stampede show; good value;
free Wi-Fi. **Cons:** rather standard rooms; sits right along
main drag with heavy traffic. ▣*3755 Pkwy.* ☎*865/453–
5538 or 800/232–5656* ⇗*198 rooms, 3 suites* ⌂ *In-room:
refrigerator, Wi-Fi. In-hotel: pools, Wi-Fi, parking (free),
no-smoking rooms* ▭*AE, D, MC, V* ⍏*CP.*

WHERE TO CAMP

$$$–$$$$ ⛺ **Waldens Creek Campground.** Pigeon Forge's newest campground is within the town limits and has 35 sites on concrete pads, with easy access to hiking and fishing. There's a supermarket within walking distance. It is located west of the main drag, just off Wears Valley Road. **Pros:** showers available; tents allowed along the creek. **Cons:** no swimming; sites are close together. ✉ *2485 Henderson Springs Rd.* ☎ *865/908–2727 or 877/908–2727* ⊕ *www. waldenscreekcampground.com* ⇌ *35 sites* ♿ *Flush toilets, full hookups, drinking water, guest laundry, showers, fire pits, picnic tables, electricity, Wi-Fi* ⊟ *AE, D, MC, V.*

NIGHTLIFE & THE ARTS

Pigeon Forge has a host of theaters, with many concentrated around the 2000 block of Parkway.

The **Comedy Barn** (✉ *2775 Pkwy. 37863* ☎ *865/428–5222 or 800/295–2844* ⊕ *www.comedybarn.com*) presents a family variety show.

The **Country Tonite Theater** (✉ *129 Showplace Blvd.* ☎ *865/ 453–2003 or 800/792–4308* ⊕ *www.countrytonitepf.com*) has foot-stompin' country music.

Hearty country dinners are accompanied by a colorful, Western-theme musical show and rodeo at Dolly Parton's **Dixie Stampede** (✉ *3849 Pkwy. 37863* ☎ *865/453–4400 or 800/356–1676* ⊕ *www.dixiestampede.com*), located at the south end of town.

SHOPPING

Every imaginable outlet store can be found somewhere in the maze of outlet centers at the heart of Pigeon Forge.

The massive indoor **Belz Factory Outlet World** (✉ *2655 Teaster La. 37863* ☎ *865/453–7316*) has over 75 stores offering major brands of clothes, shoes, and accessories.

The **Pigeon Forge Factory Outlet Mall** (✉ *2850 Pkwy.* ☎ *865/ 428–2828*) has housewares as well as clothes and shoes.

The **Shoppes of Pigeon Forge** (✉ *161 E. Wears Valley Rd.* ☎ *865/428–7002*) has stores including Liz Claiborne, Tommy Hilfiger, and Nautica.

For mountain crafts, stop at **Old Mill Village** (⊠*175 Old Mill Ave., off Pkwy., turn east at traffic light No. 7*), whose shops include **Pigeon River Pottery** (☎*865/453–1104*) and **Old Mill General Store** (☎*865/453–4628*).

GATLINBURG

8 mi southeast of Pigeon Forge.

Gateway city to Great Smoky Mountains National Park, Gatlinburg, popular with honeymooners and families, has steadily expanded from a remote little town with a sprinkling of hotels, chalets, and mountain crafts shops to a tourist town packed with attractions, including an aquarium, ski resort, amusement park, and "shoppes" peddling souvenirs and fudge. During the summer, the town is clogged with tourists, complete with the annoyances of traffic jams and packed restaurants. Nevertheless, Gatlinburg is an enduringly popular mountain resort town, with more visitors than Great Smoky Mountains National Park.

GETTING HERE & AROUND

Gatlinburg is directly outside the entrance to the national park, where U.S. 441 becomes Parkway. Heading out of town to the north, U.S. 321 splits to the northeast, and after a few miles, Glades Road branches off and swiftly leaves behind the commercialism of Gatlinburg for a winding journey past bucolic mountain landscapes and log cabins interspersed with the workshops of local artisans. Parkway is the main drag running through town.

ESSENTIALS

Visitor Information **Gatlinburg Chamber of Commerce** (⊠*811 E. Pkwy., Gatlinburg, TN* ☎*800/568–4748* ⊕*www.gatlinburg.com*).

EXPLORING GATLINBURG

Arrowmont School of Arts & Crafts (⊠*556 Pkwy.* ☎*865/436–5860*) is a nationally known visual arts complex.

The **Gatlinburg Sky Lift** (☎*865/436–4307* ⊕*www.gatlinburgskylift.com*), via which you can reach the top of Crockett Mountain, makes a fun outing for the family.

The **Ober Gatlinburg Tramway** (☎*865/436–5423* ⊕*www.obergatlinburg.com*) whisks visitors to a mountaintop amusement park, ski center, and restaurants.

CLOSE UP

The State of Franklin

If the gears of history had turned a little differently, you might have entered the western side of the Great Smokies through the state of Franklin, instead of the state of Tennessee. What is now Sevier County, Tennessee, where the towns of Gatlinburg, Pigeon Forge, and Sevierville are located, was for a few years in the late 18th century part of the autonomous State of Franklin. In the years following the American Revolution, the frontier people of what was then the far western tip of North Carolina became dissatisfied with their government far away in eastern North Carolina. They called for the establishment of a separate state. On August 23, 1784, delegates from several counties convened in the town of Jonesborough and declared themselves independent of North Carolina. Then, in 1785, a delegation

from these counties submitted a petition for statehood to the United States Congress. Seven states voted to admit the new state under the proposed name Frankland. In an effort to gain the approval of more states and to curry the favor of Benjamin Franklin, leaders changed the proposed name to Franklin. However, the vote still fell short of the two-thirds majority required to admit a territory to statehood under the Articles of Confederation. By 1790, the government of the State of Franklin had collapsed and the territory was taken back under the control of North Carolina. Not long after, North Carolina ceded Franklin to the federal government to form the Southwest Territory, and what was the short-lived State of Franklin became part of Tennessee, which was admitted to the Union in 1796.

5

WHERE TO EAT

¢ ✕**Pancake Pantry.** *American.* This restaurant, with its century-old brick, polished-oak paneling, rustic copper accessories, and spacious windows, is a family favorite for breakfast and lunch. Austrian apple-walnut pancakes covered with apple cider compote, black walnuts, powdered sugar, and whipped cream are a house specialty. Other selections include omelets, sandwiches, and fresh salads. The line often stretches out the door. ✉*628 Pkwy.* ☎*865/436–4724* ⌖*Reservations not accepted* ▬*No credit cards* ⊘*No dinner.*

$-$$ ✕**Smoky Mountain Trout House.** *Seafood.* This restaurant is a throwback to traditional mountain vacation eateries, with pine paneling, checkered tablecloths, and stuffed fish mounted on the walls. Of the 15 distinctive trout prepara- tions to choose from at this cozy restaurant, an old favorite is trout Eisenhower: pan-fried, with cornmeal breading and served with bacon-and-butter sauce. Steaks, country ham, and grilled chicken are also on the menu. There is no designated parking for the restaurant, but the attendant at the paid lot across the street should be able to give you a ticket which the restaurant will reimburse. ⊠ *410 Pkwy.* ☎ *865/436–5416* ⚖ *Reservations not accepted* ▭ *AE, D, DC, MC, V* ⊘ *No lunch.*

WHERE TO STAY

$ 🛏**Best Western Twin Islands Motel.** This chain motel is located in the thick of the tourist strip, beside the Little Pigeon River and in between Ripley's Aquarium of the Smokies and Gatlinburg's Hard Rock Cafe. Rooms have balconies over- looking the river, and you can fish on the motel property. **Pros:** comfortable rooms; an easy walk to all Gatlinburg attractions; free Wi-Fi. **Cons:** in a high-traffic area with lots of noise; no restaurant. ⊠ *539 Pkwy.* ☎ *865/436–5121 or 800/223–9299* ⊕ *www.bestwestern.com* ⤹ *92 rooms, 20 suites* ⚖ *In-room: refrigerator, Wi-Fi. In-hotel: pool, no- smoking rooms* ▭ *AE, D, MC, V.*

★ Fodor'sChoice 🛏**Buckhorn Inn.** This charming country inn is
$ set on 40 acres of remote woodlands about 5 mi outside Gatlinburg. Guests—including seclusion-seeking diplomats, government officials, and celebrities—have been coming here since 1938. The views of Mt. LeConte and the Great Smokies are spectacular, and the Great Smoky Arts and Crafts Community is nearby. A nature trail winds through the property, and guests may spot ducks, birds, or bears nearby. Rooms are spread among the main inn building, three guesthouses, and seven cottages. The inn has wicker rockers, paintings by local artists, a huge stone fireplace, and French doors that open onto a large stone porch. All rooms are spacious, and some have balconies and gas fireplaces. Full breakfasts are included in the rate. A four- course gourmet dinner ($35) is served nightly at 7. **Pros:** peaceful setting; away from the bustle of Gatlinburg. **Cons:** Wi-Fi not available throughout entire property; two-night minimum required on weekends. ⊠ *Off U.S. 321 and Buck- horn Rd., 2140 Tudor Mountain Rd.* ☎ *865/436–4668 or 866/941–0460* ⊕ *www.buckhorninn.com* ⤹ *19 rooms, 4 suites* ⚖ *In-room: no phone, kitchen (some), refrigerator*

(some), DVD. In-hotel: restaurant, gym, parking (free), no-smoking rooms ⊟*D, MC, V* ⏐◎⏐ *BP.*

¢ ⚄ **Garden Plaza Hotel.** Two impressive indoor pools provide
☾ ample recreation opportunities for families. There's also a game room with video games and ping pong. The hotel is actually a multi-building complex located a short distance from the main drag on a mountain road. A breakfast buffet is included with room rates. **Pros:** concierge; conveniently located near Gatlinburg attractions; free Wi-Fi. **Cons:** no public Internet terminal; no restaurant. ⊠*520 Historic Nature Trail* ☎*865/436–9201 or 800/435–9201* ⊕*www.4lodging.com/gattn* ⇗*400 rooms* ⎉*In-room: refrigerator, Wi-Fi. In-hotel: bar, pools, gyms, coin laundry, public Wi-Fi, some pets allowed, no-smoking rooms* ⊟*AE, D, MC, V* ⏐◎⏐*BP.*

¢–$ ⚄ **Park Vista Resort Hotel.** Set on a mountain ledge with
☾ spectacular views, this large hotel has modern, lavishly decorated public areas and spacious, elegant guest rooms. Each room has a balcony overlooking colorful gardens, the town of Gatlinburg, the Little Pigeon River, and the mountains beyond. Nonetheless, this green, semicircular contemporary tower is a jarring sight in the Great Smoky Mountains. There's a playground and game room for the kids. **Pros:** balconies off every room; downtown trolley stops at hotel. **Cons:** not aesthetically pleasing; not within walking distance to downtown. ⊠*705 Cherokee Orchard Rd.* ☎*865/436–9211 or 800/421–7275* ⊕*www.parkvista. com* ⇗*307 rooms, 5 suites* ⎉*In-room: refrigerator (some), Wi-Fi. In-hotel: restaurant, room service, bar, pool, gym, laundry service, Wi-Fi, parking (free), some pets allowed, no-smoking rooms* ⊟*AE, D, MC, V.*

WHERE TO CAMP

$$$$ ⛺ **Twin Creek RV Resort.** This RV resort offers large sites along a mountain stream. Located northeast of downtown, just past the turnoff for Glades Road, it is a short drive from beautiful mountain scenery and the workshops of the Great Smoky Arts and Crafts Community. Cabins are available for rent as well. **Pros:** lots of amenities and activities; good for RVs. **Cons:** no tents allowed; not within walking distance of Gatlinburg attractions. ⊠*1202 E. Pkwy.* ☎*865/436–7081 or 800/252–8077* ⊕*www.twincreekrvresort.com* ⇗*72 RV sites* ⎉*Flush toilets, full hookups, drinking water, guest laundry, showers, fire pits, grills, picnic tables, electricity,*

general store, play area, swimming (pool), Wi-Fi ▭MC, V ☉Closed Nov.–mid-Mar.

NIGHTLIFE & THE ARTS

Sweet Fanny Adams Theatre and Music Hall (⊠*461 Pkwy.* ☎*877/388–5784 or 865/436–4039* ⊕*www.sweetfanny-adams.com*) stages original musical comedies, Gay '90s revues, and old-fashioned sing-alongs. Reservations are advised.

SPORTS & THE OUTDOORS

Bent Creek Golf Resort (⊠*3919 E. Pkwy.* ☎*865/436–2875* ⊕*www.bentcreekgolfcourse.com*) has an 18-hole, par-72 course that is open to the public.

SHOPPING

The mountain towns of East Tennessee are known for Appalachian folk crafts, especially wood carvings, cornhusk dolls, pottery, dulcimers, and beautiful handmade quilts. The **Great Smoky Arts and Crafts Community** is a collection of 80 shops and craftspeople's studios along 8 mi of rambling country road. Begun in 1937, the community includes workers in leather, pottery, weaving, hand-wrought pewter, stained glass, quilt making, hand carving, marquetry, and more. Everything sold here is made on the premises by the community members. Also here is the popular tearoom and lunch spot, **Wild Plum Tearoom**, on Buckhorn Road near the Buckhorn Inn. ⊠*Off U.S. 321 on Glades Rd., 3 mi east of Gatlinburg* ⊕*Box 807, Gatlinburg 37738* ☎*865/671–3600 or 800/565–7330* ⊕*www.gatlinburgcrafts.com.*

TOWNSEND

33 mi southeast of Knoxville, 26 mi west of Gatlinburg/ Pigeon Forge.

Townsend, population about 250, sits in a mist-shrouded valley about an hour south of Knoxville. Like Gatlinburg, Townsend is right outside the entrance to Great Smoky Mountains National Park, but there the similarities end: it has a minuscule amount of tourist development, with only a handful of shops, restaurants, and motels.

GETTING HERE & AROUND

To get to Townsend from downtown Knoxville, take U.S. 129 off I–40, exit 387, to Alcoa/Maryville, where U.S. 321/TN 73 leads to Townsend. Once in Townsend, the road continues through town to the entrance to Great Smoky Mountains National Park, while another road branches off and heads east to Pigeon Forge, about 20 mi away.

Great Smoky Mountains Heritage Center is just about a mile inside Townsend from the entrance to the national park. The beautiful, scenic Cades Cove is under 10 mi down the road into the park.

ESSENTIALS

Visitor Information Smoky Mountains Visitors Center (⊠ *7906 E. Lamar Alexander Pkwy., Townsend, TN* ☎ *865/448–6134 or 800/525–6834* ⊕ *www.smokymountains.org*).

EXPLORING TOWNSEND

Great Smoky Mountains Heritage Center has exhibits on Native American and pioneer culture, giving visitors a look at daily life, recreation, and spirituality. There is also a log cabin and other historic buildings. ⊠ *123 Cromwell Dr.* ☎ *865/448–0044* ⊕ *www.gsmheritagecenter.org* ⊠ *$6* ⊙ *Tues.–Sat. 10–5, Sun. 1–5.*

Tuckaleechee Caverns features impressive, well-lit formations. Most stunning of all is the "big room" with massive stalagmites and stalactites. Visitors also see a stream flowing through the cavern and a "fairyland" of dramatic formations. Guided tours depart roughly every 15 minutes. ⊠ *825 Cavern Rd.* ☎ *865/448–2274* ⊕ *www.tuckaleecheecaverns. com* ⊠ *$14* ⊙ *Daily 10–5.*

WHERE TO STAY & EAT

$–$$ ✕ **Carriage House Restaurant.** *American.* This restaurant has a simple, down-home ambience and is frequented by locals as well as tourists. The simple but extensive menu has everything from New York strip steak and fried chicken to grilled salmon and veggie burgers. The restaurant is very convenient to the Smokies, at just over a mile up the road from the national park entrance. ⊠ *8310 TN 73* ☎ *865/448–2263* ⊟ *AE, D, MC, V* ⊙ *Closed mid-Nov.–mid-Mar.*

¢ ✕ **Sister Cats Cafe.** *American.* This cozy lunch spot has an eclectic menu of sandwiches and salads, such as a Hawaiian panini with ham, pineapple, and roasted red pepper. Daily specials may include quiche or spinach enchiladas. The dining room features Persian rugs and walls cluttered with bric-a-brac. ⊠ *7327 E. Lamar Alexander Pkwy. (TN 73)* ☎*865/448–0033* ⊕*sistercatscafe.com* ⊟*D, MC, V* ⊘*No dinner. Closed Sun. and Wed.*

$ ⊞**Talley Ho Inn.** Next door to the Carriage House restaurant, this low-key motel on the main road has rooms in a variety of sizes. Many rooms have balconies and gas fireplaces. Family-owned since the 1950s, it sits just over a mile from the national park entrance. **Pros:** amazing views of the mountains; discount available at adjacent restaurant. **Cons:** no fitness center or business center; Wi-Fi service can be sporadic. ⊠*8314 TN 73* ☎*865/448–2465 or 800/448–2465* ⊕*www.talleyhoinn.com* ⊅*48 rooms* ⊜*In-room: refrigerator (some), Wi-Fi. In-hotel: pool, Wi-Fi, parking (free), no-smoking rooms* ⊟ *D, MC, V.*

Asheville and Other North Carolina Towns

WORD OF MOUTH

"Take a day and go down to Chimney Rock and Lake Lure. It is a beautiful area and Chimney Rock Park has incredible hiking trails and the views are incredible. Weather permitting, you have to take the kids on the Lake Lure boat tour."

—Traci The Lake Lure Gal

By Lan
Sluder

ASHEVILLE, THE HUB OF WESTERN North Carolina and about an hour from the east side of the Smokies, is one of the biggest small cities you'll ever visit, with the artsy élan and dynamic downtown of a much larger burg. Set in a valley surrounded by the highest mountains in Eastern America, Asheville is a base for exploring the park, but it is also a destination in itself. Here you can tour America's largest home, the Biltmore Estate, and discover why Asheville has a national reputation for its arts, crafts, and music scenes. Coffee houses, brewpubs, sidewalk cafés, boutiques, antiques shops, clubs, and galleries are everywhere in the city's art deco downtown. Just a short drive away are inviting small mountain towns, mile-high vistas that will take your breath away, and enough high-energy outdoor fun to keep your heart rate up.

Around the eastern edge of the park are a number of small Carolina towns. Hendersonville is known for its 10 blocks of antiques stores and galleries on historic Main Street. Flat Rock began as a summer resort town and includes poet Carl Sandburg's home. Brevard is another small, walkable town, located near the Pisgah Forest. The Cherokee reservation and town of Cherokee mark the North Carolina entrance to the park and have much to offer, from the Oconaluftee Indian Village to Harrah's Casino. One of the lesser-known gateways to the park, Bryson City, lies along the Nantahala River, which is great for river rafting trips. Robbinsville and Lake Santeetlah are near Fontana Lake and good fishing. Sylva and Waynesville are short on glitz but long on charm. The towns all share the same backdrop, the beautiful mountains.

ABOUT THE RESTAURANTS

At many places, the emphasis is on "slow food," made with locally grown, often organic, ingredients. Asheville is the place to go for innovative cuisine, but the smaller mountain towns turn out reliable and hearty mountain favorites.

ABOUT THE HOTELS

You can find the usual chain motels and hotels here, though less than on the Tennessee side of the park. Bed-and-breakfasts bloom in the mountains like wildflowers; Asheville alone has more than three dozen. There are also a few large resorts, including the Grove Park Inn Resort & Spa.

WHAT IT COSTS				
¢	$	$$	$$$	$$$$
RESTAURANT				
under $10	$10–$14	$15–$19	$20–$24	over $24
HOTEL				
under $100	$100–$150	$151–$200	$201–$250	over $250
CAMPING				
under $10	$10–$14	$15–$19	$20–$24	over $24

Restaurant prices are for a main course at dinner. Hotel prices are for two people in a standard double room in high season. Camping prices are for a standard campsite per night.

ASHEVILLE

6

Asheville is the hippest city in the South. At least that's the claim of Asheville's fans, who are legion. Visitors flock to Asheville to experience the arts and culture scene, which rivals that of Santa Fe, and to experience the city's blossoming downtown, with its myriad restaurants, coffeehouses, museums, galleries, bookstores, antiques shops, and boutiques.

Named "the best place to live" by many books and magazines, Asheville is also the destination for retirees escaping the cold North, or of "halfbacks," those who moved to Florida but who are now coming half the way back to the North. Old downtown buildings have been converted to upmarket condos for these affluent retirees, and, despite the housing slowdown, new residential developments are springing up south, east, and west of town. As a result of this influx, Asheville has a much more cosmopolitan population than most cities of its size (70,000 people in the city, about 400,000 in the metro area).

Asheville has a diversity you won't find in many cities in the South. There's a thriving gay community, many aging hippies, and young alternative-lifestyle seekers. People for the Ethical Treatment of Animals (PETA) has named Asheville the most vegetarian-friendly city in America.

The city really comes alive at night, with the restaurants, sidewalk cafés, and coffeehouses; so visit after dark to see it at its best. Especially on warm summer weekends, Pack Square, Biltmore Avenue, Haywood Street, Wall Street, and Battery Park Avenue are busy until well after midnight.

GETTING HERE & AROUND

From the east and west, the main route to Asheville is I–40. The most scenic route to Asheville is via the Blue Ridge Parkway, which meanders between the Shenandoah National Park in Virginia and the Great Smoky Mountains National Park near Cherokee, North Carolina. Interstate 240 forms a freeway perimeter around Asheville, and Pack Square is the center of the city.

While a car is virtually a necessity to explore Asheville thoroughly, the city does have a metropolitan bus system with 24 routes radiating from the Transit Center in downtown. Asheville also has a sightseeing trolley service; tickets are available at the Asheville Convention and Visitors Bureau. Asheville is highly walkable, and the best way to see downtown is on foot.

ESSENTIALS

Visitor Information **Asheville Convention and Visitors Bureau** (⊠ *36 Montford Ave., Box 1010* ☎ *828/258–6101 or 888/247–9811* ⊕ *www.exploreasheville.com*).

DOWNTOWN ASHEVILLE

A city of neighborhoods, Asheville rewards careful exploration, especially on foot. You can break up your sightseeing with stops at the more than 50 restaurants in downtown alone, and at any of hundreds of unique shops.

Downtown Asheville has the largest extant collection of art deco buildings in the Southeast outside of Miami Beach, most notably the S&W Cafeteria (1929), Asheville City Hall (1928), First Baptist Church (1927), and Asheville High School (1929). It's also known for its architecture in other styles: Battery Park Hotel (1924) is neo-Georgian; the Flatiron Building (1924) is neoclassical; the Basilica of St. Lawrence (1909) is Spanish Renaissance; and Pack Place, formerly known as Old Pack Library (1925), is in the Italian-Renaissance style.

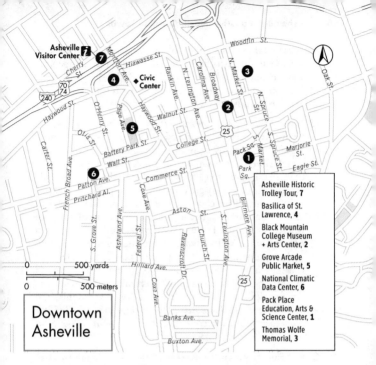

Downtown Asheville

TOP ATTRACTIONS

❹ Basilica of St. Lawrence. A collaboration between Biltmore House's head architect Richard Sharp Smith and the Spanish engineer-architect Rafael Gustavino, this elaborate Catholic basilica was completed in 1909. It follows a Spanish Renaissance design, rendered in brick and polychrome tile, and has a large, self-supporting dome with Catalan-style vaulting. ⊠ *97 Haywood St., Downtown* ☎ *828/252–6042* ⊞ *Free* ⊙ *Weekdays 9–4.*

❷ Black Mountain College Museum + Arts Center. Famed Black Mountain College (1933–57), 16 mi east of Asheville, was important in the development of several groundbreaking 20th-century art, dance, and literary movements. Some of the maverick spirits it attracted in its short lifetime include artists Willem and Elaine de Kooning, Robert Rauschenberg, Josef and Anni Albers, Ben Shahn, M.C. Richards, and Franz Kline; dancer Merce Cunningham; musician John Cage; filmmaker Arthur Penn; and writers Kenneth Noland, Charles Olson, and Robert Creeley. A museum and gallery dedicated to the history of the radical college occupies a small space in downtown Asheville. It puts on occasional exhibits and publishes material about the college. Call ahead to find out what's currently happening. ✉ *54 Broadway, Downtown* ☎ *828/299–9306* 🌐 *www.blackmountaincollege.org* 🎫 *Varies, depending on the exhibit; usually $5–$10* ⏲ *Wed.–Sat. noon–4.*

❺ **Grove Arcade Public Market.** When it opened in 1929, the Grove Arcade was trumpeted as "the most elegant building in America" by its builder, W. E. Grove, the man also responsible for the Grove Park Inn. With the coming of the Great Depression and World War II, the Grove Arcade evolved into a dowdy government building. In late 2002 its polished limestone elegance was restored, and it reopened as a public market patterned in some ways after Pike Place Market in Seattle. The market covers a full city block and has about 50 locally owned stores and restaurants, along with apartments and office space. A new Arts & Heritage Gallery features interactive exhibits and regional crafts and music. The building is an architectural wonder, with gargoyles galore, and well worth a visit even if you don't shop or dine here. ✉ *1 Page Ave., Downtown* ☎ *828/252–7799* 🌐 *www.grovearcade.com* 🎫 *Free* ⏲ *Mon.–Sat. 10–6, Sun. noon–5; store hrs vary.*

❶ **Pack Place Education, Arts & Science Center.** This 92,000-square-foot complex in downtown Asheville houses the **Asheville Art Museum, Colburn Earth Science Museum, Health Adventure,** and **Diana Wortham Theatre.** The **YMI Cultural Center,** also maintained by Pack Place, and focusing on the history of African-Americans in western North Carolina, is across the street. The Health Adventure has 11 galleries with hands-on exhibits, all of interest to children. The Asheville Art Museum stages major exhibits several times a year, with some highlighting regional artists. The Colburn Earth Science Museum displays local gems and minerals. The intimate 500-seat Diana Wortham Theatre hosts musical concerts and dance and theater performances year-round. ✉ *2 S. Pack Sq., Downtown* ☎ *828/257–4500* 🌐 *www.packplace.org* 🎫 *Art museum $6, Health Adventure $8.50, earth science museum $4, YMI Cultural Center $5* ⏲ *Tues.–Sat. 10–5, Sun. 1–5 (art museum open until 8 Fri.).*

★ Fodor'sChoice **Thomas Wolfe Memorial.** Asheville's most famous
❸ son, novelist Thomas Wolfe (1900–38), grew up in a 29-room Queen Anne–style home that his mother ran as a boardinghouse. The house, a state historic site, was badly

damaged in a 1998 fire (a still-unsolved case of arson); it reopened in mid-2004 following a painstaking $2.4 million renovation. Though about one-fourth of the furniture and artifacts were lost in the fire, the house—memorialized as "Dixieland" in Wolfe's novel *Look Homeward, Angel*— has been restored to its original 1916 condition, including a light canary-yellow paint on the exterior. You'll find a visitor center and many displays, and there are guided tours of the house and heirloom gardens. The admission, at only a dollar, is one of the best bargains in town. *⊠52 Market St., Downtown ☎828/253–8304 ⊕www.wolfememorial. com ☜$1 ☉Tues.–Sat. 9–5, Sun. 1–5.*

WORTH NOTING

❼ Asheville Historic Trolley Tour. A motorized trolley bus takes you to the main points of interest around Asheville, including the Grove Park Inn, Biltmore Village, the Thomas Wolfe Memorial, the Montford area, the River Arts District, and Pack Square and downtown. You can buy tickets and board the trolley at the Asheville Convention and Visitors Bureau and get on or off at any stop on this 80-minute narrated tour. Reservations are available but usually aren't necessary. Ghost Tours on Saturday nights at 7:30 from March to November explore Asheville's supernatural side. They take you past spooky sights like the notorious murder site at Battery Park, and phantoms on Church Street *⊠Asheville Convention and Visitors Bureau, 36 Montford Ave., ☎888/667–3600 ⊕www.ashevilletrolleytours.com ☜$19; ghost tours, $20.*

❻ National Climatic Data Center (NCDC). The world's largest active archive of global weather data, the National Climatic Data Center provides weather data to researchers all over the world. The NCDC gathers and maintains weather data from some 10,000 weather stations around the United States, and some of its historical data goes back over 200 years. Users of the data range from large engineering firms planning energy-efficient development to individuals planning a retirement move. ■TIP→ At present, only group tours of the center are available, and must be arranged in advance. *⊠Federal Plaza, 151 Patton Ave., Downtown ☎828/271– 4800, 828/271–4203 for group tours ⊕www.ncdc.noaa. gov ☜Free ☉Weekdays 8–4:30.*

GREATER ASHEVILLE

North Asheville, the historic Montford section (home to more than a dozen B&Bs), and the Grove Park neighborhood all have fine Victorian-era homes, including many remarkable Queen Anne houses. Biltmore Village, across from the entrance to the Biltmore Estate, was constructed at the time that Biltmore House was being built, and is now predominantly an area of retail boutiques and galleries. The River District, along the French Broad River, is an up-and-coming arts area, with many studios and lofts. Across the river, West Asheville has suddenly become the hottest part of the city, with its main artery, Haywood Road, sporting new restaurants, edgy stores, and popular clubs, though much of West Asheville retains its low-key, slightly scruffy, 1950s ambience.

WORD OF MOUTH. "Well, I seldom post anything on the US board, but just had to comment on the Biltmore. We went for a long weekend the first weekend in Dec because I wanted to be there during the Christmas season. We stayed at the Inn and everything about the trip exceeded my expectations. Staying at the Inn with the Christmas package we were able to enter the home as much as we wanted to. This is a destination in itself." —mimipam

TOP ATTRACTIONS

★ Fodor's Choice **Biltmore Estate.** Built in the 1890s as the private home of George Vanderbilt, the astonishing 250-room French-Renaissance château is America's largest private residence. (Some of Vanderbilt's descendants still live on the estate, but the bulk of the home and grounds are open to visitors.) Richard Morris Hunt designed it, and Frederick Law Olmsted landscaped the original 125,000-acre estate (now 8,000 acres), which faces Biltmore Village. It took 1,000 workers five years to complete the gargantuan project. On view are the priceless antiques and art collected by the Vanderbilts, including notable paintings by Renoir and John Singer Sargent, along with 75 acres of gardens and formally landscaped grounds. You can also see the state-of-the-art winery and an 1890s-era farm, River Bend. Candlelight tours of the house are offered at Christmastime. Also on the grounds are a deluxe hotel, five restaurants open to the public, and an equestrian center. Each year in August, Biltmore Estate hosts music concerts with nationally known entertainers such as B.B. King and

REO Speedwagon. Biltmore House's fourth floor, whose rooms are now open to the public, includes an observatory with sweeping views of the surrounding landscape, an architectural model room housing Hunt's 1889 model of the house, and servants' bedrooms and meeting hall, so you can see how the staff lived. Most people tour the house on their own, but guided tours are available ($15 additional). Note that there are a lot of stairs to climb, but much of the house is accessible for guests in wheelchairs or with limited mobility. ■TIP→ **If possible, avoid visiting on weekends during fall color season and the weeks between Thanksgiving and Christmas, when crowds are at their largest. Save by booking online rather than buying at the gate.** Saturday admission prices are higher than weekday rates, but, if you come back, the second visit in two days is only $10. The best deal is the annual pass, allowing unlimited admission for a year and costing only about twice as much as a one-day admission. ⊠*Exit 50 off I–40, South Metro* ☎*828/255–1700 or 800/411–3812* ⊕*www.biltmore.com* ☎*$47 Sun.–Fri.; $51 Sat.; $59 flex ticket for any day of the year; $99 unlimited visit annual pass; $15 extra for guided group tours of the house; $150 extra for premium tour with personal guide and visits to areas not normally open to the public.* ☉*Admission gate and reception and ticket center: Jan.–Mar., daily 9–4; Apr.–Oct., daily 8:30–5; Nov. and Dec., daily 8:30–8.*

Biltmore Village. Across from the Biltmore Estate, Biltmore Village is a highly walkable collection of restored English village–style houses, now mostly shops and galleries. Badly flooded in 2004, with many buildings damaged and shops closed, the Village has come back to life, with nearly all shops now reopened. Of particular note is **All Souls Cathedral,** one of the most beautiful churches in America. It was designed by Richard Morris Hunt following the traditional Norman cross plan and opened in 1896. ⊠*3 Angle St., South Metro* ☎*828/274–2681* ☎*Free* ☉*Daily, hrs vary.*

★ Fodor'sChoice **North Carolina Arboretum.** Part of the original
♻ Biltmore Estate, these 434 acres completed Frederick Law Olmsted's dream of creating a world-class arboretum in the western part of North Carolina. Highlights include southern Appalachian flora in stunning settings, such as the Blue Ridge Quilt Garden, with bedding plants arranged in patterns reminiscent of Appalachian quilts, and sculptures set among the gardens. An extensive network of trails is available for walking or mountain biking. A bonsai exhibit

CLOSE UP

Biltmore Boasts

The Biltmore Estate is North Carolina's leading tourist attraction and boasts many superlatives. Biltmore Estate:

■ Is the largest private home in America, with 250 rooms in 175,000 square feet of living space.

■ Is America's most-visited historic house, followed by Mount Vernon, Hearst Castle, and Graceland, with more than 1 million visitors annually.

■ Has appeared in over a dozen movies, including *The Swan* (1956), *Richie Rich* (1994), *Forrest Gump* (1994), *Patch Adams* (1998), and *Hannibal* (2001).

■ Has been visited by U.S. presidents William McKinley, Woodrow Wilson, and Richard Nixon.

■ Had many innovations rarely seen at the time, including fire alarms, elevators, an intercom system, and centrally controlled clocks.

■ Has its own bowling alley, 70,000-gallon indoor swimming pool, 10,000-volume library, and fully equipped gym.

■ Has more than 1,600 employees, making it one of Asheville's largest private employers.

---

features miniature versions of many native trees. The 16,000-square-foot Baker Exhibit Center, which opened in late 2007, hosts traveling exhibits on art, science, and history. ■ TIP→ **For an unusual view of the arboretum, try the Segway tour, where you can glide through the forest for two hours on the gyroscopically controlled "Human Transporter" invented by Dean Kamen.** The cost ($45 weekdays, $55 Saturdays) includes training on the Segway. Riders must be at least 18 years old and weigh between 80 and 250 pounds. Tours are at 10 and 2 Monday–Saturday. ✉ *100 Frederick Law Olmsted Way, 10 mi southwest of downtown Asheville, at Blue Ridge Pkwy. (MM 393), near I–26 and I–40, South Metro* ☎ *828/665–2492* ⊕ *www.ncarboretum.org* 🚗 *$6 per car parking fee; free Tues.* ⊙ *Visitor education center: Mon.– Sat. 9–5, Sun. noon–5. Gardens and grounds: Apr.–Oct., daily 8 AM–9 PM; Nov.–Mar., daily 8 AM–7 PM.*

WNC Farmers Market. The highest-volume farmers' market in North Carolina is a great place to buy local jams, jellies, honey, stone-ground grits and cornmeal, and, in season, local fruits and vegetables. In spring look for ramps, a wild cousin of the onion with a very strong odor. A

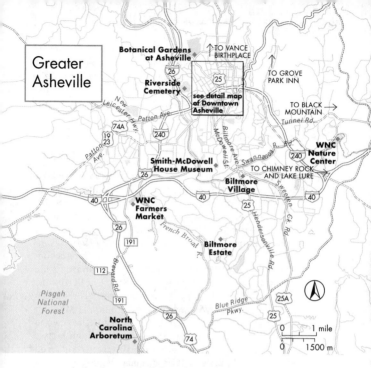

see detail map of Downtown Asheville

wholesale section below the main retail section (both are open to all) offers produce in bulk. ✉*570 Brevard Rd., 5 mi southwest of downtown Asheville, off I–40, South Metro* 🕾*828/253–1691* 🎟*Free* ☉*Apr.–Oct., daily 8–6; Nov.–Mar., daily 8–5.*

WORTH NOTING

Asheville Urban Trail. This 1.7-mi walk developed by the City of Asheville has about 30 "stations," with plaques marking places of historical or architectural interest. The self-guided tour begins at Pack Place Education, Arts & Science Center. ■TIP→**To enhance your walking experience, rent an audio guide at the Asheville Art Museum, which is part of the Pack Place complex.** From April to November, guided group tours leaving from Pack Place are usually scheduled at 10:30 and 3 on Saturday, weather permitting. ✉*2 S. Pack Sq., at Pack Place, Asheville Art Museum* 🕾*828/258–0710* ⊕*www.urbantrails.net* 🎟*Audio guide $5, tour $5.*

Botanical Gardens at Asheville. Adjoining the University of North Carolina at Asheville campus, this 10-acre site has walking trails and displays of native plants, including a bog with carnivorous plants such as Venus flytraps, pitcher plants, and sundew. ■TIP→ **It's a fine place for a picnic, and not far from the busy downtown.** ✉ *151 Weaver Blvd., at Broadway, 2 mi north of downtown Asheville, North Metro* ☎ *828/252–5190* ⊕ *www.ashevillebotanicalgardens.org* ✆ *Free* ☉ *Daily dawn–dusk.*

★ **Grove Park Inn.** This large resort overlooking Asheville is well worth a visit even if you don't stay here, as eight U.S. presidents have. The oldest section was built in 1912–13 using huge, locally mined granite stones, some weighing 10,000 pounds. It was modeled after the grand railroad hotels in the American West. Inside there's the largest collection of Arts and Crafts furniture in the world. On the grounds are two small but interesting museums. The **North Carolina Homespun Museum** (⊕ *www.grovewood.com/ homespun_museum.php*) tells the story of a training school established by the Vanderbilt family (of Biltmore Estate fame) to revive interest in native crafts. A collection of antique cars assembled by a local car dealer is the main feature of the **Estes-Winn Memorial Automobile Museum** (⊕ *www.grovewood.com/car_museum.php*). Grovewood Gallery, also on the resort grounds in a 1917 English-style cottage, showcases the work of some 500 craftspeople and artists. ■TIP→ **If you visit in the cooler months, be sure to warm yourself in front of the two enormous stone fireplaces in the inn's lobby.** ✉ *290 Macon Ave., North Metro* ☎ *800/438–5800 or 828/252–2711* ⊕ *www.groveparkinn.com* ✆ *Free* ☉ *Hotel daily 24 hrs; Homespun Museum and Estes-Winn Automobile Museum Apr.–Dec., Mon.–Sat. 10–5, Sun. 11–5.*

Riverside Cemetery. Authors Thomas Wolfe and O. Henry are buried here, along with about 13,000 others, including some of Asheville's most prominent citizens. The 87-acre cemetery, overlooking the French Broad River in the historic Montford area, has flower gardens and ancient oaks and poplars. ■TIP→ **Take the drive through the cemetery, where signs direct you to the graves of noted people.** ✉ *Birch St. off Pearson Dr., North Metro* ☎ *828/258–8480.*

Smith-McDowell House Museum. This is the oldest surviving brick house in Asheville, dating from 1840. The grounds were designed by Frederick Law Olmsted in 1900. The interior has much of the house's original Greek-revival woodwork, and restored rooms date from 1840 to 1900. Exhibits in the gallery focus on Asheville's early history. On the grounds is the Buncombe County Civil War Memorial, listing the names of the 551 soldiers from Buncombe County who died in the war. From mid-November to early January, the house has Victorian Christmas displays, and it also hosts the campy Aluminum Christmas Tree Museum, a collection of pop-culture trees from the 1950s and '60s. ⊠*283 Victoria Rd., East Metro* ☎*828/253–9231* ⊕*www. wnchistory.org* ☜*$7 Jan.–Nov., $10 Dec.* ⊙*Thurs.–Sat. 10–4; extended hours during Christmas season.*

Vance Birthplace. A reconstructed pioneer cabin and outbuildings mark the childhood home of Zebulon Vance, three-time governor of North Carolina and United States senator from 1879 to 1894. You can tour the site, which is representative of more prosperous mountain homesteads during the early 19th century. ⊠*911 Reems Creek Rd., 13 mi north of downtown Asheville, North Metro* ☎*828/645–6706* ☜*Free* ⊙*Apr.–Oct., Tues.–Sat. 9–5; Nov.–Mar., Tues.–Sat. 10–4.*

☾ **WNC Nature Center.** On a 42-acre Natural Heritage site, the WNC Nature Center is one of the region's most popular attractions for kids. It's basically a zoo focusing on animals native to the region, with cougars, bobcats, black bears, white-tailed deer, gray and red wolves, and gray and red foxes in natural-like settings. The center also has an excellent area on native reptiles and amphibians, plus a petting zoo. ⊠*75 Gashes Creek Rd., East Metro* ☎*828/298–5600* ⊕*www.wildwnc.org* ☜*$7* ⊙*Daily 10–5.*

WHERE TO EAT

Because of the large number of visitors to Asheville and the many upscale retirees who've moved here, the city has a dining scene that's much more vibrant and varied than its size would suggest. You'll find everything from Greek to Vietnamese, Moroccan to Southern soul food, and barbecue to sushi. Asheville has more vegetarian restaurants per capita than any other city, and there are coffeehouses on many corners.

DOWNTOWN

$$$ ✕**Bistro 1896.** *Seafood.* Bistro 1896 (in a building on Pack Square dating from that year) focuses on seafood but also offers other dishes. Start with oysters on the half shell, so fresh you can smell the salt air, or fried calamari, then jump to seafood-stuffed salmon or sesame-encrusted tuna. The bistro look comes from the period photos on the walls and glass-top tables with fresh flowers. On Sunday there's a

brunch with a build-it-yourself Bloody Mary bar. Sidewalk seating lets you take in the street performers on bustling Pack Square. ⊠*7 Pack Sq., Downtown* ☎*828/251–1300* ⊟*AE, MC, V.*

¢ ✕**Doc Chey's.** *Asian.* "Peace, love, and noodles" is the theme at this outpost of an Atlanta noodle house, with Vietnamese, Thai, Japanese, and Chinese noodle bowls and rice plates served fast, cheap, and tasty. It's always packed. ⊠*37 Biltmore Ave., Downtown* ☎*828/252–8220* ⊟*AE, MC, V.*

$ ✕**Early Girl Eatery.** *Southern.* Named after an early-maturing tomato variety, Early Girl Eatery is casually Southern, with a cheerfully chic twist. A wall of south-facing windows provides wonderful light most of the day. No white tablecloths here: you eat on brown butcher paper. The dinner menu runs to items like seared duck breast with collard greens. At breakfast, choose huge stacks of buttermilk pancakes or Creole catfish and stone-ground grits. ⊠*8 Wall St. Ave., Downtown* ☎*828/259–9592* ⊟*MC, V.*

$ ✕**Greenlife.** *Eclectic.* Asheville's wildly popular organic and
★ natural foods grocery is *the* place to stock up on healthful, delicious picnic supplies. In addition to groceries, Greenlife has an extensive prepared-food and takeout section, featuring a variety of soups of the day (including several vegan soups), hot lunch items, fresh sushi, and made-to-order sandwiches on organic breads. Greenlife also has the friendliest employees in town. ⊠*70 Merrimon Ave., Downtown* ☎*828/254–5440* ⊟*MC, V.*

¢–$ ✕**Laughing Seed Café.** *Vegetarian.* You'll get more than brown rice and beans at this vegetarian eatery with a bold mural on one wall and a bar. The extensive menu ranges from fruit drinks to sandwiches and pizzas to dinner specialties influenced by the flavors of India, Thailand, Mexico, and Morocco. Fruits and vegetables come from local organic farms during the growing season. Breads are baked daily on premises. There's outdoor dining on charming Wall Street. ⊠*40 Wall St., Downtown* ☎*828/252–3445* ⊟*AE, D, MC, V* ☻*Closed Tues.*

$$$$ ✕**The Market Place.** *Modern Southern.* Clean lines, neutral colors, and brushed-steel mobiles create a sophisticated style at one of Asheville's longest-lived fine-dining establishments. (It opened in 1979.) The food offers refreshing twists on ingredients indigenous to the mountains, such as

game and trout, and the South in general. Possible entrées are pan-seared red trout with corn fritters and squash slaw, and wood-grilled pork chop with sautéed greens, herbed quinoa, and strawberry-ginger compote. Iron gates open onto an exterior courtyard and dining patio. On the casual side of the restaurant, Bar 100 offers a bar menu of snacks and lighter dishes, all made with ingredients from within 100 mi of Asheville. ⊠*20 Wall St., Downtown* ☎*828/252–4162* ⚒*Reservations essential* ⊟*AE, MC, V* ⊙*Closed Sun. No lunch.*

$-$$ ✕**Mela Indian Restaurant.** *Indian.* Mela opened in 2005 and
★ quickly established itself as the best Indian restaurant in the city. Rather than specialize in one type of Indian cuisine, it offers dishes from across the country. The tandoori dishes (chicken, salmon, or lamb) are especially delicious. Entrées are served with basmati rice, lentil stew, and *papadum* (lentil wafers). Portions are large, making this one of the best values downtown. The space is unexpectedly modern, with rough tile walls and a high ceiling, though accented with woodwork, doors, and furnishings from India. ⊠*70 N. Lexington, Downtown* ☎*828/225–8880* ⊟*AE, D, MC, V.*

¢ ✕**Old Europe.** *Eastern European.* The Hungarian owners, Zoltan and Melinda Vetro, bring a European sensibility to this immensely popular pastry shop and coffeehouse. It's often jammed; the crowd spills over to the courtyard, slurping coffee—served with a piece of chocolate—and liqueurs and downing delicious tortes, cakes, and other European pastries. Although full meals are served, you're better off sticking to the desserts and coffees. There's live entertainment on weekends, in a nightclub upstairs. ⊠*41 N. Lexington Ave., Downtown* ☎*828/252–0001* ⊟*MC, V.*

¢–$ ✕**Salsa's.** *Latin-American.* In an expanded space with a slightly retro-hippie look, you'll find spicy and highly creative Mexican and Caribbean fare in huge portions. Pan-fried fish tacos, roast pumpkin empanadas, and organic chicken enchiladas are among the recommended entrées. ⊠*6 Patton Ave., Downtown* ☎*828/252–9805* ⊟*AE, D, MC, V* ⊙*Closed Sun.*

$–$$ ✕**Tupelo Honey Café.** *Southern.* Hello, darlin'! This is the
♺ place for down-home Southern cooking with an uptown twist. Owner Sharon Schott delivers a lot more than grits, with dishes like seared salmon with corn bread, and hormone-free pork chop with mashed sweet potatoes. Break-

fast is served anytime and there is a jar of tupelo honey available on every table. The atmosphere is loud and a little funky and there's often a line. Kids are welcome; they can entertain themselves by drawing on the paper tablecloths. ⊠*12 College St., Downtown* ☎*828/255–4863* ⌸*Reservations not accepted* ⊟*AE, MC, V* ⊗*Closed Mon. No lunch Fri. and Sat.*

$$–$$$ ✕**Zambras.** *Spanish.* Sophisticated tapas selections, such
★ as grilled scallops with parsnip-potato gratin, prosciutto-wrapped medjool dates with goat cheese, pan-seared local trout with hazelnuts and oranges, and steamed mussels make this one of the most interesting restaurants in the mountains. There are also several varieties of paella and other dishes, many influenced by the cuisine of Mediterranean Spain and North Africa, and a wine list featuring unusual Spanish wines and sherries. Voluptuous Moorish colors and live gypsy music (and belly dancers on weekends) lend an exotic air. ⊠*85 Walnut St., Downtown* ☎*828/232–1060* ⌸*Reservations essential* ⊟*AE, D, MC, V* ⊗*No lunch.*

GREATER ASHEVILLE

$–$$ ✕**12 Bones Smokehouse.** *Barbecue.* You'll recognize this spot by the long line of customers snaking out the door. Open only weekdays 11 to 4, the wait to place your order is often a half hour. True to the barbecue joint ethos, with concrete floors and old Formica-top tables, 12 Bones has no atmosphere. What it does have is the smokiest baby back ribs you've ever tasted, and delicious sides including collard greens, corn pudding, and "mashed sweet taters." The crowd ranges from hippie potters from the River District art-studio scene to downtown suits—the staff will call you "Sweetie." ⊠*5 Riverside Dr., River District* ☎*828/253–4499* ⊟*MC, V* ⊗*Closed weekends. No dinner.*

$–$$ ✕**Asheville Pizza and Brewing Company.** *Pizza.* Locally known as the "Brew 'n View," this funky brewery-cum-eatery-cum-movie theater is extremely popular. Grab a microbrew beer and a pizza with portobello mushrooms and fresh spinach, and watch *Pink Floyd The Wall* from the comfort of a sofa in the recently redone theater. ⊠*675 Merrimon Ave., North Metro* ☎*828/254–1281* ⊟*MC, V.*

★ **Fodor's**Choice✕**Gabrielle's.** *Continental.* From the moment
$$$$ you're met at the door, offered an ice-cold martini, and invited to stroll the lovely Victorian gardens while your table is readied, you suspect that dinner at Gabrielle's

is going to be one of your best dining experience in the mountains—and chances are it will be. The best does come at a price, however. The five-course tasting menu, which changes frequently, is $79, or $139 with paired wines. The somewhat less expensive (around $60) prix-fixe menu has items such as wild Alaskan halibut dusted with fennel pollen, served with local foraged mushrooms and grilled ramps (a wild onion-like vegetable) and rack of Kurabuto pork with heirloom corn hominy. The near-perfect service and the setting in an elegant, art-filled 19th-century cherry-panel space, with piano music in the background, make for a memorable splurge. Executive chef Perry Hendrix, stolen away by Robert Redford when Redford was filming in Asheville a few years ago, returned to Gabrielle's in 2008. ✉*87 Richmond Hill Dr., at Richmond Hill Inn, North Metro* ☎*828/252–7313 or 800/545–9238* ⌂*Reservations essential* ⊟*AE, MC, V* ⊘ *No lunch.*

¢–$ ✕**Sunny Point Café and Bakery.** *American.* In a restored storefront in up-and-coming West Asheville, Sunny Point lives up to its name with bright, cheerful decor. It's a good spot for breakfast, where free-range pork sausage shares the menu with granola, herbed potatoes, and some of the biggest biscuits in town. Now open for dinner, it experiments a little at this meal, with dishes like chicken-fried tofu. In good weather the best tables are outside on the patio. ✉*626 Haywood Rd., West Metro* ☎*828/252–0055* ⊟*MC, V* ⊘*Closed Sun. and Mon.*

BILTMORE VILLAGE

$$$–$$$$ ✕**Fig Bistro.** *French.* Fig many be tiny in size, with only around 15 tables, but it's big in creativity. Most dishes are at least vaguely French, as the chef trained in France. The menu changes frequently, but the scallops, cod, snapper, and other seafood are a delight. When available, the duck—grilled with a sweet potato puree, as a confit salad, or in pâté mousse—is also terrific. Fig has a true bistro ambience, with hardwood floors, pressed tin ceilings, black chairs, a near floor-to-ceiling wall of windows (though the view is of a commercial street), and exposed brick. In good weather, there's seating in an outdoor courtyard. Light drinkers can order half glasses of wine. ✉*18 Brook St., Biltmore Village* ☎*828/277–0889* ⊟*AE, D, MC, V* ⊘*Closed Sun.*

$$$ ✕**Rezaz.** *Mediterranean.* With abstract art displayed on the ★ cinnamon- and apricot-color walls and waiters dressed in black rushing around pouring wine, you'd never know this

sophisticated Mediterranean restaurant is in the site of a former hardware store. Try the veal osso buco milanese or the arborio-crusted sea scallops. There are daily specials, such as goat cheese ravioli on Monday and seared ahi tuna on Friday. You enter the restaurant through Enoteca, Rezaz's wine bar, which serves panini sandwiches, antipastos, and other less-expensive fare in a casual setting. ✉28 *Hendersonville Rd., Biltmore Village* ☎828/277–1510 ☐*AE, MC, V* ⊘*Closed Sun.*

WHERE TO STAY

The Asheville area has a nice mix of B&Bs, motels, and small owner-operated inns. There are more than three dozen B&Bs, one of the largest concentrations in the South. Most are in the Montford area near downtown and the Grove Park area north in the city. At least eight B&Bs in the area promote themselves as gay-owned and actively seek gay and lesbian guests, and an equal number advertise that they are gay-friendly. More than 100 chain motel properties are dotted around the metropolitan area, with large clusters on Tunnel Road near the Asheville Mall, on U.S. Highway 25 and Biltmore Avenue near the Biltmore Estate, and southwest near Biltmore Square Mall. Also, you'll find inns and boutique hotels, both downtown and around the city. In rural areas around the city are a few lodges and cabin colonies.

DOWNTOWN

$$$–$$$$ ⌨**Haywood Park Hotel.** Location is the main draw of this downtown hotel, which was once a department store. Ensconced in a suite here, you're within walking distance of many of Asheville's shops, restaurants, and galleries. The lobby has golden oak woodwork accented with gleaming brass. The suites are spacious, with baths done in Spanish marble. The long-popular Flying Frog Café, with an astonishingly eclectic menu—mixing French, Indian, and German cuisine—is in the hotel. There's a small shopping galleria in the atrium, and a very popular sidewalk café. **Pros:** great central downtown location; expansive suites. **Cons:** limited parking (valet); somewhat outdated decor in rooms and lobby; service sometimes spotty; no pool. ✉*1 Battery Park Ave., Downtown* ☎828/252–2522 *or* *800/228–2522* ⊕*www.haywoodpark.com* ⋟*33 suites* ⌂*In-room: safe (some), refrigerator, Wi-Fi. In-hotel: restaurant, room service, bar, gym, laundry service, no-smoking rooms* ☐*AE, D, DC, MC, V* ⓘ*BP.*

NORTH METRO

★ Fodor's Choice 🖾 **1900 Inn on Montford.** Guests are pampered at
$$$–$$$$ this Arts and Crafts–style B&B, where most rooms have
whirlpool baths, some have big-screen plasma TVs, and all
have fireplaces. There are lots of nooks and corners in the
expansive public spaces for snuggling up with a book. The
inn has a social hour every evening. Innkeepers Ron and
Lynn Carlson say that the Cloisters—a 1,300-square-foot
suite in their carriage house out back—is the largest suite
in Asheville. Younger children are discouraged in the main
house. **Pros:** well-run and deluxe B&B; antiques but also
modern amenities. **Cons:** not for families with small chil-
dren. ✉296 Montford Ave., North Metro ☎828/254–9569
or 800/254–9569 ⊕www.innonmontford.com ⬱5 rooms,
3 suites ⌂In-room: refrigerator (some), DVD, Internet,
Wi-Fi. In-hotel: Wi-Fi, no kids under 12, no-smoking rooms
⊟AE, D, MC, V ⊙BP.

$$$–$$$$ 🖾 **Albemarle Inn.** Famed Hungarian composer Béla Bar-
★ tók lived here in the early 1940s, creating his third piano
concerto, the "Asheville Concerto." You can stay in his
room on the third floor, although Juliet's Chamber, with
its private balcony overlooking lovely gardens, may appeal
more to modern Romeos. Owners Cathy and Larry Sklar
left their jobs as lawyers in Connecticut in order to turn
this 1907 Greek-revival mansion in a quiet North Asheville
residential area into one of the top B&Bs in the region.
Some rooms have working fireplaces and canopied beds.
Gourmet breakfasts are prepared by the inn's chef. **Pros:**
delightfully upscale B&B; lovely residential neighborhood;
excellent breakfasts. **Cons:** old-fashioned claw-foot tubs
in some rooms make showering difficult. ✉86 Edgemont
Rd., 1 mi north of I–240, North Metro ☎828/255–0027
or 800/621–7435 ⊕www.albemarleinn.com ⬱10 rooms,
1 suite ⌂In-room: Wi-Fi. In-hotel: no kids under 12, no-
smoking rooms ⊟D, MC, V ⊙BP.

$$$–$$$$ 🖾 **Black Walnut Inn.** The Biltmore House supervising architect
Richard Sharp Smith built this 1899 home in Asheville's
Montford section. Today it's a B&B on the National Reg-
ister of Historic Places. Most of the rooms—all redone
in 2004 by owners Peter and Lori White—have working
fireplaces. Parts of the 2000 movie 28 Days were filmed
here. (The star, Sandra Bullock, stayed in the Dogwood
Room.) **Pros:** a gem of a B&B; charming antique-filled
house; excellent breakfast and afternoon wine and appe-
tizer hour included. **Cons:** grounds are not large, with

only a small garden. ⊠*288 Montford Ave., North Metro* ☎*828/254–3878 or 800/381–3878* ⊕*www.blackwalnut. com* ⌐*6 rooms, 1 cottage* ♿ *In-hotel: Wi-Fi, no-smoking rooms* ▭*D, MC, V* ⫯*BP.*

$$$$ 🏨**Grove Park Inn Resort & Spa.** Asheville's premier large resort
★ is an imposing granite edifice that dates from 1913 and has panoramic views of the Blue Ridge Mountains. Henry Ford, F. Scott Fitzgerald (who stayed in room 441), and Michael Jordan, as well as eight U.S. presidents from Woodrow Wilson to George H. W. Bush, have stayed here. It's furnished with oak antiques in the Arts and Crafts style, and the lobby fireplaces are as big as cars. Four restaurants offer plenty of choices. The spa is one of the finest in the country. As the hotel's main focus is on group meetings, alas, sometimes individual guests get short shrift. Rooms in the original section are mostly smaller but have more character than those in the newer additions. **Pros:** imposing historical hotel; wonderful setting; magnificent mountain views; first-rate spa and golf course. **Cons:** individual guests sometimes play second fiddle to large group meetings. ⊠*290 Macon Ave., North Metro* ☎*828/252–2711 or 800/438–5800* ⊕*www. groveparkinn.com* ⌐*498 rooms, 12 suites* ♿*In-room: Internet, Wi-Fi. In-hotel: 4 restaurants, bars, golf course, tennis courts, pools, gym, spa, laundry service, Wi-Fi, no-smoking rooms* ▭*AE, D, DC, MC, V* ⫯*EP.*

$$–$$$ 🏨**The Lion and the Rose.** One of the characters in Thomas
★ Wolfe's *Look Homeward, Angel* lived in this house, an 1898 Queen Anne–Georgian in the historic Montford Park area near downtown. It couldn't have looked any better then than it does now. A special detail is a 6-foot Palladian-style stained-glass window at the top of oaks stairs. Innkeepers Jim and Linda Palmer keep the heirloom gardens and five guest rooms looking gorgeous. The landscaping around the house is striking. For snacks and wine, guests have 24-hour access to a well-stocked pantry. For the most privacy, choose the Craig-Toms suite, which occupies the entire third floor. **Pros:** comfortable small B&B; impressively landscaped grounds; good value. **Cons:** like all the B&Bs in Montford, it's a bit of a walk to downtown. ⊠*276 Montford Ave., North Metro* ☎*828/255–6546 or 800/546– 6988* ⊕*www.lion-rose.com* ⌐*4 rooms, 1 suite* ♿*In-room: refrigerator (some), DVD, Wi-Fi. In-hotel: Wi-Fi, no kids under 12, no-smoking rooms* ▭*D, MC, V* ⫯*BP.*

★ **Fodor's**Choice ✕ **Richmond Hill Inn.** Once a private residence,
$$$–$$$$ this elegant Victorian mansion is on the National Register of Historic Places. Many rooms in the mansion are furnished with canopy beds, Victorian sofas, and other antiques, while the more modern cottages have contemporary pine poster beds. Although Richmond Hill does not enjoy the panoramic views of Asheville's other top hotels, and the immediate neighborhood is not exactly upscale, the 46-acre grounds are stunning, with ever-changing gardens. Its dinner restaurant, Gabrielle's, is one of the best in the region. **Pros:** outstanding historical inn; beautiful grounds; excellent service. **Cons:** location isn't ideal; lacks stunning mountain views; no pool. ✉*87 Richmond Hill Dr., North Metro* ☎*828/252–7313 or 888/742–4536* ⊕*www.richmondhillinn.com* ⌂*24 rooms, 3 suites, 9 cottages* ⏚*In-room: Internet. In-hotel: 2 restaurants, no-smoking rooms* ▤*AE, MC, V* ⧾*BP* ⊘*Closed Jan.*

SOUTH METRO

$$$–$$$$ ✕ **Bohemian Hotel.** You can't stay any closer to the Biltmore Estate than at this hotel, unless you are on the Estate grounds. New in late 2008, the Bohemian is steps from the Estate's main gate, and close to all the shops and restaurants in Biltmore Village. The down side is that this is a congested area, with frequent delays due to a nearby train track crossing on Biltmore Avenue; you'll need the hotel's valet parking. The Tudor style of the hotel is designed to blend with the architecture of Biltmore Village, though some say it reminds them of Hogwarts school in the Harry Potter movies and novels. Spacious rooms have sumptuous velvet fabrics, antique mirrors, and plasma TVs. **Pros:** new upscale hotel; at Biltmore Estate gate, near Biltmore Village. **Cons:** located in a congested area with heavy traffic. ✉*11 Boston Way, South Metro* ☎*828/505–2949* ⊕*www.bohemianhotelasheville.com* ⌂*104 rooms* ⏚*In-room: refrigerator (some), Wi-Fi. In-hotel: restaurant, bar, gym, spa, Wi-Fi, no-smoking rooms* ▤*AE, D, MC, V.*

★ **Fodor's**Choice ✕ **Inn on Biltmore Estate.** Many people who visit
$$$$ the Biltmore mansion long to stay overnight; if you're one of them, your wish is granted in the form of this posh hilltop property. The hotel mimics the look of Biltmore House with natural stone and copper. French manor houses inspired the interior. Nice touches include afternoon tea in the library. The dining room, reserved for hotel guests only, is bookended by large windows with mountain views and a massive fireplace. Menus deftly blend local and inter-

national ingredients. Available packages include admission to Biltmore Estate for the length of your stay, and free shuttles to all parts of the estate. **Pros:** deluxe hotel on Biltmore Estate grounds; exclusive restaurant; top-notch service. **Cons:** very expensive; atmosphere can be a bit formal. ⊠*Biltmore Estate, Exit 50 off I–40, South Metro* ☎*800/922–0084* ⊕*www.biltmore.com/inn* ↪*204 rooms, 9 suites* ⚐*In-room: refrigerator (some), Internet, Wi-Fi. In-hotel: restaurant, room service, bar, pool, spa, gym, bicycles, Wi-Fi, no-smoking rooms* ⊟*AE, D, DC, MC, V* ❑*EP.*

▦ **The Residences at Biltmore.** Located not far from the gates of Biltmore Estate, these suites-style accommodations are some of the most luxe in Asheville. Studio and one-bedroom condo apartments (some two- and three-bedroom units are available), tastefully decorated with Arts and Crafts touches, have fully equipped kitchens with granite countertops and stainless steel appliances, stacked stone gas fireplaces, hardwood floors, wall-mounted flat-screen TVs, and washers and dryers. Most units have whirlpool baths. **Pros:** luxury suites with fully equipped kitchens; convenient location near both Biltmore Estate and downtown Asheville; well-managed with helpful staff. **Cons:** on-site restaurant planned but not yet open; a bit of a hike to restaurants in Biltmore Village. ⊠*700 Biltmore Ave., South Metro* ☎*828/350–8000 or 866/433–5594* ⊕*www. residencesatbiltmore.com* ↪*55 suites* ⚐*In-room: kitchen, DVD, Wi-Fi. In-hotel: pool, gym, Wi-Fi, no-smoking rooms* ⊟*AE, D, MC, V.*

NEARBY ASHEVILLE

▦ **Pisgah View Ranch.** Saddle up! In the same family since 1790, this 2,000-acre dude ranch may suit you if you're looking for a rural mountain experience and a family atmosphere, with plenty of ranch-style food, homey activities like square dancing and cookouts, and unlimited horseback riding. Cottages, which vary considerably in size and appeal, are functional rather than fancy. On an all-inclusive basis, with all meals and activities including horseback riding, rates are $320 per day double occupancy ($220 without the horseback riding) plus 11% tax and 15% gratuity. Camping and RV sites also available. **Pros:** beautiful mountain setting on 2,000 acres; ride horses to your heart's content on miles of riding trails; filling country food served family-style. **Cons:** simple cabin accommodations are far from deluxe; may be too "Andy Griffith" for some.

✉70 Pisgah View Ranch Rd., 16 mi west of Asheville,
Candler ☎828/667–9100 or 866/252–8361 ⊕www.pis-
gahviewranch.net ⇗39 cottages ♿In-room: no phone, no
TV (some). In-hotel: restaurant, pool ▤D, MC, V ⊗Closed
Nov.–Apr. ▯◯▯AI.

$$ ▭ **Sourwood Inn.** Two miles from the Blue Ridge Parkway,
★ down a narrow winding road, sits one of the most stunning
small inns in the mountains. The inn is constructed of stone
and cedar, in the Arts and Crafts style. Twelve large rooms
each have a real wood-burning fireplace, a bathtub with
a view (there's also a separate shower), and French doors
that open onto a private balcony. ▮TIP→**Unfortunately, the inn
doesn't have air-conditioning. Even at 3,000 feet it can be a little
warm at times in summer.** Sassafras Cabin is a private retreat
about 100 yards from the inn. **Pros:** stunning mountain-side
setting; handsome rooms; bathrooms with views. **Cons:**
requires a 20-minute drive to get to downtown Asheville
and to restaurants; no air-conditioning. ✉810 Elk Moun-
tain Scenic Hwy. ☎828/255–0690 ⊕www.sourwoodinn.
com ⇗12 rooms, 1 cabin ♿In-room: no a/c, no phone, no
TV (some). In-hotel: restaurant, no-smoking rooms ▤AE,
MC, V ⊗Closed Jan. and weekdays in Feb. ▯◯▯BP.

WHERE TO CAMP

$$$$ ⚠ **Campfire Lodgings.** If you brave the narrow, twisting last
half-mile drive to the top of a mountain ridge just north of
Asheville, you're repaid with stunning mountain views and
an appealing campground. Located on about 100 acres,
Campfire Lodgings has tent sites, RV and trailer sites, cab-
ins, and yurts (round, soft-sided structures based on ancient
Asian designs, with conical roofs and set on platforms).
The best campsites are the five premium RV sites (P1–5),
all of which have great views over the French Broad River
Valley. They cost a rather pricey $50 per night or $350 per
week. Shower and bath facilities for the campsites and yurts
are in four "bath suites," rather than in communal bath-
houses. **Pros:** beautiful mountain views; variety of camping
and lodging options. **Cons:** access road to campground is
narrow, winding and fairly steep. ✉116 Appalachian Vil-
lage Rd. 28804 ☎828/658–8012 or 800/933–8012 www.
campfirelodgings.com ⇗10 RV/trailer sites, 9 tent sites,
2 cabins, 1 house, 3 yurts ♿Flush toilets, full hookups,
drinking water, guest laundry, showers, fire rings, electricity,
public telephone, fishing pond, Wi-Fi ▤MC, V.

NIGHTLIFE & THE ARTS

For the latest information on nightlife, arts, and entertainment in the Asheville area, get a copy of *Take 5,* an entertainment tabloid in Friday's *Asheville Citizen-Times,* or the weekly free newspaper, *Mountain Express.*

THE ARTS

The Asheville area has about 40 theaters and theater companies. Asheville also has a vibrant art and crafts gallery scene, with about two dozen galleries. Most of the galleries are within a block or two of Pack Square, while some, especially working studios, are in the River District. Biltmore Village also has several galleries.

One of the oldest community theater groups in the country, **Asheville Community Theatre** (✉*35 E. Walnut St., Downtown* ☎*828/254–1320*) stages professional plays year-round in its own theater building. The biggest art gallery in town, with 14,000 square feet of exhibit space, **Blue Spiral 1** (✉*38 Biltmore Ave., Downtown* ☎*800/291–2513*) has about 30 exhibits of sculpture, paintings, and photographs each year.

In the Pack Place complex, the 500-seat **Diana Wortham Theatre** (✉*2 S. Pack Sq., Downtown* ☎*828/257–4530*) is home to more than 100 musical and theatrical events each year. As the headquarters of the prestigious craft group, the Southern Highland Craft Guild, the **Folk Art Center** (✉*Blue Ridge Pkwy., MM 382* ☎*828/298–7298*) regularly puts on exceptional quilt, woodworking, pottery, and other crafts shows and demonstrations. This is a top spot to purchase very high-quality (and expensive) traditional crafts, such as quilts, baskets, and pottery. In a 1928 landmark building decorated with polychrome terra-cotta tile, **Kress Emporium** (✉*19 Patton Ave., Downtown* ☎*828/281–2252*) is a place for more than 75 craftspeople to show and sell their crafts. The space is not air-conditioned and can be hot in summer. Owned by arts entrepreneur John Cram, **New Morning Gallery** (✉*7 Boston Way, Biltmore Village* ☎*828/274–2831 or 800/933–4438*) has 12,000 square feet of exhibit space, focusing on more popular ceramics, garden art, jewelry, furniture, and art glass. In a tiny, 99-seat theater, **North Carolina Stage Company** (✉*33 Haywood St., Downtown* ☎*828/350–9090*) is a professional company that puts on edgy, contemporary plays. With professional summer theater that often celebrates mountain culture, **Southern Appalachian Repertory Theatre (SART)** (✉*Owen Hall,*

Mars Hill College ☎828/689–1239) produces plays such as William Gregg and Perry Deane Young's *Mountain of Hope,* about the 1835 controversy over whether or not Mt. Mitchell is the highest peak east of the Rockies. In a 1938 building that housed a five-and-dime, **Woolworth Walk** (✉25 *Haywood St., Downtown* ☎828/254–9234) features the work of 150 crafts artists, in 20,000 square feet of exhibit space on two levels, and there's even a soda fountain, built to resemble the original Woolworth luncheonette.

The 2,400-seat **Thomas Wolfe Auditorium** (✉87 *Haywood St., Downtown* ☎828/259–5736), in the Asheville Civic Center, hosts larger events including traveling Broadway shows and performances of the Asheville Symphony. The Civic Center, which is showing its age, is looking at a $140 million expansion to include a new performing-arts theater.

NIGHTLIFE

More than a restaurant, more than a movie theater, **Asheville Pizza and Brewing Company** (✉675 *Merrimon Ave.* ☎828/254–1281), also called Brew 'n' View, is a wildly popular place to catch a flick while lounging on a sofa, drinking a microbrew, and scarfing a veggie pizza. In a renovated downtown appliance store, the ever-popular **Barley's Taproom** (✉42 *Biltmore Ave.* ☎828/255–0504) has live bluegrass and Americana music three or four nights a week. The bar downstairs has about two dozen microbrew beers on draft, and you can play pool and darts upstairs in the Billiard Room. Billed as a "listening room," **Grey Eagle** (✉185 *Clingman Ave.* ☎828/232–5800) in the River Arts District area, features popular local and regional bands four or five nights a week, with contra dancing on some other nights.

The camp decor at **Club Hairspray** (✉38 *N. French Broad Ave.* ☎828/258–2027) will make you feel like you're back in 1961, though the music is contemporary. The crowd is diverse but predominantly gay. **The Orange Peel Social Aid and Pleasure Club** (✉101 *Biltmore Ave.* ☎828/225–5851) is far and away the number one nightspot in downtown Asheville. Bob Dylan, Hootie and the Blowfish, and Steve Winwood have played here in an intimate, smoke-free setting for audiences of up to 950. In 2008, Rolling Stone named it one of the top five rock clubs in the United States. For smaller events, it also has a great dance floor, with springy wood slats.

6

Asheville's best-known gay and lesbian club, **Scandals** (✉11 *Grove St.* ☏828/252–2838), has a lively dance floor and drag shows on weekends. In a 1913 downtown building, the jazz and blues club **Tressa's** (✉28 Broadway ☏828/254–7072) is nominally private, but lets nonmembers in for a small cover charge. There's a quieter, no-smoking room upstairs. In happening West Asheville, the smoke-free **Westville Pub** (✉777 Haywood Rd. ☏828/225–9782) has about 50 different beers on the menu, and a different band plays nearly every night.

SPORTS & THE OUTDOORS

BASEBALL

A Class A farm team of the Colorado Rockies, the **Asheville Tourists** (✉McCormick Pl., off Biltmore Ave. ☏828/258–0428) play April to early September at historic McCormick Field, which opened in 1924. McCormick Field appears briefly in the 1987 movie *Bull Durham,* starring Kevin Costner and Susan Sarandon. Many well-traveled baseball fans consider McCormick Field one of the most appealing minor league stadiums in the country.

GOLF

Asheville Municipal Golf Course (✉226 *Fairway Dr.28805* ☏828/298–1867) is a par-72, 18-hole public municipal course designed by Donald Ross. Affordable fees start at $30. **Broadmoor** (✉101 *French Broad La., Fletcher* ☏828/687–1500), 15 mi south of Asheville, is a public Scottish-style links course, playing to 7,111 yards, par 72. **Apple Valley at Colony Lake Lure Golf Resort** (✉201 Blvd. of the *Mountains, Lake Lure* ☏828/625–2888 or 800/260–1040), 25 mi from Asheville, has two 18-hole, par-72 courses known for their beauty.

Grove Park Inn Resort (✉290 *Macon Ave.28804* ☏828/252–2711 Ext. 1012 or 800/438–5800) has a par-70 course that's more than 100 years old. You can play the course ($85 if you start after 2 PM) even if you're not a guest at the hotel. **Southern Tee** (✉111 Howard Gap Rd., Fletcher ☏828/687–7273) is an 18-hole, par-3 course with attractive rates—$22 with cart even on weekends in peak season.

HORSEBACK RIDING

Cataloochee Ranch (✉119 Ranch Rd., Maggie Valley ☏828/926–1401 or 800/868–1401) allows riders to explore the property's mile-high vistas on horseback. Trail rides are offered by stables throughout the region between April and November, including **Pisgah View Ranch** (⊠*Pisgah View Ranch Rd., Candler* ☎*828/667–9100*), where you can gallop through the wooded mountainside.

LLAMA TREKS

Avalon Llama Trek (⊠*450 Old Buckeye Cove Rd., Swannanoa* ☎*828/299–7155*) leads llama trips on the lush trails of the Pisgah National Forest.

SKIING

In addition to having outstanding skiing, **Cataloochee Resort** (⊠*Rte. 1, Maggie Valley* ☎*828/926–0285 or 800/768–0285*) hosts lots of different activities for the whole family. **Fairfield-Sapphire Valley** (⊠*4000 U.S. 64W, Sapphire Valley* ☎*828/743–3441 or 800/533–8268*) offers basic skiing despite minimal snowfall. You can "Ski the Wolf" at **Wolf Ridge Ski Resort** (⊠*578 Valley View Circle, Mars Hill* ☎*828/689–4111 or 800/817–4111*), which has night skiing and excellent snowmaking capabilities.

SHOPPING

Biltmore Village (⊠*Hendersonville Rd.* ☎*828/274–5570*), across from the Biltmore Estate, is a cluster of specialty shops, restaurants, galleries, and hotels in an early-20th-century-English-hamlet style. You'll find everything from children's books to music, antiques, and wearable art. **New Morning Gallery**, a jewelry, crafts, and art gallery at 7 Boston Way attracts customers from all over the Southeast.

Shopping is excellent all over **Downtown Asheville**, with at least 200 stores, including about 30 art galleries and over a dozen antiques shops. Several streets, notably **Biltmore Avenue, Lexington Avenue**, and **Wall Street** are lined with small, independently owned stores.

The **Grove Arcade Public Market** (⊠*1 Page Ave., Downtown* ☎*828/252–7799*), one of America's first indoor shopping centers, originally opened in 1929. The remarkable building, which covers an entire city block, was totally redone and reopened in 2002 as a collection of some 50 local specialty shops and restaurants.

Grovewood Gallery at the Homespun Shops (⊠*111 Grovewood Rd.*, ☎*828/253–7651*), adjacent to the Grove Park Inn and established by Mrs. George Vanderbilt, sells furniture and contemporary and traditionally crafted woven goods made on the premises.

SIDE TRIPS FROM ASHEVILLE

BLACK MOUNTAIN

16 mi east of Asheville via I–40.

Black Mountain is a small town that has played a disproportionately large role in American cultural history, because it's the site of Black Mountain College. For 20 years in the middle of the 20th century, from its founding in 1933 to its closing in 1957, Black Mountain College was one of the world's leading centers for experimental art, literature, architecture, and dance, with a list of faculty and students that reads like a *Who's Who* of American arts and letters.

On a different front, Black Mountain is also the home of evangelist Billy Graham. The Graham organization maintains a training center near Black Mountain, and there are several large church-related conference centers in the area, including Ridgecrest, Montreat, and Blue Ridge Assembly. Downtown Black Mountain is small and quaint, with a collection of little shops and several B&Bs.

★ Fodor'sChoice Originally housed in rented quarters at nearby Blue Ridge Assembly, in 1941 **Black Mountain College** moved across the valley to its own campus at Lake Eden, where it remained until it closed in 1957. The school's buildings were originally designed by the Bauhaus architects Walter Gropius and Marcel Breuer, but at the start of World War II the college turned to an American architect, Lawrence Kocher, and several intriguing buildings resulted, including one known as "The Ship," which still stands, with murals by Breuer. Among the students who enrolled at Black Mountain College in the 1940s were Arthur Penn, Kenneth Noland, Robert Rauschenberg, and James Leo Herlihy. Today, the site is a privately owned 550-acre summer camp for boys. ∎TIP➔ **Although the site of Black Mountain College usually is closed to the public, during the Lake Eden Festival, a music and arts festival in mid-May and mid-October, you can visit the grounds, either on a one-day pass or for weekend camping.** Other times of the year, you can rent a cabin on the grounds for overnight stays. The Ship building and other campus buildings are viewable from Lake Eden Road. There's a small museum devoted to Black Mountain College in Asheville. ✉*375 Lake Eden Rd., 5 mi west of Black Mountain* ☎*828/686–3885.*

WHERE TO STAY & EAT

¢–$ ✕**Verandah Café.** *American.* With its gingham curtains and checkered tablecloths, the atmosphere is cozy and small-townish, and the food is unpretentious and tasty at this popular café in the heart of downtown Black Mountain. The grilled cheese sandwich with fresh tomato is a winner. ⊠*119 Cherry St.* ☎*828/669–8864* ☐*MC, V* ⊘*Closed Sun.*

$–$$ ☷ **Red Rocker Inn.** A dozen red rocking chairs line the front porch of this inn in a quiet residential area two blocks from downtown. Your room (some are on the small side and most are ready for an update) may have a golf theme (the Pinehurst Room) or skylights, a fireplace, and a claw-foot tub (the Garrett Room). The restaurant ($$$–$$$$) is open to the public for breakfast and dinner by reservation. At dinner, you'll enjoy heaping portions of Southern food, served by candlelight. **Pros:** pleasant small inn; in charming small town; filling Southern breakfasts. **Cons:** smallish rooms; not much public space; could use some updating. ⊠*136 N. Dougherty St.* ☎*888/669–5991 or 828/669–5991* ⊕*www. redrockerinn.com* ⏎*17 rooms* &*In-room: safe, no TV. In-hotel: restaurant, no-smoking rooms* ☐*MC, V* ⦿*BP.*

SPORTS & THE OUTDOORS

Black Mountain doesn't have the plethora of golf courses that some other mountain towns do, but **Black Mountain Golf Course** (⊠*Black Mountain* ☎*828/669–2710*), a par-72, 6,215-yard public course, boasts the longest par 6 in the country, the 747-yard 17th hole.

SHOPPING

Part authentic small-town hardware store and part gift shop, **Town Hardware & General Store** (⊠*103 W. State St.,* ☎*828/669–7723*) sells hard-to-find tools like scythes and push plows, along with cast-iron cookware, Case knives, and Radio Flyer red wagons.

CHIMNEY ROCK & LAKE LURE

24 mi southeast of Asheville on U.S. 64/74A; 20 mi southeast of Black Mountain.

Chimney Rock and neighboring Lake Lure—both popular day trips from Asheville—were the dream projects of a single man, Dr. Lucius Morse. In the early 1900s he bought and began developing Chimney Rock, and in 1926 he dammed the Rocky Broad River to create Lake Lure. In 2007, the Morse descendants sold Chimney Rock

Park to the state of North Carolina, which is turning it, along with other nearby land, into a 3,260-acre state park. Although the scenery, particularly when viewed from atop Chimney Rock, is spectacular—several movies have been filmed here—the commercial development along parts of Hickory Nut Gorge is not so appealing. Lake Lure, with 27 mi of shoreline, is one of the most beautiful lakes in the mountains.

At **Chimney Rock Park**, currently operated by a private contractor while the state of North Carolina integrates it into a new state park, an elevator travels through a 26-story shaft of rock for a staggering view of Hickory Nut Gorge and the surrounding mountains. Trails, open year-round, lead to 400-foot Hickory Nut Falls, where the 1992 movie *The Last of the Mohicans* was filmed. ⊠*U.S. 64/74A* ☎*828/625–9611 or 800/277–9611* ⊕*www.chimneyrockpark.com* ⊠*$14* ⊙*May–Oct., daily 8:30–5:30; Nov.–Apr., daily 8:30–4:30.*

WHERE TO STAY

$$$$ ⌆**The Lodge on Lake Lure.** Originally built in the 1930s as a
★ retreat for the North Carolina Highway Patrol, this lodge is a place to slow down and enjoy life at the lakeside. All but three of the inn's 17 rooms have lake views, and the others have views of the well-tended gardens, with azaleas, rhododendrons, and other flowers and shrubs. The "gathering room" in the main lodge has soaring ceilings, with rare chestnut paneling, and a rock fireplace whose centerpiece is a huge millstone. Rooms are beautifully furnished with antiques. Rates include a full breakfast, afternoon tea and pastries, and evening hors d'oeuvres and wine. **Pros:** relaxing lakeside lodge; a comfy getaway. **Cons:** no restaurant for dinner; a long drive from other restaurants; thin walls, so you may hear your neighbors. ⊠*361 Charlotte Dr., Lake Lure* ☎*828/625–2789 or 800/733–2785* ⊕*www.lodgeonlakelure.com* ⇱*12 rooms in main lodge, 5 rooms in cottage* ⌂*In-hotel: no-smoking rooms* ▤*AE, D, MC, V* ⏐◯⏐*BP.*

SPORTS & THE OUTDOORS

The 720-acre **Lake Lure** (⊠*U.S. 64/74A* ☎*877/386–4255 or 828/625–1373* ⊕*www.lakelure.com*) draws the region's water-sports enthusiasts. You can rent boats (from kayaks and water bikes to pontoon boats) at the marina, water ski, swim, and fish. ▪TIP➜ **A small sandy beach on Lake Lure is open Memorial Day to Labor Day. Admission is $5.**

HENDERSONVILLE

23 mi south of Asheville via I–26.

Hendersonville, with about 11,000 residents, has one of the most engaging and vibrant downtowns of any small city in the South. Historic Main Street, as it's called, extends 10 serpentine blocks, lined with flower boxes and about 40 shops, including many antiques stores, galleries, and restaurants. Each year from April through October Main Street has displays of public art. Within walking distance of downtown are several B&Bs.

The Hendersonville region is North Carolina's main apple-growing area, and some 200 apple orchards dot the rolling hills around town. An Apple Festival, attracting some 200,000 people, is held each year in August.

☺ The **Holmes Educational State Forest,** a 235-acre state forest, has "talking trees," a fun way for kids to learn about the forests of western North Carolina—just punch a button on a hickory or poplar, and a recording tells you about the tree. ⊠*Crabtree Rd., 9 mi from downtown Hendersonville* ☎*828/692–0100* ⊒*Free* ☉*Mid-Mar.–mid-Nov., Tues.–Fri. 9–5, weekends 11–8.*

☺ The **Historic Johnson Farm,** a 19th-century tobacco farm that is now operated by Henderson County Public Schools, has the original farmhouse, barn, outbuildings, and a museum with about 1,000 artifacts typical of farm life of the time. ⊠*3346 Haywood Rd., 4 mi north of downtown Hendersonville* ☎*828/697–4733* ⊒*Guided tours $3* ☉*Tues.–Fri. 9–2:30; closed on school holidays.*

THOMAS WOLFE'S ANGEL. In his novel *Look Homeward, Angel,* Asheville-born Thomas Wolfe makes many references to an angel statue. The famous angel, in real life carved from Italian marble by Wolfe's father, W. O. Wolfe, stands in Hendersonville's Oakdale Cemetery, marking the graves of a family named Johnson, to whom the senior Wolfe sold the statue. The statue is protected by an iron fence. ⊠*U.S. 64, just west of downtown Hendersonville.*

6

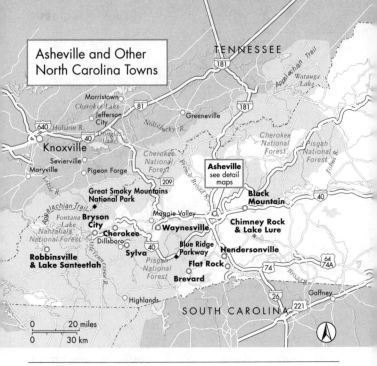

Asheville and Other
North Carolina Towns

WHERE TO STAY & EAT

$$–$$$ ×**Bistro 502.** *American.* The walls are a sedate beige, but the food here is anything but. For lunch, there's a nice selection of panini and other sandwiches. At dinner, moderately priced entrées (mostly $15–$20, with a choice of salad or soup) include fresh fish and some comfort foods, such as seared pork loin and meat loaf. There's local art on the walls, and the tables at the front are good for people watching on Main Street. You're invited to post your comments in a spiral bound notebook at each table, and the musings of previous guests are fun to read. ⊠*502 N. Main St.* ☎*828/697–5350* ⊟*AE, MC, V* ⊘*Closed Sun.*

$$–$$$ ×**Flight Wood Grill & Wine Bar.** *American.* Located in a 1920s-era bank building complete with the old vault, your best investments here include the many items grilled over local apple wood, including lamb chops (four for $28), chicken breast with salsa verde ($19), and the mixed grill ($22–$34 depending on which items you order). Wood-grilled pizzas ($10–$12) also are good choices. About 300 birds soar in a mobile around the ceiling. The staff is perky and pour some

40 wines by the glass. ⊠*401 N. Main St.* ☎*828/694–1030* ⊟*AE, MC, V* ☉*Closed Sun. No lunch.*

$$$–$$$$ ⚿**Waverly Inn.** On a warm afternoon, you'll love to "sit a spell" in a rocking chair on the front porch of Hendersonville's oldest inn. All 14 rooms in the 1898 three-story Victorian, two blocks from downtown, are named after native flowers and shrubs and outfitted with antique furnishings. The Mountain Magnolia suite has a king canopy bed, and the Silverbell room, painted an airy yellow and white, has a four-poster bed and a claw-foot bathtub. **Pros:** historic small inn; walking distance of downtown; friendly and very well run. **Cons:** quite a bit of traffic in area; some rooms are on small side. ⊠*783 N. Main St.* ☎*828/698–9193 or 800/537–8195* ⊕*www.waverlyinn.com* ↩*13 rooms, 1 suite* ⚿*In-room: DVD (some), Wi-Fi. In-hotel: Wi-Fi, no-smoking rooms* ⊟*AE, D, DC, MC, V* ⓞ*BP.*

NIGHTLIFE & THE ARTS

The Skyland Hotel is one of the places where Jazz Age novelist F. Scott Fitzgerald stayed when he visited his wife in a mental institution in Asheville, and the building is now the **Arts Center** (⊠*538 N. Main St.* ☎*828/693–8504*), a nonprofit organization that puts on art exhibits and other cultural programs.

While local nightlife is limited, you can hear live music on weekend nights and enjoy one of about 125 types of beer at **Hannah Flanagan's Pub** (⊠*300 N. Main St.* ☎*828/696–1665*).

SPORTS & THE OUTDOORS

Among the five golf courses in Hendersonville, the 6,719-yard, par-71, private **Champion Hills Golf Club** (⊠*1 Hagen Dr.* ☎*828/693–3600*) is the home course of famed golf-course designer Tom Fazio. An enjoyable public course is **Crooked Tree Golf Club** (⊠*764 Crooked Tree Rd.* ☎*828/692–2011*), where the clubhouse was once a corporate retreat owned by Warner Bros., the movie company.

SHOPPING

If you like to shop, you'll enjoy browsing the 40 shops on **Historic Main Street**, including several antiques stores, a branch of Mast General Store, and local boutiques.

FLAT ROCK

3 mi south of Hendersonville; 26 mi south of Asheville via I–26.

Flat Rock has been a summer resort since the early 19th century. It was a favorite of wealthy planters from Charleston, eager to escape the Low Country heat. The trip from Charleston to Flat Rock by horse and carriage took as long as two weeks, so you know there must be something here that made the long trek worthwhile.

☾ The **Carl Sandburg Home National Historic Site** is the spot to
★ which the poet and Lincoln biographer Carl Sandburg moved with his wife, Lillian, in 1945. Guided tours of their house, Connemara, where Sandburg's papers still lie scattered on his desk, are given by the National Park Service. In summer, the productions *The World of Carl Sandburg* and *Rootabaga Stories* are presented at the amphitheater. Kids enjoy a walk around the grounds of the farm, which still maintains descendants of the Sandburg family goats. ✉*1928 Little River Rd.* ☎*828/693–4178* ⊕*www.nps.gov/ carl* ☞*$5* ☉*Daily 9–5.*

The **Flat Rock Playhouse** has a high reputation for summer stock theater. The season runs from May to mid-December. ✉*2661 Greenville Hwy.* ☎*828/693–0731* ⊕*www.flatrock-playhouse.org.*

BREVARD

40 mi southwest of Asheville on Rte. 280.

With its friendly, highly walkable downtown, Brevard is Mayberry RFD transported to the Pisgah National Forest. In fact, a popular toy store in town is called O. P. Taylor's—get it?

Brevard residents go nuts over the white squirrels, which dart around the town's parks. These aren't albinos, but a variation of the eastern gray squirrel. About one-fourth of the squirrels in town are white. The white squirrels are thought to have come originally from Hawaii by way of Florida; they possibly were released in Brevard by a visitor in the 1950s. Whatever the truth, today Brevard capitalizes on it by holding a White Squirrel Festival in late May. One of the best places to see the little devils is on the **Brevard College** (✉*400 N. Broad St. 28712*) campus.

The oldest frame house in western North Carolina, the **Allison-Deaver House** was built in the early 1800s, and has been renovated and expanded several times. ⊠*N.C. Hwy. 280, Pisgah Forest, near Forest Gate Shopping Center* ☎*828/884–5137* ☜*Donations accepted* ☉*Apr.–Oct., Fri. and Sat. 10–4, Sun. 1–4.*

☺ Nearby Pisgah National Forest has the **Cradle of Forestry in**
★ **America National Historic Site,** the home of the first forestry school in the United States, with a 1-mi interpretive trail, the school's original log buildings, and a visitor center with many hands-on exhibits of interest to kids. The road from Brevard to the Cradle of Foresty, a scenic byway, continues on to connect with the Blue Ridge Parkway near Mt. Pisgah. ⊠*1001 Pisgah Hwy., U.S. 276* ☎*828/884–5823* ⊕*www.cradleofforestry.com* ☜*$5* ☉*Mid-Apr.–early Nov., daily 9–5.*

The newest addition to nature sites near Brevard is **DuPont State Forest,** which was established in 1996 and expanded in 2000. You'll find 10,400 acres with four waterfalls and 80 mi of old dirt roads to explore, with ideal conditions for biking or horseback riding. ⊠*U.S. 64 and Little River Rd.* ☎*828/877–6527* ⊕*www.dupontforest.com* ☜*Free.*

Near the road and easy to get to, **Looking Glass Falls** is a classic, with water cascading 60 feet into a clear pool. ⊠*Pisgah National Forest, north of Brevard, off U.S. 276* ☜*Free.*

☺ At the **Pisgah Center for Wildlife Education** the fish hatchery produces more than 400,000 brown, rainbow, and native brook trout each year for release in local streams. You can see the fish up close in tanks called raceways and even feed them (approved trout feed is sold for a quarter). There's also a small visitor center with information about the life cycle of trout and an educational nature trail. ⊠*Rte. 475 off U.S. 276 in Pisgah National Forest* ☎*828/877–4423* ☜*Free* ☉*Daily 8–5.*

☺ At **Sliding Rock** in summer you can skid 60 feet on a natural waterslide. Wear old jeans and tennis shoes and bring a towel. ⊠*Pisgah National Forest, north of Brevard, off U.S. 276* ☎*828/877–3265* ☜*$3 per car* ☉*Late May–early Sept., daily 10–5:30.*

6

WHERE TO STAY & EAT

¢   ✕**Cardinal Drive-In.** *American.* The cheeseburgers are just
fair and the onion rings are like fried cardboard, but this is
an authentic piece of Americana—a real drive-in, with car
hops and everything. ⊠*7328 S. Broad St.* ☎*828/884–7085*
⊟*No credit cards.*

$$$ ✕**Hobnob.** *Eclectic.* You can hobnob with old and new
friends at this casual spot in a colorfully painted house near
downtown. The co-owners, who formerly ran a restaurant
in Charleston, have brought a Low Country edge to dining
in Brevard, with dishes like Carolina crab cake on sweet
corn salad. Other dishes have a French influence. ⊠*226
Main St.* ☎*828/966–4662* ⊟*AE, MC, V.*

$–$$ ⛺**Red House Inn.** One of the oldest houses in Brevard, the
Red House Inn was built in 1851 as a trading post and
later served as a courthouse, tavern, post office, and school.
Now it's an unpretentious but pleasant B&B four blocks
from the center of town. There are four rooms in the main
house and an efficiency cottage. **Pros:** B&B in historic
house; comfortable; friendly hosts. **Cons:** not for swing-
ing singles. ⊠*412 W. Probart St.* ☎*828/884–9349* ⊕*www.
brevardbedandbreakfast.com* ↪*4 rooms, 1 cottage* ♿*In-
room: refrigerator (some), Wi-Fi. In-hotel: no-smoking
rooms* ⊟ *MC, V* �llⵏ*BP.*

NIGHTLIFE & THE ARTS

The nationally known **Brevard Music Center** (✉*Box 312*
☎*828/884–2011* ⊕*www.brevardmusic.org*) has a seven-
week music festival each summer, with about 80 concerts
from mid-June to early August. Keith Lockhart is the prin-
cipal conductor.

Formerly the Jim Bob Tinsley cowboy museum, the **Transyl-
vania Heritage Museum** (⊠ *W. Jordan St.* ☎*828/884–2347*)
has displays on the Brevard area and also on the life and
interests of Brevard native Tinsley, a musicologist and
author of 10 books who played with Gene Autry.

MOUNTAIN BIKING. **The North Carolina Mountains offer some of
the best mountain biking in the East. Among the favorite places
for mountain biking are Tsali, a peninsula sticking out into Lake
Fontana near Bruston City, in the Nantahala National Forest;
Dupont State Forest, just south of Brevard; and the Bent Creek,**

Davidson River, and Mills River sections of the Pisgah Ranger District of the Pisgah National Forest.

SPORTS & THE OUTDOORS

Catch rainbow, brown, or brook trout on the Davidson River, named one of the top 100 trout streams in the United States by Trout Unlimited. **Davidson River Outfitters** (⊠*26 Pisgah Forest Hwy.* ☎*828/877–4181*) arranges trips and also has a fly-fishing school and a fly shop.

Etowah Valley Country Club and Golf Lodge (⊠*U.S. 64, Etowah* ☎*828/891–7141 or 800/451–8174*) has three very different (one par-72, two par-73) 18-hole courses and offers good package deals.

♻ Western North Carolina's largest indoor skateboard, skating, and BMX biking facility is **Zero Gravity Skatepark** (⊠*1800 Old Hendersonville Hwy.* ☎*828/862–6700*), with fun boxes, ramps, launch boxes, ledges, roll-ins, and a pyramid and bowl.

CHEROKEE

178 mi east of Charlotte; 51 mi west of Asheville; 109 west of Brevard via U.S. 64; 2 mi from entrance to Great Smoky Mountains National Park.

The 56,000-acre Cherokee reservation is known as the Qualla Boundary, and the town of Cherokee is its capital. Truth be told, there are two Cherokees. There's the Cherokee with the sometimes tacky pop culture, designed to appeal to the masses of tourists. But there's another Cherokee that's a window onto the rich heritage of the tribe's Eastern Band. Although now relatively small in number—tribal enrollment is 12,500—these Cherokee and their ancestors have been responsible for keeping alive the Cherokee culture. They are the descendants of those who hid in the Great Smoky Mountains to avoid the Trail of Tears, the forced removal of the Cherokee Nation to Oklahoma in the 19th century. They are survivors, extremely attached to the hiking, swimming, trout fishing, and natural beauty of their ancestral homeland. The reservation is dry, with no alcohol sales anywhere, even at the casino. This also means that there are few upscale restaurants in the area (since they depend on wine and cocktail sales for much of their profits), just fast-food and mom-and-pop places.

GETTING HERE & AROUND

The Blue Ridge Parkway's southern terminus is at Cherokee, and the Parkway is by far the most beautiful route to Cherokee and to the Great Smoky Mountains National Park. A faster option is U.S. 23 and U.S. 74/U.S. 441 connecting Cherokee with I–40 from Asheville or from Franklin in the south. The least pleasant route is U.S. 19 from I–40, a mostly two-lane road pocked with touristy roadside shops.

ESSENTIALS

Cherokee Visitors Center (⊠*U.S. 441 Business* ☎*828/497–9195 or 800/438–1601* ⊕*www.cherokee-nc.com*).

EXPLORING CHEROKEE

The **Museum of the Cherokee Indian,** with displays and artifacts that cover 12,000 years, is one of the best Native American museums in the United States. Computer-generated images, lasers, specialty lighting, and sound effects help re-create events in the history of the Cherokee: for example, you'll see children stop to play a butter bean game while adults shiver along the snowy Trail of Tears. The museum has an art gallery, a gift shop, and an outdoor living exhibit of Cherokee life in the 15th century. ⊠*U.S. 441 at Drama Rd.* ⌂*Box 1599* ☎*828/497–3481* ⊕*www.cherokeemuseum. org* ⊑*$9* ☉*June–Aug., Mon.–Sat. 9–8, Sun. 9–5; Sept.– May, daily 9–5.*

� At the historically accurate, re-created **Oconaluftee Indian Village,** guides in native costumes will lead you through a village of 225 years ago while others demonstrate traditional skills such as weaving, pottery, canoe construction, and hunting techniques. ⊠*U.S. 441 at Drama Rd., 28719* ☎*828/497–2315* ⊕*www.cherokee-nc.com* ⊑*$9* ☉*Mid-May–mid-Oct., daily 9:30–5:30.*

☁ Every mountain county has significant deposits of gems and minerals, and at the **Smoky Mountain Gold and Ruby Mine,** on the Qualla Boundary, you can search for gems such as aquamarines. Children love panning precisely because it can be wet and messy. Here they're guaranteed a find. Gem ore can be purchased, too, for $4–$10 per bag: gold ore costs $5 per bag. ⊠*U.S. 441 N* ☎*828/497–6574* ⊑*$4–$10, depending on gems* ☉*Mar.–Nov., daily 10–6.*

WHERE TO STAY

$-$$ ⌨**Fairfield Inn & Suites.** This three-story chain motel is directly across from Harrah's Casino, so you can walk to the casino without worrying about parking. Rooms here are typical of the Fairfield Inn chain—comfortable and clean but not deluxe. **Pros:** convenient to casino; usual chain motel amenities. **Cons:** like all Fairfield motels. ✉*568 Painttown Rd.28719* ☎*828/497–0400* 📠*828/497–4242* ⊕*www.marriott.com* ⬙*96 rooms, 4 suites* ♿*In-room: refrigerator, Wi-Fi. In-hotel: pool, laundry facilities, laundry service, parking (free), no-smoking rooms* ▭*AE, D, DC, MC, V* ℍ*CP.*

$$$-$$$$ ⌨**Harrah's Cherokee Casino Hotel.** The 15-story hotel, which opened in 2002 and doubled in size with an addition in 2005, towers over the mom 'n' pop motels nearby and the casino next door, to which it is umbilically attached via a series of escalators and walkways. The lobby and other public areas incorporate Cherokee traditional art themes. Rooms are large, about 500 square feet, and have 32-inch TVs. For high-rollers, there are suites on the top floor. The Selu Garden Café in the hotel and the Seven Sisters restaurant in the casino are handy after a day of playing the slots. Restaurants and the casino do not offer alcoholic drinks, as the sale of alcohol is prohibited on the Cherokee reservation. A $650 million expansion that will bring the total of hotel rooms here to over 1,000 and also add new restaurants, shops, and a spa and increase the number of video gaming machines to over 5,000 is expected to be completed by 2012. **Pros:** supersized hotel; convenient to casino. **Cons:** hotel often fully booked due to comps and deals for gamblers; no booze. ✉*U.S. 19 at U.S. 441 Business28719* ☎*800/427–7247 or 828/497–7777* ⊕*www.harrahs.com* ⬙*576 rooms* ♿*In-room: refrigerator (some), Wi-Fi. In-hotel: 5 restaurants, pool, gym, no-smoking rooms* ▭*AE, D, DC, MC, V* ℍ*EP.*

WHERE TO CAMP

$$$$ ⛺**Yogi Bear's Jellystone Park.** This large commercial campground has just about every amenity you could want, from a heated swimming pool to an outdoor movie theater (bring your own lawn chairs). In addition to 152 campsites, Jellystone has 31 air-conditioned cabins for rent on a daily or weekly basis. The campground has about 1,500 feet of frontage on the Raven Fork River, a stocked trout stream

(NC fishing license required). You can also wade or tube in the river. **Pros:** woodsy, riverside location; full range of amenities. **Cons:** most campsites are best suited for travel trailers and pop-ups, rather than for large RVs. ⊠*317 Galamore Bridge Rd.* ☎*828/497–9151 or 877/716–6711* ⊕*www.jellystone-cherokee.com* ⊅*152 RV/trailer sites, 31 cabins* &*Flush toilets, full hookups, dump station, drinking water, guest laundry, showers, fire rings, electricity, public telephone, general store, play area, swimming creek, pool, Wi-Fi* ⊟*MC, V.*

NIGHTLIFE & THE ARTS

Unto These Hills (⊠*Mountainside Theater on Drama Rd., off U.S. 441 N* ☎*828/497–2111 or 866/554–4557*) is a colorful and well-staged history of the Cherokee from the time of Spanish explorer Hernando de Soto's visit in 1540 to the infamous Trail of Tears. The show runs from mid-June to late August, and tickets start at $18 ($8 for children 12 and under). The drama was updated in 2006 with a new script and new costumes.

Owned by the Eastern Bank of the Cherokee, **Harrah's Casino** (⊠*777 Casino Dr., U.S. 19 at U.S. 441 Business* ☎*828/497–7777 or 800/427–7247*) has more than 3,600 video-gaming machines in a casino the size of more than three football fields. Digital blackjack and digital baccarat combine live dealers with digital cards. Some gamblers complain about stingy video machine payouts and the fact that alcohol is not served. Big-name stars such as Wayne Newton, Jay Leno, and Willie Nelson provide entertainment at the casino, which has a theater seating 1,500. A $650 million expansion is underway that will increase the number of gaming machines to over 5,000 and add a larger theater.

SPORTS & THE OUTDOORS

There are 30 mi of regularly stocked trout streams on the **Cherokee Indian Reservation** (☎*828/497–5201 or 800/438–1601*). To fish in tribal water, you need a tribal fishing permit, available at nearly two dozen reservation businesses. The $7 permit is valid for one day and has a creel limit of 10. A five-day permit is $28. Fishing is permitted from late March to October.

A five-minute hike from the **Mingo Falls Campground** (⊠*Big Cove Rd., about 4 mi north of Acquoni Rd.*) will reward you with a view of the 120-foot-high Mingo Falls. In the downtown area you can cross the Oconaluftee River on a footbridge to **Oconaluftee Islands Park & Trail** (⊠*Off U.S. 441, across from Cherokee Elementary School*) and walk a trail around the perimeter of the park, which also has picnic facilities.

SHOPPING

The **Qualla Arts and Crafts Mutual** (⊠*U.S. 441 at Drama Rd., 28719* ☎828/497–3103), across the street from the Museum of the Cherokee Indian, is a cooperative that displays and sells items created by 300 Cherokee craftspeople. The store has a large selection of high-quality baskets, masks, and wood carvings, which can cost hundreds of dollars.

BRYSON CITY

65 mi east of Asheville; 11 mi southwest of Cherokee.

Bryson City is a little mountain town on the Nantahala River, one of the lesser-known gateways to the Great Smokies. The town's most striking feature is a city hall with a four-sided clock. Since becoming the depot and headquarters of the Great Smoky Mountains Railroad, the downtown shopping area has been rejuvenated, mostly with gift shops and ice cream stands.

GETTING HERE AND AROUND

Bryson City is a 15-minute drive from Cherokee on U.S. 19. Near Bryson City are two entrances to the Great Smokies.

EXPLORING BRYSON CITY

The most popular river in western North Carolina for rafting and kayaking is **Nantahala River,** which races through the scenic Nantahala Gorge, a 1,600-foot-deep gorge that begins about 13 mi west of Bryson City on U.S. 19. Class III and Class IV rapids (Class V are the most dangerous) make for a thrilling ride. Several outfitters run river trips or rent equipment. Happily, the severe drought that reduced water flow on many other rivers in the region doesn't affect the Nantahala, due to daily dam releases. ■TIP→**At several points along the river you can park your car and watch rafters run the rapids—on a summer day you'll see hundreds of rafts** and kayaks going by. ⊠*U.S. 19, beginning 13 mi west of Bryson City*.

The popular train rides of the **Great Smoky Mountains Railroad** include excursions from Bryson City, and several special trips. Diesel-electric or steam locomotives go along the Nantahala Gorge. Open-sided cars or standard coaches are ideal for picture taking as the mountain scenery glides by. Some rides include a meal: on some Friday evenings there's a mystery theater train with dinner, and on Saturdays a gourmet dinner train. ⊠*225 Everett St., Suites G and H, Bryson City* ☎*800/872–4681* ⊕*www.gsmr.com* ☎*$34–$53 for standard seating; upgraded seating $12–$20 additional; rates plus $3 parking fee; most tickets include admission to the Smoky Mountain Model Railroad Museum.*

♻ Somewhat overly commercial and overpriced, the **Smoky Mountain Model Railroad Museum** nevertheless appeals to kids or anyone with a fond memory of model trains. More than 2,500 model trains are displayed around two model railroad operating layouts. This is also a retail store selling model trains of all kinds. ⊠*100 Greenlee St., near Great Smoky Mountains Railroad Depot* ☎*828/488–5200 or 866/914–5200* ⊕*www.smokymtntrains.com* ☎*$9* ⊙*Mon.– Sat. 8:30–5:30.*

WHERE TO STAY & EAT

$ ✕**River's End at Nantahala Outdoor Center.** *American.* The casual riverbank setting and high-energy atmosphere at NOC's eatery draws lots of hungry people just returned from an invigorating day of rafting. There are salads, soups, and sandwiches during the day and fancier fixin's in the evening. The chili's a winner—there are black- and white-bean versions ($5.25 for a bowl). For more upscale fare at NOC, try Relia's Garden, which specializes in steak and trout (closed Monday–Wednesday). ⊠*13077 Hwy. 19 W28713* ☎*828/488–2176* ⊟*MC, V* ⊙*Closed Nov.–Mar.*

$–$$ ⊞**Fryemont Inn.** An institution in Bryson City for eight decades, the Fryemont Inn is on the National Register of Historic Places. The lodge exterior is bark, rooms in the main lodge are paneled in real chestnut, and the lobby has a fireplace big enough for 8-foot logs. If you need more luxury, choose one of the suites with fireplaces and air-conditioning. The restaurant ($$–$$$), serving Southern fare, is open to the public for breakfast and dinner. **Pros:** historic inn; comfortably rustic; charming restaurant with wholesome, simple food. **Cons:** rooms in main lodge are far from posh; can be warm on a summer day; no swimming pool; restaurant does not serve lunch. ✉*245 Fryemont St., Bryson City28713* ☎*828/488–2159 or 800/845–4879* ⊕*www.fryemontinn.com* ➳*37 rooms, 3 suites, 1 cabin* ♿*In-room: no a/c (some), no phone, no TV (some). In-hotel: restaurant, pool* ⊟*D, MC, V* ⊠*MAP.*

$–$$ 🏨**Hemlock Inn.** This folksy, friendly mountain inn on 50 acres above Bryson City is the kind of place where you can rock, doze, and play Scrabble. Even if you're not a guest at the inn, you can make a reservation for dinner Monday through Saturday and for lunch on Sunday. The all-you-can-eat meals (breakfast included in the rates, dinner packages available) are prepared with regional foods and served family-style on lazy Susans at big round tables. Fly-fishing and river rafting–kayaking and other packages are available. **Pros:** unpretentious, family-oriented inn; delicious Southern-style food; like a visit to grandma's. **Cons:** no modern conveniences like Wi-Fi, TVs, or in-room phones; family-style meals may not suit everyone; no alcohol served; no swimming pool. ✉*Galbraith Creek Rd.* ⌖*Box 2350* ♁*1 mi north of U.S. 19* ☎*828/488–2885* ⊕*www.hemlockinn. com* ➳*22 rooms, 3 cottages* ♿*In-room: no a/c, no phone, no TV. In-hotel: restaurant* ⊟*D, MC, V* ⊠*BP.*

WHERE TO CAMP

$$$–$$$$ ⛺**Deep Creek Tube Center & Campground.** The draw here is ☻ the tubing on Deep Creek, which is fun for kids, though the water is cold even in the middle of summer. The campground's general store rents tubes. The best campsites are the 9 creek-side ones, but these are too small for big RVs; larger rigs will have to use the 7 mountain-view sites. There are 10 small, rustic cabins. One, called Cataloochee Camper ($65 a night), is a restored 1886 log cabin made of wormy chestnut logs from the Cataloochee area. **Pros:** easy access to Deep Creek for tubing. **Cons:** camp sites are on the small side, and the sites for larger RVs are in full sun with little or no shade. ✉*1090 West Deep Creek Rd., 28713* ☎*828/488–6055* ⊕*www.deepcreekcamping. com* ➳*33 RV/trailer sites, 13 tent sites, 10 cabins* ♿*Flush toilets, full hookups, dump station, drinking water, guest laundry, showers, fire rings, electricity, public telephone, general store, play area, swimming creek, Wi-Fi* ⊟*MC, V* ⊙*Closed mid-Dec.–Mar.*

$$$–$$$$ ⚠️**Tumbling Waters Campground.** This small, family-run campground doesn't have a lot of frills, but it has a lovely setting mid-way between Bryson City and Fontana Dam with easy access to Fontana Lake, the Nantahala River, the Appalachian Trail, and the Tsali mountain biking area. There's a small stream and a trout pond. The owners are friendly and the bathhouse is very clean with hot showers. Ice and firewood are available, but little else, so bring supplies. **Pros:** quiet, comfortable spot to enjoy the mountains; good access to mountain biking, rafting, and hiking. **Cons:** simple place with no frills. ✉*1612 Panther Creek Rd., Almond* ☎*828/479-3814* ⊕*www.tumblingwaters.com* ⤳*4 tent sites, 8 RV/trailer sites, 1 cabin, 1 rental trailer* ⚿*Flush toilets, full hookups, dump station, drinking water, guest laundry, showers, fire rings, electricity, swimming creek, fishing pond* ⊟*MC, V* ☉*Closed Dec.–Feb.*

SPORTS & THE OUTDOORS

Privately owned **Deep Creek Stables** (✉*Deep Creek Picnic Area, near Bryson City entrance to Great Smokies National Park* ☎*828/488–8504*) offers trail riding in the Smokies.

Nantahala Outdoor Center (NOC) (⌂*13077 Hwy. 19 W* ☎*800/232-7238* ⊕*www.noc.com*) guides more than 30,000 rafters every year on the Nantahala and eight other rivers: the Chattooga, Cheoah, French Broad, Nolichucky, Ocoee, Gauley, New, and Pigeon. Due to the severe regional drought in 2007–2008, the French Broad River was at its lowest flow level in more than 100 years, and as of this writing most rafting trips on the French Broad have been discontinued. ■TIP→**The Cheoah River has reopened for rafting and kayaking, after being dammed and closed for years, but only for about 17 days a year. Serious rafters and kayakers looking for a challenge on Class IV/IV+ rapids should consider the Cheoah.** NOC also rents kayaks, ducks, and other equipment. The NOC complex on the Nantahala River is virtually a tourist attraction in itself, especially for young people, with three restaurants, cabin and campground rentals, an inn, a stop for the Great Smokies Railroad, and an outdoor store.

The par-71, 5,987-yard course at semiprivate **Smoky Mountain Country Club** (✉*1112 Conley Creek Rd., Whittier* ☎*828/497–4653 or 800/474–0070*) has 400 feet of elevation change over the 18 holes, not to mention stunning views of the mountains.

ROBBINSVILLE & LAKE SANTEETLAH

98 mi southwest of Asheville; 35 mi southwest of Bryson City.

If you truly want to get away from everything, head to the area around Robbinsville in the far southwest corner of North Carolina, a little south of the southern edge of the Great Smokies. The town of Robbinsville offers little, but the Snowbird Mountains, Lake Santeetlah, Fontana Lake, the rugged Joyce Kilmer–Slickrock Wilderness, and the Joyce Kilmer Memorial Forest, with its giant virgin poplars and sycamores, definitely are highlights of this part of North Carolina.

More than 29 mi long, **Fontana Lake & Dam** borders the southern edge of the Great Smokies. Unlike most other lakes in the mountains, Fontana has a shoreline that is almost completely undeveloped, since about 90% of its 240 mi are owned by the federal government. Fishing here is excellent, especially for small-mouth bass, muskie, and walleye. On the downside, the Tennessee Valley Authority (TVA) manages the lake for power generation, and at peak visitor time in the fall the lake is drawn down, leaving large areas of mudflats. Fontana Dam, completed in 1944, at 480 feet is the highest concrete dam east of the Rockies. The Appalachian Trail crosses the top of the dam. ⊠*Fontana Dam Visitor Center, off Rte. 28, 3 mi from Fontana Village* ☎*865/632–2101 TVA* ⊠*Free* ☉*Visitor center May–Nov., daily 9–7.*

★ **Fodor's**Choice One of the few remaining sections of the original Appalachian forests, **Joyce Kilmer Memorial Forest,** a part of the 17,000-acre Joyce Kilmer–Slickrock Wilderness, has 400-year-old yellow poplars that are as much as 20 feet in circumference, along with huge hemlocks, oaks, sycamores, and other trees. If you haven't seen a true virgin forest, you can't imagine what America must have looked like in the early days of settlement. A 2-mi trail takes you through wildflower- and moss-carpeted areas of incredible beauty. The forest is named for the early-20th-century poet, killed in World War I, who is famous for the lines "I think I shall never see / A poem lovely as a tree." ■TIP➔**During June, the parking lot of the Joyce Kilmer Memorial Forest is an excellent spot to see the light shows of the synchronous fireflies (*Photinus carolinus*), which blink off and on in unison.** ⊠*15 mi west of Robbinsville, off Cherohala Skyway via Hwy. 143* *and Kilmer Rd.* ☎828/479–6431 *Cheoah Ranger District* ⚑*Free.*

Formed in 1928 with the construction of the Santeetlah Dam, **Lake Santeetlah,** meaning "blue waters" in the Cherokee language, has 76 mi of shoreline, with good fishing for crappie, bream, and lake trout. The lake is managed by Alcoa as a hydroelectric project, but most of the land is owned by the federal government as part of the Nantahala National Forest. ✉*Cheoah Point Recreation Area, Rte. 1145 off U.S. 129, about 7 mi north of Robinsville* ☎828/479–6431 *Nantahala National Forest/Cheoah Ranger District* ⚑*Free.*

WHERE TO STAY

$$ 📺**Blue Boar Inn.** On the outside, it looks like a lodge for bear and wild boar hunters, which it was—it was built in 1950 by a Cincinnati beer magnate as a hunting lodge. Today, inside, it has been totally redone, with upscale modern furnishings, including air-conditioning and TVs. Each spacious room has a porch. Up a hillside above the main lodge, privately owned cottages (plans are for 10 of them eventually) are available for rent for $250–$325 nightly. The 1,000-square-foot cottages each have two bedrooms, two baths, kitchen, hot tubs, and fireplaces. You can kayak or canoe on nearby Lake Santeetlah, and a stocked trout pond is on the lodge grounds. A delicious full breakfast is included (for lodge rooms only), and dinner is available at an extra charge. BYOB, as no wine or other alcohol is sold. **Pros:** peaceful mountain retreat; large rooms with upscale furnishings; self-catering cabins an option. **Cons:** no alcohol sold; no swimming pool; remote location. ✉*1283 Blue Boar Rd., Robbinsville* ☎828/479–8126 *or* 866/479–8126 ⊕*www.blueboarinn.com* ⮕8 *rooms, 3 two-bedroom cottages* ⬙*In-room: kitchen (some), refrigerator. In-hotel: restaurant, no-smoking rooms* ⊟*AE, D, MC, V* ⊙*Closed late Nov.–late Mar.* ⦾*BP.*

★ **Fodor's**Choice 📺**Snowbird Mountain Lodge.** When it's 95°F and $$$–$$$$ the paperwork is piling up, Snowbird is the kind of mountain lodge you daydream about. The main lodge, built in 1941 and now in the National Register of Historic Places, has two massive stone fireplaces, solid chestnut beams across the ceiling, and beautiful views across the valley. If you run out of things to do, there are 10,000 books in the library and 100 acres of grounds to explore. The restaurant serves "rustic" meals like fresh trout with grilled vegetable salsa, and the wine list is the size of a small telephone directory. For more luxury than the main lodge rooms offer, choose a room in the Chestnut Lodge or a king suite in a separate cottage. Some rooms have whirlpool baths and fireplaces. **Pros:** gorgeous mountainside setting; excellent food; huge wine list. **Cons:** remote; no swimming pool. ⊠*4633 Santeetlah Rd., Robbinsville* ☎*828/479–3433 or 800/941–9290* ⊕*www.snowbirdlodge.com* ⇒*21 rooms, 2 suites in separate cottage* ⚷*In-room: no a/c (some), no phone, refrigerator (some), no TV. In-hotel: restaurant, tennis courts, Internet terminal, Wi-Fi, no kids under 12, no-smoking rooms* ▤*MC, V* ⊗❮◯❯*MAP.*

SYLVA

48 mi southwest of Asheville; 2 mi east of Dillsboro via U.S. 23; 50 mi east of Robbinsville via U.S. 74.

Sylva, population 2,300, is the county seat of Jackson County. It has a classic small-town Main Street with stores selling furniture, hardware, watches, books, beer, and other necessities. The domed Jackson County courthouse, built in 1914 in the Beaux Arts style, overlooks the downtown from a nearby hilltop. Noted author John Parris was a native of Sylva.

Mountain Heritage Center. In wormy chestnut–paneled quarters at Western Carolina University, this museum maintains and displays the heirlooms of hundreds of mountain families, from butter churns to baby bassinets. Most exhibits rotate, but the permanent exhibit "Migration of the Scotch-Irish People" describes the history and culture of the English and Scottish people of Northern Ireland, known as Ulster Scots, who settled the Carolina mountains in the 18th century. ⊠*150 H.F. Robinson Bldg., Western Carolina University,Cullowhee* ☎*828/227–7129* ⊕*www.wcu.edu/ mhc* ▣*Free* ⊗*Weekdays 8–5; also Sun. 2–5 in Oct. only; closed during some college holiday periods.*

WHERE TO STAY & EAT

$–$$ ✕**Jarrett House.** *American.* The food here may not win any awards for creative cooking, but folks love the mountain trout ($15.95), country ham with red-eye gravy ($15.95), and fried chicken ($13.95) at the Jarrett House, in continuous operation since 1884 and now on the National Register

BARD OF THE MOUNTAINS

John Parris (1914–99), a native of the small town of Sylva, has been called the "Bard of the Mountains." In the course of four decades of writing the daily newspaper column "Roaming the Mountains" for the *Asheville Citizen*, Parris gathered and published more on mountain traditions and culture and language than perhaps any other writer who ever lived. Some of his daily columns were collected in five books, including *My Mountains, My People*. Sometimes sentimental, but always full of authentic detail, his daily stories were prose poems about the mountains he loved. These lines from *Mountain Cooking* exemplify his style:

"An old farmhouse with a fire blazing on the hearth has a way of conjuring up memories.

This is particularly so when the first icy winds come prowling under the eaves and there's a smell of frost in the air.

It is then that the memories come flooding back...."

of Historic Places. Jarrett House is best known for its dining, but you can also stay here. Rooms (¢) in this three-story country inn, with porches on all three levels, are small and unpretentious, but you can't beat the location right across from Dillsboro's shops. ⊠*Box 219, U.S. 441, Dillsboro* ☎*828/586–0265 or 800/972–5623* ⊕ *www.jarretthouse. com* ⊟*No credit cards* ⊘*Closed Jan.–Apr.*

\$–\$\$ ▦**Balsam Mountain Inn.** A stay here is like going back 75 years in time, when folks rocked and chatted on the front porch, went to bed at 10 PM, and hotels didn't have amenities like air-conditioning, room TVs, swimming pool, fitness center, or, heaven forbid, Internet connections. In this rambling old wood-frame inn, the floors creak and you may overhear your neighbors through paper-thin walls. But if you can buy into the back-in-time premise, Balsam Mountain Inn is a delight, with a cozy library, friendly staff, and a wonderfully unpretentious restaurant. The rooms, most not overly large, have been redone, but old-fashioned elements such as claw-foot tubs remain. You'll enjoy the included breakfast served in the sun porch. **Pros:** friendly, down-home, old mountain inn; delicious food. **Cons:** rooms vary, and some are small, with thin walls; lights out at 10. ⊠*68 Seven Springs Dr., Balsam* ☎*800/224–9498* ⊕*www.balsammountaininn.com* ⊷*41 rooms, 9 suites* ⚬*In-room: no a/c, no phone, no TV. In-hotel: restaurant* ⊟*AE, D, MC, V* ⊚⏐*BP.*

SPORTS & THE OUTDOORS

On the Tuckaseegee River, much gentler than the Nantahala River, **Tuckaseegee Outfitters** (☒*U.S. 74/441* ☎*800/539–5683*) offers nonguided trips by tube, raft, and inflatable kayak.

SHOPPING

Nearby Dillsboro has a cluster of mostly tourist-oriented shops, in the several blocks adjoining the Great Smokies Railroad tracks. A co-op of more than 80 area artisans owns and runs **Dogwood Crafters** (☒*90 Webster St.* ☎*828/586–2248*), where you can purchase pottery, rugs, baskets, and other crafts. You can see potters throwing pots at **Mountain Pottery** (☒*152 Front St., 28725* ☎*828/586–9183*), where pottery, including ceramics made in the Japanese raku style, by about 75 different local potters are for sale.

WAYNESVILLE

6

17 mi east of Cherokee on U.S. 19; 17 mi northeast of Sylva via U.S. 23.

This is where the Blue Ridge Parkway meets the Great Smokies. Pretty, arty Waynesville is the seat of Haywood County. About 40% of the county is occupied by the Great Smoky Mountains National Park, Pisgah National Forest, and the Harmon Den Wildlife Refuge. The town of Waynesville is a rival of Blowing Rock and Highlands as an upmarket summer and vacation home retreat for the well-to-do, though the atmosphere here is a bit more countrified. A Ramp Festival, celebrating the smelly local cousin of the onion, is held in Waynesville annually in early May. New B&Bs are springing up around Waynesville like wildflowers after a heavy rain. Local restaurants celebrated in 2008, when the town voted to allow liquor by the drink. Ghost Town, a Wild West theme park popular with kids, is nearby, in Maggie Valley.

The **Museum of North Carolina Handicrafts,** in the Shelton House (circa 1875), has a comprehensive exhibit of 19th-century heritage crafts. ☒*307 Shelton St.* ☎*828/452–1551* ☒*$5* ☉*May–Oct., Tues.–Fri. 10–4.*

Cold Mountain, the vivid best-selling novel by Charles Frazier, has made a destination out of the real **Cold Mountain.** About 15 mi from Waynesville in the Shining Rock

Wilderness Area of Pisgah National Forest, the 6,030-foot rise had long stood in relative anonymity. But with the success of Frazier's book, people want to see the region that Inman and Ada, the book's Civil War–era protagonists, called home.

For a view of the splendid mass—or at least of the surrounding area—stop at any of a number of overlooks off the Blue Ridge Parkway. Try the Cold Mountain Parking Overlook, just past mile marker 411.9; the Wagon Road Gap parking area, at mile marker 412.2; or the Waterrock Knob Interpretative Station, at mile marker 451.2. You can climb the mountain, but beware, as the hike to the summit is strenuous. No campfires are allowed in Shining Rock, so you'll need a stove if you wish to cook. Inform the **ranger station** (☎828/877–3350) if you plan to hike or camp.

☾ **Ghost Town in the Sky** is a Wild West theme park on top of a mountain. Originally opened in 1961, it closed in 2002 but came back to life in 2007 under new ownership. You ride up 3,300 feet in a chairlift or an inclined railway. At the top, you're greeted by gunslingers who stage O.K. Corral–style gunfights. One cowhand says he's been in more than 50,000 gunfights at Ghost Town. There are 40 replica buildings meant to represent an 1880s Western town. Also at the park are thrill rides, including the new "Cliff Hanger" roller coaster. ⊠*16 Fie Top Rd., Maggie Valley* ☎*828/926–1140* ⊕*www.ghosttowninthesky.com* ⊠*$30 ($24 if purchased online)* ☉*Early May and early Sept.–early Nov., Fri-Sun. 10–6; mid-May–early Sept., daily 10–6.*

WHERE TO STAY & EAT

✕**Lomo Grill.** *Argentine.* Waynesville's best restaurant combines Mediterranean-style ingredients with the chef-owner's Argentine background. The grilled steaks are perfectly prepared and served with delicately cooked, fresh local vegetables. Many of the fruits and vegetables are grown in the chef's garden. In a 1920s downtown space with a high, crimson-red ceiling, Lomo Grill has superlative servers, efficient and friendly without being obsequious. Try the key lime pie—it's the best in the mountains. ⊠*44 Church St.* ☎*828/452–5222* ▤*AE, D, DC, MC, V* ☉*Closed Sun. and Mon. No lunch.*

$$$$ 🏨**The Swag Country Inn.** This exquisite, rustic inn sits at
★ 5,000 feet, high atop the Cataloochee Divide overlooking a swag—a deep depression in otherwise high ground. Its 250

wooded acres share a border with Great Smoky Mountains National Park and have access to the park's hiking trails. Guest rooms and cabins were assembled from six authentic log structures and transported here. All have exposed beams and wood floors and are furnished with early American crafts. New beds and other upgrades were added in 2008. Dinners here are social events, with hors d'oeuvres, conversation, and an option of family-style or individual seating. There's a two-night minimum stay; bring your own beverages, as the inn is in a dry county. **Pros:** small inn with personality; fabulous location on a nearly mile-high mountain top; delicious meals included. **Cons:** remote; expensive; no TV. ⊠ *2300 Swag Rd.* ☎ *828/926–0430 or 800/789–7672* ⊕ *www.theswag.com* ☞ *16 rooms, 3 cabins* ⚄ *In-room: no TV, no a/c. In-hotel: restaurant, no-smoking rooms* ═ *AE, D, MC, V* ⊘ *Closed Nov.–Mar.* ⧀ *FAP.*

$$$-$$$$ 🖼 **The Yellow House on Plott Creek Road.** Just outside town, this lovely two-story Victorian sits on a low knoll, with gorgeous, colorful surrounding gardens. The hotel strives for an impressionist feel, with light, dappling pastoral colors. The rooms and suites are named for and decorated to evoke other destinations, from Savannah to the Caribbean island of Saba to E'staing, France. Most rooms have fireplaces, and some suites have whirlpool baths. Honeymoon and anniversary packages include fresh flowers, a picnic hamper, and a book of poetry. **Pros:** well-run B&B; lovely grounds; personal service. **Cons:** not a place for singles looking for the action. ⊠ *89 Oak View Dr., at Plott Creek Rd., 1 mi west of Waynesville* ☎ *828/452–0991 or 800/563–1236* 🖷 *828/452–1140* ⊕ *www.theyellowhouse. com* ☞ *4 rooms, 6 suites* ⚄ *In-room: refrigerator (some), no TV, Wi-Fi. In-hotel: no kids under 13, no-smoking rooms* ═ *MC, V* ⧀ *BP.*

SPORTS & THE OUTDOORS

If you want to fly-fish for rainbow, brown, or native brook trout, try **Lowe Fly Shop and Guide Service** (⊠ *15 Woodland Dr.* ☎ *828/452–0039*), which runs wading and floating trips on area streams and lakes. The owner has written two books on fly-fishing. A full-day wade trip for two with guide costs around $300.

A public course at the Methodist conference center, **Lake Junaluska Golf Course** (⊠ *19 Golf Course Rd.* ☎ *828/456–5777*), is short but surprisingly tricky, due to all the trees.

At **Waynesville Country Club Inn** (✉*176 Country Club Dr.* ☎*828/452–4617*), you can play three 9-hole Donald Ross–designed courses in any combination.

SHOPPING

The **Downtown Waynesville** (✉*Main St.*) shopping area stretches three blocks from the city hall to the Haywood County courthouse, with a number of small boutiques, bookstores, and antiques shops.

Travel Smart Great Smoky Mountains National Park

GETTING HERE & AROUND

▌ BY AIR

Although there are small general aviation airports for private airplanes at towns near the Great Smoky Mountains National Park, including the Gatlinburg/Pigeon Forge (GKT) Airport in Sevierville, most visitors who arrive by air fly into one of the region's larger airports and make the last leg of the trip by car.

Airlines & Airports **Airline and Airport Links.com** (⊕www.airline-andairportlinks.com).

Airline Security Issues **Transportation Security Administration** (⊕www.tsa.gov).

AIRPORTS

The nearest airports with national air service are McGhee Tyson Airport (TYS) in Knoxville, about 45 mi west of the Gatlinburg entrance to the park, and Asheville Regional Airport (AVL), 60 mi east of the Cherokee entrance.

Charlotte Douglas International Airport (CLT) in Charlotte, a major hub for US Airways, about 160 mi east of the Cherokee entrance, is the closest large national and international airport.

Airport Information **Asheville Regional Airport** (AVL ☎928/556–1234 ⊕www.flyavl.com). **Charlotte Douglas International Airport** (CLT ☎704/359–4910 ⊕www.charlotte-airport.com). **Gatlinburg/Pigeon Forge Airport** (GKT ☎865/453–

8393). **McGhee Tyson Airport** (TYS ☎865/342–3000 ⊕www.tys.org).

FLIGHTS

Allegiant, American, Continental, Delta, United, and US Airways serve Knoxville, with nonstop service to and from around 20 cities, including Atlanta, Charlotte, Chicago, Dallas-Fort Worth, Denver, LaGuardia New York, Newark, Philadelphia, and Tampa.

Continental, Delta, and US Airways fly into Asheville, with nonstop service to and from seven cities including Atlanta, Charlotte, Detroit, Houston, Minneapolis, and Newark.

US Airways is the dominant carrier at Charlotte Douglas; Air Canada, AirTran, American, Continental, Delta, JetBlue, Lufthansa, and United also serve Charlotte. Airlines have nonstop service to and from more than 125 cities, including several destinations in Europe and the Caribbean.

Airline Contacts **American Airlines** (☎800/433–7300 ⊕www.aa.com). **Continental Airlines** (☎800/523–3273 for U.S. and Mexico reservations, 800/231–0856 for international reservations ⊕www.continental.com). **Delta Airlines** (☎800/221–1212 for U.S. reservations, 800/241–4141 for international reservations ⊕www.delta.com). **United Airlines** (☎800/864–8331 for U.S. reservations, 800/538–2929 for international reservations

⊕www.united.com). **US Airways** (☎800/428–4322 for U.S. and Canada reservations, 800/622–1015 for international reservations ⊕www.usairways.com).

▌ BY BUS

There's no public bus transportation to the Great Smokies. Greyhound provides bus service to Asheville and Waynesville on the North Carolina side and to Knoxville on the Tennessee side. Schedules change frequently; call or check the Web site for information.

Cherokee Trails, operated by the Eastern Band of Cherokee Indians Public Transit, runs a shuttle bus between Cherokee and Gatlinburg/Pigeon Forge, with two to four trips daily May–November, and limited service at other times. The cost is $12–$14, round-trip.

Gatlinburg has a trolley service with 20 trolley-style buses that travel to some 100 locations in Gatlinburg and surrounding areas. From June through October trolleys make runs into the western edge of the park, starting at the Gatlinburg Mass Transit Center on Parkway (U.S. 441) in downtown Gatlinburg at stoplight number 5, with stops at the Sugarlands Visitor Center, Laurel Falls parking area, and Elkmont campground before returning to Gatlinburg. The trip lasts about 1½ hours. The cost is $2, and exact change is required. Trolley maps are available at Gatlinburg welcome centers.

Bus Information Cherokee Trails (☎ 828/497–5296 ⊕www.cherokeetransit.com). **Gatlinburg Mass**

Transit (☎ 865/436–0535 ⊕www.ci.gatlinburg.tn.us/transit/trolley.htm). **Greyhound** (☎800/231–2222 ⊕www.greyhound.com).

▌ BY CAR

Most of the Great Smokies' scenic highlights are many miles apart, and a car is essential for touring the park.

Coming either from the east or west, I–40 is the main access route to the Great Smokies; from the north and south, I–75, I–81, and I–26 are primary arteries. A scenic option from the northeast is the Blue Ridge Parkway, which runs about 469 mi from Virginia, ending at Cherokee about ½ mi from the main eastern entrance to the Smokies.

The closest sizeable cities to the park are Knoxville on the west and Asheville on the east. Knoxville is about 45 mi northwest of Gatlinburg and Sugarlands Visitor Center. Knoxville is 35 mi north of the Townsend entrance to the park, a little less than an hour away by car.

Asheville is about 50 mi east of Cherokee and the Oconaluftee Visitor Center. It takes a little over an hour to get from Asheville to the Cherokee entrance of the park (or about two hours via the winding Blue Ridge Parkway).

GASOLINE

There are no gas stations or other automotive services in the park. Numerous service stations are in Bryson City, Cherokee, Gatlinburg, Pigeon Forge, Townsend, and other towns around the park.

RENTAL CARS

If you're flying in, you will almost certainly need a rental car to visit the Great Smokies. National car rental companies are located at the Asheville, Knoxville, and Charlotte commercial airports, and the Gatlinburg/Pigeon Forge general aviation airport has one car rental company.

ROAD CONDITIONS

As the old saying goes, you can go down a mountain road too slowly a thousand times, but you can go down too fast only once. Driving in the mountains can pose difficulties you may not face back home: steep grades of 6%, 8%, or even 10% or more are not uncommon. While these are probably not a problem for most modern cars, heavy RVs and vehicles towing trailers run a risk of overheating when going up and burning out brakes when coming down. Even in a car, you should shift to a lower gear when going downhill to save your brakes. Blind curves and switchbacks can be scary even for experienced drivers, especially at night when your visibility may be limited and you run the risk of hitting a deer or other animal. Nor will keeping to the interstates necessarily work. For example, I–40 between Canton, NC, and the Tennessee line is notorious for severe accidents. This section of I–40 is heavily used by big tractor-trailer trucks, it is curvy, with narrow or no breakdown lanes, and fog is common; it has twice the fatality rate of any other interstate in North Carolina. This highway is also known for rockslides. One particularly bad slide in 1997 closed I–40 for six months.

Still, most roads in the Smokies and elsewhere in the mountains are well maintained, and warning signs alert you to dangerous curves and steep grades. With all these factors in play, you need to allow more time for driving in the mountains. The Blue Ridge Parkway, for example, has a 45-MPH speed limit, and on many curvy sections you will average much less than that. In the Smokies, the main road through the park, Newfound Gap Road (U.S. 441), also has a 45-MPH speed limit (lower in some places). Some secondary roads in the park have speed limits of only 10 or 15 MPH.

Newfound Gap Road through the park and higher elevation sections of the Blue Ridge Parkway are often closed in winter due to snow and ice. Some secondary roads, including Balsam Mountain Road, Roaring Fork Motor Nature Trail, and Parson Branch Road, are closed all winter.

ROADSIDE EMERGENCIES

In the event of a roadside emergency, call 911. Depending on the location, either the state police, local police in Cherokee or Gatlinburg, or a county sheriff's department will respond. To reach park rangers, call ☎ *865/436–9171*. You can call rangers to report problem bears, animals hit by cars, injured or lost hikers, a car breakdown or accident in the park, and other emergencies. Rangers are also available to answer specific questions about park sites, destinations, and regulations.

RVS

RVs and travel trailers are, up to a point, welcomed in the Smokies. Only one small campground, Deep Creek, doesn't permit RVs and trailers, but except for Look Rock all the other campgrounds have length limitations for RVs and trailers, ranging from 12 to 40 feet. Three large campgrounds, Elkmont and Cades Cove on the Tennessee side and Smokemont on the North Carolina side, are the most RV-friendly, with easy access and a sizeable percentage of RV sites.

Most of the larger campgrounds have dump stations, but none have electrical, water, or sewer hookups. You'll be boondocking here. Note too that several of the campgrounds restrict the use of generators from May through October, typically prohibiting the running of generators in certain sections of the campground.

Many private campgrounds are located near entrances to the park. On the North Carolina side, there are numerous campgrounds in Cherokee, Bryson City, and elsewhere. On the Tennessee side, there are at least 50 campgrounds around Pigeon Forge, Gatlinburg, Sevierville, and Townsend. Nearly all commercial campgrounds have 30 or 50 amp electrical, sewer, and water hookups, restrooms, showers, and dump stations. Many have cable TV and Internet connections. Some have swimming pools.

The National Park Service prohibits RVs, trailers, and buses on some secondary roads in the park, including Balsam Mountain Road, Greenbrier Road past the ranger station, Heintooga Ridge Road, Roaring Fork Motor Nature Trail, Rich Mountain Road, and the road exiting the park at Metcalf Bottoms Picnic Area. Some other roads, such as the unpaved road leading into Cataloochee Valley, permit RVs, trailers, and buses, but because these roads are narrow (one lane in places) and with many blind curves, extreme caution is advised.

If you don't own an RV or trailer but want to try out traveling in one, you can rent one. Typically, you'll pay around $75 to $150 a night, plus a mileage fee of around 30¢ to 35¢ a mile, which doesn't include your gas. (Many RVs get just 6 to 10 miles a gallon, so fuel can be a major expense.) Off-season and longer-term rental specials may offer some bargains. One of the largest and best-known rental outfits is Cruise America, with about 125 locations nationwide including three in North Carolina and three in Tennessee.

RV Rentals Cruise America (☎800/671–8042 ⊕www.cruiseamerica.com).

▌ BY TRAIN

Amtrak train stations closest to the Great Smokies are in Greenville and Spartanburg, South Carolina, about 100 mi southeast or two hours by car from the Cherokee entrance to the park. Amtrak's Crescent offers service between New York and New Orleans, with stops in those two cities and also Charlotte.

The Great Smoky Mountains Railroad has excursions along the southwestern edge of the park and into the Nantahala National Forest. A 4½-hour, 44-mi (round-trip) excursion from Bryson City travels along the Tuckasegee River, crosses the Fontana Lake Trestle, and goes into the Nantahala Gorge.

Train Information Amtrak (☎800/872-7245 ⊕www.amtrak. com). **Great Smoky Mountains Railroad** (☎800/872-4681 ⊕www. gsmr.com).

ESSENTIALS

▌ ACCESSIBILITY

Wheelchair access in the park varies from excellent to non-existent. All of the visitor centers are accessible, but most of the historic buildings in the park, including the old structures in Cades Cove and Cataloochee, are not. Several of the larger frontcountry campgrounds, including Cades Cove, Cosby, Elkmont, and Smokemont, have wheelchair-accessible restrooms, and three—Cades Cove, Elkmont, and Smokemont—have paved and wheelchair-accessible campsites. They have also been modified with special tables and fire grills. Big Creek horse camp has an accessible campsite and restroom. Most trails in the park are steep, rugged, and unpaved. However, an accessible .5-mi paved trail is located on Newfound Gap Road, just south of Sugarlands Visitor Center.

If you have a physical disability, including a temporary disability, or are accompanying someone who needs accessible parking, you may get a temporary parking permit at Sugarlands or Oconaluftee visitor centers.

▌ ACCOMMODATIONS

Inside the park, there is only one hotel, the rustic hike-in LeConte Lodge. Other than that, the park has 10 frontcountry campgrounds with nearly 950 campsites and more than 100 backcountry campsites and shelters.

Outside the park there is a wide variety of lodging options. All of the towns at the edge of the park, including Gatlinburg, Pigeon Forge, Townsend, and Sevierville on the Tennessee side and Cherokee, Bryson City, and Waynesville on the North Carolina side have many motels, both chain and independent. An even bigger selection is available in the nearby larger cities of Knoxville and Asheville.

⇨ *For detailed information on lodging outside the park, see Chapters 5 and 6.*

BED-AND-BREAKFASTS

For bed-and-breakfast accommodations, the largest selection by far is in Asheville, with more than three dozen in the metropolitan area. However, B&Bs can be found in towns all around the park. The Asheville Bed & Breakfast Association manages 12 properties with many in-town and some in the mountains. Romantic Asheville provides an online directory of 29 B&Bs in the Asheville area. The Smoky Mountain Bed and Breakfast Association manages reservations for 20 B&Bs on the Tennessee side, with properties in Gatlinburg, Pigeon Forge, Townsend, Sevierville, Cosby, Newport and Dandridge.

Reservation Services and Directories Asheville Bed & Breakfast Association (☎877/262–6867 ⊕www.ashevillebba.com). **Romantic Asheville** ⊕ www.romanticasheville.com). **Smoky Mountain Bed & Breakfast Association** (⊕www.smokymountainbb.com).

CABINS & COTTAGES
If you're looking for lodging that's more comfortable than camping but more private than a motel, hotel, or B&B, a rental cabin or cottage may be the answer. Mountain cabin rentals are available around the park. They range from deluxe private homes with several bedrooms and amenities including hot tubs, fireplaces, air-conditioning, and big-screen TVs to simple cottages. Some rent on a nightly basis, and others weekly. Many are offered by individuals who have only one or at most a few cabins for rent. Check with the chambers of commerce in towns around the park (⇨*see the Visitor Information section below*) for a list of rentals. **Vacation Rentals by Owner** (⊕*www.vrbo.com*) is another great resource.

CAMPGROUNDS
There are 10 developed campgrounds with 947 tent and RV campsites as well as over 100 backcountry campsites and shelters in the park. Backcountry campsites and shelters are free and developed campsites cost up to $23 per night. Campgrounds at Cades Cove, Cosby, Elkmont, and Smokemont as well as horse camps and some backcountry sites and shelters accept reservations. The rest are first-come, first-served. ⇨*See Chapter 4: Lodging & Dining in the Park for more information on campgrounds in the park.*

COMMERCIAL CAMPGROUNDS
About 75 commercial campgrounds are located around the park. Unlike campgrounds in the park, most of these offer hookups and showers, and some have amenities like swimming pools. Smoky Mountains RV Campgrounds lists 31 commercial RV campgrounds in eastern Tennessee. Your Smokies lists more than 100 commercial RV campgrounds in western North Carolina.

Campground Information Smoky Mountains RV Campgrounds (⊕www.smokymountains-rv-campgrounds.com). **Your Smokies: Camping in NC Smoky Mountains** (⊕www.yoursmokies.com/smokies-campingnc.html).

RESORTS & LODGES
Small mountain lodges and inns, along with some upscale resorts, dot the mountains outside the park, especially on the North Carolina side. These resorts and lodges offer a different, more personalized experience than a hotel or motel, and they often have stunning views and superior dining. The Resorts and Lodges Web site is a good resource for scouting out the many options available.

Resort & Lodge Information Resorts and Lodges (⊕www.resortsandlodges.com).

▌ADMISSION FEES
Unlike at most other national parks, admission to the Great Smokies is free. Admission to all historical and natural sites within the park is also free. Picnicking and backcountry

camping are free. Only the front-country developed campgrounds charge a nightly fee.

ADMISSION HOURS

The Great Smoky Mountains National Park is open 24 hours, seven days a week, year-round. However, many campgrounds and other visitor facilities close in winter; exact closing dates vary. Some secondary roads also close in winter. Many picnic areas close at dusk, some campgrounds limit access to only registered campers after a certain time of night, and some secondary roads in the park have gates that are closed at dusk.

COMMUNICATIONS

INTERNET

Most hotels and motels in the region outside the park offer some kind of high-speed Internet or Wi-Fi connection. There is no Internet access at any of the park campgrounds or at LeConte Lodge.

PUBLIC TELEPHONES

There are public telephones at all visitor centers and most front-country campgrounds. Cell-phone reception is spotty or non-existent in many areas of the park.

EATING OUT

Other than a snack bar at Cades Cove campground, and a few vending machines, there is no food service in the park. You can picnic at 11 developed picnic areas or trailside in the backcountry. Restaurants of all kinds, from fast food chains to sophisticated chef-owned

> ### WORD OF MOUTH
>
> Was the service stellar or not up to snuff? Did the food give you shivers of delight or leave you cold? Did the prices and portions make you happy or sad? Rate restaurants and write your own reviews in Travel Ratings or start a discussion about your favorite places in Travel Talk on ⊕ www.fodors.com. Your comments might even appear in our books. Yes, you, too, can be a correspondent!

bistros, abound in the towns around the park.

EMERGENCIES

In case of a fire, crime, or medical emergency, dial 911. To report a security or other problem, contact the Park Rangers (☎ 865/436–9171). Emergency medical services are available 24 hours a day at hospitals near the park, including Blount Memorial Hospital in Maryville, Fort Sanders Sevier Medical Center in Sevierville (a new hospital, LeConte Medical Center, is expected to replace the existing medical center in late 2009), Swain County Hospital in Bryson City, and Haywood Regional Medical Center in Clyde near Waynesville. Mission Hospitals in Asheville and the University of Tennessee Medical Center in Knoxville are leading regional medical centers.

Contacts **Blount Memorial Hospital** (⊠907 E. Lamar Alexander Pkwy., Maryville, TN ☎865/983–7211). **Emergencies** (☎911). **Fort Sanders Sevier Medical Center** (⊠709 Middle Creek Rd.,

Sevierville, TN ☎865/429–6100).
Haywood Regional Medical Center (⊠262 Leroy George Dr., Clyde, NC ☎828/456–7311). **Mission Hospitals** (⊠ 509 Biltmore Ave., Asheville, NC ☎828/213–1111). **Swain County Hospital** (⊠45 Plateau St., Bryson City, NC ☎828/488–2155). **University of Tennessee Medical Center** (⊠ 1924 Alcoa Hwy., Knoxville, TN ☎865/305–9000).

▎MONEY

Although there are no banks or ATMs in the park, there are dozens of bank offices with ATMs in the towns around the park. Wells Fargo (which purchased Wachovia in 2008), Bank of America, and First Citizens are among major banks in western North Carolina; First Tennessee and SunTrust are major banks in east Tennessee.

▎PACKING

While you don't want to overpack, you need to be prepared for a variety of weather conditions in the park and surrounding mountains. Elevations in the Smokies and the mountains around the park vary from under 2,000 feet to well over 6,000 feet; temperatures and precipitation are elevation-dependent. Temps at Clingmans Dome may be 10 to 20 degrees lower than in Gatlinburg or Cherokee, and precipitation at higher elevations can be twice or more than that at lower elevations. Weather is especially variable in the spring and summer. One day it may be near 80° and the next it could be snowing. Therefore, you need to pack

with a mind to dressing in layers: it's a better idea to bring several layers of shirts and fleeces in different weights rather than just one bulky sweater or coat. Wear fast-drying synthetics instead of cotton for hiking and camping trips. In winter you'll need to be prepared for temperatures below freezing, and even below zero at high elevations. Remember to pack rain gear, especially in spring and summer.

Bring sturdy footwear for hiking or walking. If you're hiking in the backcountry you'll want boots with good ankle support. You may want to coat your boots with silicone, as trails may be muddy. Wicking socks, in wool rather than cotton, are also a good idea as they will keep your feet warm and dry. Depending on your interests, you may also want to pack fly-fishing gear and a field manual to help you identify wildflowers, birds, and other flora and fauna.

If you're tubing, rafting, or swimming, bring a backpack or large fanny pack for carrying food, water, snacks, insect repellent, sunscreen, a first aid kit, and other items you may want on hand.

For backcountry trips, bring plenty of drinking water and a purification system suitable for killing *Giardia* bacteria. Flashlights or head lamps are a must. Remember a camera and lightweight binoculars for wildlife viewing. For serious backpacking treks, GORP has an extensive packing list at ⊕*gorp.away.com/gorp/gear/ practical-advice/backpacking-packing-list.html*.

When not hiking or camping, casual outdoor wear is appropriate almost everywhere. The exceptions are a few upscale restaurants in Asheville and Knoxville, where shorts and T-shirts will look out of place at dinner. Pack at least one business-casual outfit if you think you'll be going out for a nice meal.

PERMITS

Camping and overnight hiking in the backcountry require a permit. Backcountry permits are free. To camp in the backcountry, you must complete a permit at one of the 14 self-registration stations in and near the park, which are available 24 hours a day. You cannot get a permit by mail, telephone, or online. Your permit must designate the campsite or shelter at which you will stay for each night of your trip. Keep the permit with you and drop the top copy in the registration box. Most backcountry campsites are first-come, first-served, but a few campsites and all shelters require an advance reservation. Download a park trail map at ⊕ *www.nps.gov/grsm/planyourvisit/backcountry-camping.htm* to get the locations of all reserved and non-reserved backcountry campsites and shelters. Day hikes do not require a permit.

Information Backcountry Information Office (☏865/436–1297 daily 9–noon ⊕www.nps.gov/grsm/planyourvisit/backcountry-camping.htm).

PETS

Pets are permitted in some areas of the park but strictly prohibited in others. Dogs and other pets are allowed in frontcountry campgrounds, picnic areas, and along roads, but they must be kept on a leash at all times. The leash cannot be longer than 6 feet. Pets are not allowed on park trails, except the Gatlinburg and the Oconaluftee River trails, and they are not permitted anywhere in the backcountry. Pet excrement must be immediately collected and disposed of in a trash can.

RESTROOMS & SHOWERS

All visitor centers, campgrounds, and picnic areas have restrooms. Most have flush toilets and running water. There are no showers at the campgrounds or anywhere else in the park. Showers are available at most commercial campgrounds around the park.

SAFETY

The Great Smoky Mountains National Park is a wilderness area, and as such there are inherent risks. Hiking or camping in the backcountry requires you to exercise good judgment: don't hike alone; let a responsible person know your plans and get a backcountry permit if required; bring a trail map, flashlights, compass, and adequate water; check the weather in advance; dress appropriately and wear hiking boots or shoes that offer good ankle support; and follow park guidelines for avoiding problems with bears, snakes, and insects such as yellow jackets. ⇨ *See The Bear Facts in Chapter 1: Welcome to the Great Smoky Mountains for information on what to do if you come into contact with a bear.*

Crime is generally not a problem in the park, and the towns around the edge of the park are mostly small with moderate to low crimes rates. However, serious crimes including rapes and murders have occurred in and around the park, so you should use the same common sense approaches to avoid crime that you would use anywhere else.

One flashpoint for property crime in the park is trailhead parking. Thieves may observe you parking at a trailhead and know that you'll be away from your vehicle for a long period. Although trailheads are patrolled regularly, there are things you can do to protect your vehicle: look around the trailhead parking lot for signs of break-ins; notice other people at the trailhead—if they look like they don't belong, they probably don't; avoid leaving any visible valuables in the vehicle, and don't leave blankets or towels in the vehicle that may look like you're concealing valuables; don't do your packing at the trailhead—thieves may be watching what you put in the trunk; leave pocketbooks and wallets at home—just bring the cash you need, an ID, and perhaps one credit or debit card; check with rangers to see if there have been any break-ins recently and ask about any parking areas to avoid.

▌ TAXES

The statewide sales tax in Tennessee is 7%, except for food which has a rate of 5.5%. In addition, counties, cities, and towns may have an additional local add-on tax. The local tax is 2.5% in Gatlinburg, Pigeon Forge, and Sevierville, and 2.25% in Townsend and Knoxville, for a total of 9.25% to 9.5%.

The statewide sales tax in North Carolina is 4.25%. In addition, counties, cities, and towns may have an additional local add-on tax. The combined state and local sales tax rate in most counties on the North Carolina side of the park is 7%.

▌ TIME

The Great Smoky Mountains National Park and nearby areas are in the Eastern time zone.

Time Zones Timeanddate.com (⊕www.timeanddate.com/world-clock).

▌ TOURS

The National Park Service has looked at introducing shuttle tours in the park, but so far that doesn't seem to be a practical option. However, in fall 2008, an experimental shuttle tour of Cades Cove, supported by the Park Service, began. It is operated by Cades Cove Heritage Tours. Tours in 19-seat buses cost $13, depart from the Great Smoky Mountains Heritage Center in Townsend, and last about three hours.

Rocky Top Tours in Pigeon Forge offers bus and van tours of Newfound Gap, Cades Cove, Roaring Fork Motor Nature Trail, and sites around the park, such as Biltmore House in Asheville and Harrah's Casino in Cherokee. Rates start at $15.

Smoky Mountain Tour Connection in Pigeon Forge specializes in group tours in the Smokies. Most packages include lodging, meals, and tickets to attractions.

Tour Information **Cades Cove Heritage Tours** (✉ 123 Cromwell Dr., Townsend, TN ☎865/329-2424 ⊕www.cadescoveheritagetours.org). **Rocky Top Tours** (☎877/315-8687 or 865/429-8687 ⊕www.rockytop-tours.com). **Smoky Mountain Tour Connection** (☎800/782-1061 or 865/453-0734 ⊕www.smokymtn-tourconnection.com).

▌ VISITOR INFORMATION

All of the park visitor centers, and especially the Oconaluftee and Sugarlands visitor centers, provide excellent information about the park. Park staff at the centers offer free advice about sightseeing, camping, picnicking, and touring the Smokies. A free tabloid newspaper, *Smokies Guide*, which contains an area map and interesting articles on the park, is published four times a year (spring, summer, fall, and winter) and is available at all the visitor centers. Stores at the visitor centers sell dozens of books, maps, and pamphlets on the park. There is a good selection of brochures on activities in the park, such as day hikes, historical sites, and auto touring; these are sold in visitor centers, most for $1 each.

FODORS.COM CONNECTION

Before your trip, be sure to check out what other travelers are saying on ⊕www.fodors.com.

Brochures or booklets on touring Cades Cove, Roaring Fork, Cataloochee, and other major sites in the park are available near the entrance to these areas. The price, paid on the honor system, is usually 50¢ to $1.50.

Several Web sites are useful for trip-planning information, including the National Park Service's Great Smoky Mountains National Park Web site, which has information on fees and permits. Also try ⊕*www.gsmnp.com*, a commercial site where you'll find information on the park as well as lodging and dining. You can use the LeConte Lodge Web site to make reservations for this hike-in lodge. The park service allows camping reservations to be made online for four park campgrounds (Cades Cove, Cosby, Elkmont, and Smokemont) as well.

Chambers of commerce and tourist information offices at towns and cities around the park, and their Web sites, are also helpful. The Asheville, Bryson City, and Gatlinburg tourism offices and Web sites have the most to offer. Also, Web sites for the Blue Ridge Parkway and Pisgah and Nantahala national forests are useful in planning a visit to the mountain areas around the Great Smokies park. For information on the Qualla Boundary (the Cherokee Indian reservation) and on Cherokee culture, contact the Cherokee Welcome Center.

ONLINE TRAVEL TOOLS

All About the Great Smoky Mountains Great Smoky Mountains National Park (National Park Service) (✉ 107 Park Headquarters Rd., Gatlinburg, TN ☎865/436–1200 ⊕www.nps.gov/grsm). **Great Smoky Mountains National Park (commercial Web site)** (⊕www.gsmnp.com).

Tourist Information Asheville Convention & Visitors Bureau (✉ 36 Montford Ave., Asheville, NC ☎888/247–9811 ⊕www.explore-asheville.com). **Blue Ridge Parkway (National Park Service)** (✉199 Hemphill Knob Rd., Asheville, NC ☎828/271–4779 ⊕www.nps.gov/blri). **Bryson City & The Great Smokies** (✉ Swain County Chamber of Commerce, 210 Main St., Bryson City, NC ☎800/867–9246 ⊕www.greatsmokies.com). **Gatlinburg Visitors and Convention Bureau**(✉1011 Banner Rd., Gatlinburg, TN ☎800/588–1817 ⊕www.gatlinburg.com). **LeConte Lodge** (☎865/429–5704 ⊕www.leconte-lodge.com). **National Forests in North Carolina** (☎828/257–4200 ⊕www.cs.unca.edu/nfsnc).

Native American Information Cherokee Welcome Center (✉498 Tsali Blvd., Cherokee, NC ☎800/438–1601 ⊕www.cherokee-nc.com).

INDEX

NOTES

NOTES

ABOUT OUR WRITERS

Michael Ream is a travel writer who has chased stories through Tennessee, Mississippi, Louisiana, Texas, Arkansas, Missouri, and Kansas, as well as North Africa and South America. His writing has appeared in publications including *Southern Traveler, Saveur,* and *South American Explorer*. Previously, he contributed to *Fodor's Texas* and *Fodor's Essential USA*, where he wrote about the Ozarks.

Asheville native and former New Orleans newspaper editor Lan Sluder has written a half-dozen books, including travel guides to Belize and the coast of the Carolinas and Georgia. His articles have appeared in *Caribbean Travel & Life*, the *Chicago Tribune*, the *New York Times*, *Where to Retire,* and other publications around the world. He has also contributed to other Fodor's guides, including *Fodor's Belize* and *Fodor's The Carolinas and Georgia*. Lan's home base in North Carolina is a mountain farm near Asheville settled by his forebears in the early 1800s.